# Patents and the Measurement of International Competitiveness

D0171118

# Patents and the Measurement of International Competitiveness

New Data on the Use of Patents by Universities, Small Firms and Individual Inventors

William Kingston and Kevin Scally
*School of Business Studies, Trinity College, Dublin*

**Edward Elgar**
Cheltenham, UK • Northampton, MA, USA

Published by
Edward Elgar Publishing Limited
Glensanda House
Montpellier Parade
Cheltenham
Glos GL50 1UA
UK

Edward Elgar Publishing, Inc.
136 West Street
Suite 202
Northampton
Massachusetts 01060
USA


A catalogue record for this book
is available from the British Library

**Library of Congress Cataloguing in Publication Data**

Kingston, William.
      Patents and the measurement of international competitiveness : new data on the use of patents by universities, small firms, and individual inventors / William Kingston and Kevin Scally.
          p. cm.
    Includes bibliographical references and index.
1.    Technological innovations. 2. Competition, International. 3. Patents.
I. Scally, Kevin, 1952- II. Title.
T173.8.K57 2006
608–dc22

                            2005057709


ISBN-13: 978 1 84376 444 1
ISBN-10: 1 84376 444 X

Printed and bound in Great Britain by MPG Books Ltd, Bodmin, Cornwall

# Contents

# Preface

In 2001, the Commission of the European Communities published 'Enforcing small firms' patent rights,'[1] the research for which had been directed by one of the authors of the present book. In this research, European individuals and firms which had taken advantage of the 'Small Entity' discounts in the United States Patent and Trademark Office were a fundamental component of the database.

That research covered the years 1994 to 1997, and the resulting information proved to be so useful that it was considered worthwhile to extend it to 2003 so as to give a full ten year period of results. In doing so, its coverage was also expanded to every country in the world which had acquired a USPTO patent during the ten years. Valuable additional measures, including citations, payment of maintenance fees, differences between invention categories and the extent to which the inventions of non-American inventors are actually owned within the United States, were added.

The present book is the result and it is hoped that it will make a useful contribution to the information needed for making comparisons of inventive output internationally. Since most of this comes from the developed countries, it was first considered that comprehensive data should be provided for those countries that are members of the OECD, with summary information for all other countries. However, it was quickly discovered that Israel, although not an OECD member, has such a high level of inventive activity that it ought to be included with the advanced countries. In particular, it provides an illuminating and important point of comparison with a group of OECD countries, close to Israel in terms of GDP and population, including Denmark, Finland, Ireland, New Zealand and Norway. It is important to note, therefore, that the term OECD* is used throughout the book to mean 'OECD countries plus Israel'.

One of the surprises to emerge from the expanded data was the inventiveness of Taiwan's Individual inventors, as measured in this particular way. The total number of Small Entity patents acquired by residents of Taiwan exceeds that of any other nation, other than the US. In fact, over three quarters of all the non OECD* Small Entity patents were granted to Taiwanese residents and, crucially, the majority were in the Individual category. As will be seen, the number of Small Entity patents acquired by most countries in the non OECD* group is negligible, being typically less than one per year.

## ACKNOWLEDGMENTS

This database was made possible by the freedom of access which the United States Patent and Trademark Office provides to its information, and we are grateful to Mr Jim Hirabayashi of that office for extracting what we needed from their records so frequently and so expeditiously.

The major part of the data concerning citations accompanied the text *Patents, Citations, and Innovations* by Jaffe and Trajtenberg,[2] and we are grateful to Dr Bronwyn Hall for the additional citations data up to the end of 2002. We also acknowledge with thanks financial support provided by the Research Fund of the European Patent Office, although of course that Office bears no responsibility for the results.

William Kingston (wkngston@tcd.ie)
Kevin Scally (kscally@tcd.ie)

School of Business Studies, Trinity College, Dublin

## NOTES

1. EUR 17032. *Enforcing small firms' patents rights*. Luxembourg, Office for Official Publications of the European Communities.
2. Jaffe, A. B. and Trajtenberg, M. (2002) *Patents, Citations, and Innovations: a window on the knowledge economy*, Cambridge, MA, The MIT Press.

PART ONE


International comparisons

# 1. Introduction

In searching for means of comparing one country's technological performance with another's, it is only to be expected that scholars would want to use patent counts. Patents exist in every country of any size, are well tabulated, are easily accessible and go back to the beginning of the industrial revolution. Indeed, there have been many studies which purport to use them in this way, as well as many others which are little more than vehicles for demonstrating econometric skills, making use of the large numbers which libraries of patents can provide.

However, when such collections of data are examined carefully, they are found to be less valuable than appears at first, and their use has drawbacks which have not always been properly recognised by researchers.[1] There are several reasons for this.

First patents only protect a small part of technology. Moreover, in many areas of it, they have now become little more than a reinforcement of large firms' primary means of protecting their inventions, which is the combination of manufacturing capability and speed to the market with anything new. This has been confirmed by several large-scale empirical studies of the actual mechanisms used by firms to protect the output of their investments in research and development.[2]

Even where patents are used, some technologies use them more than others. For example, out of a total of more than 2.3 million Utility patents issued by the United States Patent and Trademark Office to the end of 2001, 44 per cent were in the Mechanical classes, 27 per cent in the Electrical and 29 per cent in Chemical classes. In recent decades Chemical patents have become more numerous than they were in earlier periods. This could be because the modern patent system's criteria were established in the US 1952 Act, which was effectively written by lawyers for the pharmaceutical industry.[3] These criteria were then copied throughout the world. Invention in chemical firms may be especially market-driven, with researchers working towards technical targets which can be specified rather precisely by their managements. This could be reinforced still further by having developed a particularly precise vocabulary, thus making the results amenable to patenting. Other fields of technology, such as mechanical engineering and electronics, may not have similarly precise language, making it more difficult for inventions in them to be described so as to 'precisely define the limits' of what is claimed as an invention, as the law requires.

Thirdly, patent *numbers* on their own mean little as indicators of patent *value*. The vast majority of issued patents are worthless, yet a tiny number of those that are valuable are extremely so. In countries where renewal fees have to be paid annually to keep patents in force, data on payment of these fees can be used as a means of measuring value very roughly. This depends on the reasonable assumption that if a renewal fee is *not* paid, the present value of the patent is considered by its owner to be less than the fee. Since, although fees do increase progressively, their cost even in the later years of a patent's life is not very great, this assumption may be taken to mean that owners have effectively written off their patents as worthless at the point where they abandon payment of renewal fees.

Unfortunately, the converse is not the case. Payment of a renewal fee may not necessarily represent an objective assessment, but may reflect undue optimism about the patent's future value on the part of its owner, which is most likely to be found in the cases of Individual or Small Firm patents. There must also be a bias *in favour* of payment of fees on portfolios of patents in large firms. Firstly, in such firms renewal payments may be routine, without any significant evaluation of the patent's present value. Secondly, the employed managers of patent departments will not be penalised for keeping worthless patents in force, but will certainly be blamed severely if they fail to renew a patent which the firm finds later on that it could have used to advantage. In these cases the risk to an individual career is perceived as a greater threat than the expenditure on maintenance.

In spite of these drawbacks, focusing attention on patents which have their renewal fees paid for the maximum possible number of years at least eliminates large numbers of valueless patents from consideration. It can fairly be assumed that all the most valuable patents will be found in this residual number. Among the studies which have used this technique are Schankerman,[4] Lanjouw, Pakes and Putnam,[5] and Scherer and Harhoff.[6] All of these writers found the distribution of patent value highly skewed, although their estimates of values varied widely.

## INTERNATIONAL COMPARISONS

When attempting to make international comparisons, a serious problem is that patents do not mean the same thing everywhere, in terms of the protection they purport to give. As a matter of policy, the protection provided by Japanese patents has until recently been narrower than that of US and European patents. Even within the range of the European patent itself, because the scope of the protection is adjudicated by national courts, a patent can mean quite different things in two member countries of the European Patent Convention.[7]

These differences are compounded by variations in the nature and quality of the examination which has led to the issuance of any particular patent. Until comparatively recently, for example, Belgian patents were not examined for anything other than conformity with formal requirements, all questions such as those of novelty or non-obviousness being left to the Courts to decide. At the other end of the scale, the examination standards of the German Office have traditionally been considered to be the highest of any of the National Offices. Standards may also change over time: for example, it is now widely held by practitioners in the United States that the great increase in patenting in recent years has been accompanied by lower patent quality, attributed to the difficulty of recruiting enough qualified examiners.

Indeed, it may well be that a simple measure of the value of any single patent cannot be achieved. Some research has attempted to establish a commercial value for patents by examining how inventors have benefited in direct financial ways through licensing their inventions to third parties or by exploiting the invention themselves. Other writers have pointed to the 'value' of patents as tactical or strategic ammunition, when used aggressively or defensively by larger firms. A startup firm seeking investment may use patents as a means of reassuring a venture capitalist or 'angel'. Even for an individual inventor, possession of a single patent in a particular field of expertise may provide additional credibility when seeking employment or consultancy work. Prospective employers are no better equipped than academics to measure the 'real' value of any patent.

In discussing patent values, account must also be taken of the way in which the recent explosion of interest in intellectual property rights has led to the use of patents strategically to *prevent* competitors putting products on the market that may not conform to the degree of closeness of substitution that the system allows. Competitors can be intimidated by implied threats to cause them large delays and costs in litigation. At the limit, such policies cause firms to avoid innovation altogether, because if they innovate, they can be sued for infringement by predators whose primary motive in obtaining patents is extortion, not innovation.[8]

It is clear that the various notions of patent value must be underpinned by some ultimate expectation, on the part of the patent holder, of future economic gain. The difficulty that writers have found in putting a precise measure on this value may be compared to the difficulties facing the accountancy profession in measuring 'goodwill' in the context of corporate investment. Nevertheless, even if arriving at an absolute measure is likely to prove difficult or impossible in individual cases, broad comparisons between groups of patents can be made if certain conditions apply.

## USE OF THE 'SMALL ENTITY' DATA

The database which the present book reveals and discusses meets these conditions. Consequently, it offers a means of throwing light on the ways in which countries differ in terms of their technological capability. It is a subset of the main database of the United States Patent and Trademark Office (USPTO) limited to patents whose applicants took advantage of a privilege which that Office offers to 'Small Entities': individuals, not for profit organisations, and small businesses. This privilege is a 50 per cent discount on the majority of fees.[9] The database contains all Small Entity patents issued from 1994 to 2003 inclusive,[10] matched with their full bibliographic data from the main US Patent database.[11]

## DEFINITIONS

The USPTO's Manual of Patent Examining Procedure, Section 1.27 (see Appendix A) provides definitions of these three types of 'Small Entity'. Individuals are self-defining, but 'Nonprofits' are not, so that a full discussion of their definition will be found at the beginning of Chapter 3, which is devoted to them. As for small businesses, to qualify under the Small Business Act, the general rule is that such a concern may not employ more than 500 staff. A firm of that size would be a substantial enterprise in most countries other than the US (the equivalent Canadian Small Entity regulation applies to firms with less than 50 staff).[12]

The USPTO's 500-employee limit for qualification of businesses as 'small' does at least serve to distinguish such firms from very large, multi-national concerns. The remission of fees is not available to an entity which would normally qualify under the regulations if it has established a contractual relationship concerning the patent with an entity not entitled to the reduction in fees. Since the penalty for wrongfully claiming the fee remission includes a complete voiding of the patent, such 'fraud on the Office' is clearly a risk not worth taking.

As a member of the Paris Convention for the Protection of Industrial Property, the United States is bound to treat patent applications from citizens of other member countries of this Convention as if they were from its own citizens: consequently, such applications, too, are entitled to claim Small Entity status if they qualify. Considerable numbers of applicants from abroad take advantage of this, so that their records in the USPTO provide a unique opportunity of making international comparisons which do not have the disadvantages touched upon in the discussion above.

Although almost all of the research and development which leads to patents today is carried out by firms, for Constitutional reasons, United States patents cannot be granted to these, but only to individuals. This makes no practical difference, since if the inventor is under a contract of employment, he will be bound to assign any patents granted to him to his employer firm. Each patent document records the names of all the individual inventors and their place of residence as well the name of the assignee, if any. In this database, the residence of the first named (or leading) inventor is designated as the patent 'source'. This is the practice followed by the USPTO when providing its own analyses of patent numbers by country of origin.

The boundary between patents belonging to individual inventors and those of small firms is inevitably fluid. All really small firms depend very largely on the entrepreneurial energy of a single individual, who may also be the firm's founder. But in terms of patent ownership, what may be called the 'exploiting entity' may appear as either that individual or his firm. In some cases, for taxation or other reasons, it may appear advantageous to such a person to have ownership of any patents kept outside the firm, in others they may be 'assigned' to the firm, and there does not seem to be any way of making useful and consistent distinctions.

## ADVANTAGES OF THE DATABASE

Use of this database allows valid and valuable comparisons between the levels of inventive activity in different countries for several reasons.

Since large multinational firms are excluded from the data both directly and indirectly, it is a reasonable assumption that organisations which avail of this remission in USPTO fees, the Small Entity patents, are more likely to represent the 'home grown' proportion of any country's 'patent-using' innovative activity, including technology startup firms.

Secondly, all of the patents in the database have been through the same examining procedure, so that to this extent, like is genuinely being compared with like.

Thirdly, at least subjectively, these patents relate to those inventions, from any country, which hold out the best prospect of being valuable. Applicants are more likely to consider that they need protection in the US for their better inventions, and also the cost of patenting in that country will deter them from making applications for their less important ones.

Fourthly, the coverage of the database can be expected to be particularly high for the inventions from the Nonprofit group – research institutes, universities, hospitals and the like. This is because any research carried on in these entities should be of global, rather than of local, significance. Consequently, if the results are considered to be patentable at all, they will have to be patented in the United States. Indeed, there is a strong case that Nonprofit Small entities should not be researching in these 'patentable' areas at all if they do not intend to look for protection in that country. This is because if their results are free to a United States firm to copy, the advantages such a firm is likely to have in terms of size, whether measured in terms of productive assets or resources for marketing, are likely to be decisive eventually in the world market as well as in the US one.

Some confirmation of this point can be found in Section 2 of the database, which deals with countries which have very few US patents. It will be noted that almost all of the patents originating from these countries are in the pharmaceutical area. This is probably because the results of pharmaceutical research are intrinsically global in their effect, corresponding to the point just made, and also because of recognition that the best hope of reward for the research results would be from a US license.

A caveat which should be kept in mind when considering the data is that although comparisons between countries other than the United States can be fairly made from the Small Entity database for the reasons just discussed, this is not the case for comparisons between any of them and the United States itself. The reason is that the self-selection process which is at work in these other countries to eliminate the less valuable patents does not apply to United States applicants. Consequently, the US figures reflect large numbers of patents that have little chance of ever being innovated, of the kind that have been filtered out from the grants to applicants from other countries by factors such as the invention being of interest only in a local market, the cost of making an application in the United States, and so on.

Another cause of difference between the United States figures and those of other countries is that so many firms in the US are in complex technologies. Since Anti-Trust policy made patent pools illegal there, it is the practice of such firms to patent 'every blade of grass' so as to develop bargaining strength which will prevent them from being locked out from using incremental innovations of their competitors.[13] Once again, these causes of distortion should apply less to the Nonprofit section than to other types of patentee.

## REFINEMENTS OF THE BASIC DATABASE

Apart from straightforward comparison between patent numbers by country, some further refinements have been incorporated into the database. The first of these adds data on patent 'citations'. Trajtenberg and others have shown that when one patent is cited as prior art during the examination of another, it shows that the later patent is building on the information in the earlier one, and hence it testifies to the quality of the latter. Citation levels may thus be an indication of value.[14] Harhoff found that each citation in a later patent of one of the most valuable German patents which he had identified in his earlier work was associated with a significant value for the earlier patent.[15] Jaffe and Trajtenberg have pointed to a correlation between the growth of investment in a specific industry and the associated growth in the number of citations of patents in that industry.[16]

Secondly, as the database covers patents issued over a full ten year period, it has been possible to incorporate information on what proportion of Small Entity patents were renewed by paying the appropriate fee after the initial four year period, and for a smaller subset of those, what proportion were renewed after eight years.

Thirdly, further insight into the relative strength of indigenous invention in different countries is provided by including the proportions of patents where the first inventor is resident in a country other than the United States, but the patent is assigned to a United States firm.

## NOTES

1. See for example, Desrochers, P. (1998) 'On the abuse of patents as economic indicators' *The Quarterly Journal of Austrian Economics* 1 (Winter) 51–74.
2. See in particular: R. Levin, et al.(1987) 'Yale study of R&D appropriability methods', *Brookings Economic Papers*; A. Arundel, A. van de Paal, and L. Soete (1995) *Innovation strategies of Europe's largest industrial firms: Results of the PACE survey*; Cohen, W., R. Nelson, and J. Walsh (2001) 'Appropriability mechanisms: use and change over time' Paper presented to the Swedish International Symposium on Law, Economics and Intellectual Property, Gothenburg, June 26–30.
3. See Judge Rich (1978) quoted in P. J. Federico, 'Origins of Section 103', in John F. Witherspoon, ed. *Nonobviousness – The Ultimate Condition of Patentability,* Bureau of National Affairs, Washington, DC, 1, 109.
4. Schankerman, M. (1998) 'How valuable is patent protection? Estimates by technology field' *Rand Journal of Economics* 29, 77–107.
5. Lanjouw, J., A. Pakes, and J. Putnam (1998) 'How to count patents and value intellectual property: the uses of patent renewal and application data' *Journal of Industrial Economics* 46, 405–432.
6. Scherer, F., and D. Harhoff (2000) 'Technology policy for a world of skew-distributed outcomes' *Research Policy* 29, 559–566.
7. Discussed in David Cohen (1998) 'Article 69 and European patent integration' *Northwestern Law Review* 92, 1083–1129.
8. Macdonald, Stuart (2004) 'When means become ends: considering the impact of patent strategy on innovation' *Information Economics and Policy* 16, 135–158.
9. See Sterba, R. (1997) 'Small Entity status: who's "small", who isn't, who should be, and why?' *American Intellectual Property Law Association Quarterly Journal* 25, 425–437.
10. Provided by the USPTO in May 2004.
11. USPTO Patents BIB for December 2003.
12. Canadian Intellectual Property Office, Glossary, accessed 22 July 2003, available at http://strategis.ic.gc.ca/sc_mrksv/cipo/patents/e-filing/gloss.htm
13. Kash, D., and W. Kingston (2001) 'Patents in a World of Complex Technologies' *Science and Public Policy* 28, 11–22.

14. Trajtenberg, M. (1990) 'A penny for your quotes. Patent citations and the value of innovations' *Rand Journal of Economics* 21, 172–187.
15. Harhoff, D., et al. (1999) 'Citation frequency and the value of patented inventions' *Review of Economics and Statistics* 81(3), 511–515.
16. Jaffe, A. B., and M. Trajtenberg (2002) *Patents, Citations, and Innovations: a window on the knowledge economy*, Cambridge, MA, The MIT Press.

# 2. OECD* Small Entity patents

This chapter provides an overview of the full database of OECD* Small Entity patents from 1994 to 2003. Later chapters will examine the three subdivisions of Nonprofits, Small Firms and Individuals. The basis for all the analysis that follows is the assessment of value. Inventors and firms, seeking to protect their new ideas, are generally faced with a decision on whether to file first for a patent under their domestic patent regime – in their 'home' country – or in some external jurisdiction. This decision will be influenced by the inventor's view of the market potential of the invention: the broader the potential market, the broader the scope of the protection required. Inventors who see that their invention is 'local' in nature, and will be limited to a particular geographic area in its future applications, will have an easy decision to make. An advantage of filing locally is that it is usually a less expensive and more convenient option than going directly to a larger or foreign jurisdiction. In any case, where the inventor's country of residence is a signatory to the Paris Convention of 1883, the invention is protected in all other signatory countries for a period of one year.[1] Therefore, even where inventors have such faith in the global marketability of their inventions that they have every intention of seeking the widest possible international patent protection, it would make sense for them to apply for a local patent first. They then have a breathing space of one year, protected by the Paris Convention, to pursue the international patents elsewhere. Anyone filing for a patent with the United States Patent and Trademark Office, for example, may claim the date of such a foreign filing as the 'priority' date; it becomes, in other words, the effective date of filing in the US.

Since it is a central argument of this analysis that USPTO patents represent (for countries other than the US itself) the selected subset of each country's patents considered to be most globally marketable, we should expect, on looking at the USPTO Small Entity patent data, to see priority dates (indicating a previous filing with the inventor's national or regional patent office) associated with the majority of the patents granted to non-US residents. Table 2.1 shows the priority data for the ten years covered by this study. The second column displays the total for Small Entity patents, followed by the number and percentage where priority was claimed in the application to the USPTO. In the case of Germany, for example, almost 90 per cent of the Small Entity patents granted by the USPTO to German resident inventors had already been filed first outside the US, generally in the German or European patent offices.

*Table 2.1    OECD\* countries; proportion of SE patents where priority was claimed under the Paris Convention, 1994 to 2003*

|    | Country | SE total | Priority claim | % Priority |
|----|---------|----------|----------------|-----------|
| 1  | Czech Republic | 47 | 44 | 93.6% |
| 2  | Austria | 1,168 | 1,079 | 92.4% |
| 3  | Portugal | 47 | 42 | 89.4% |
| 4  | Germany | 11,880 | 10,468 | 88.1% |
| 5  | Italy | 4,926 | 4,184 | 84.9% |
| 6  | France | 3,623 | 3,076 | 84.9% |
| 7  | Finland | 919 | 766 | 83.4% |
| 8  | Switzerland | 2,539 | 2,072 | 81.6% |
| 9  | Korea | 3,864 | 3,150 | 81.5% |
| 10 | Luxembourg | 26 | 21 | 80.8% |
| 11 | Japan | 12,647 | 10,188 | 80.6% |
| 12 | Spain | 1,049 | 844 | 80.5% |
| 13 | Australia | 3,262 | 2,604 | 79.8% |
| 14 | Denmark | 711 | 563 | 79.2% |
| 15 | Netherlands | 1,447 | 1,139 | 78.7% |
| 16 | Sweden | 2370 | 1848 | 78.0% |
| 17 | Ireland | 305 | 237 | 77.7% |
| 18 | UK | 6,098 | 4,712 | 77.3% |
| 19 | New Zealand | 472 | 353 | 74.8% |
| 20 | Slovakia | 18 | 13 | 72.2% |
| 21 | Belgium | 629 | 441 | 70.1% |
| 22 | Hungary | 129 | 90 | 69.8% |
| 23 | Poland | 52 | 23 | 44.2% |
| 24 | Greece | 106 | 45 | 42.5% |
| 25 | Israel | 3,791 | 1,561 | 41.2% |
| 26 | Turkey | 23 | 9 | 39.1% |
| 27 | Iceland | 39 | 13 | 33.3% |
| 28 | Mexico | 311 | 96 | 30.9% |
| 29 | Norway | 657 | 179 | 27.2% |
| 30 | Canada | 15,196 | 2,566 | 16.9% |
| 31 | US | 271,785 | 761 | 0.3% |

The German proportion, and the near 80 per cent figure for the other EU countries, tend to support the view that USPTO applications represent a subset of each nation's indigenous inventions. We reach the 22nd country on the list, Hungary, before the proportion falls below 70 per cent. So at least 70 per cent of these patents were first applied for outside the US, but were also deemed sufficiently valuable to warrant protection in the US market. In fact, as Table 2.2 shows, when the data for the US and Canada are excluded, the proportion of all other OECD\* Small Entity patents claiming priority is 79 per cent. Canada was excluded from the table because, as will be seen, Canadian inventors make minimal use of the Paris Convention. A few other countries have a low proportion of priority claims and these exceptions will be discussed next.

*Table 2.2    OECD\* (excl. US and Canada); total proportion of SE patents where priority was claimed for each year, 1994 to 2003*

| Year | SE total | Priority claim | % Priority |
|------|----------|----------------|------------|
| 1994 | 4,687 | 3,844 | 82.0% |
| 1995 | 4,795 | 3,926 | 81.9% |
| 1996 | 4,985 | 4,024 | 80.7% |
| 1997 | 5,287 | 4,243 | 80.3% |
| 1998 | 7,099 | 5,560 | 78.3% |
| 1999 | 7,140 | 5,503 | 77.1% |
| 2000 | 7,472 | 5,851 | 78.3% |
| 2001 | 7,658 | 6,058 | 79.1% |
| 2002 | 7,130 | 5,507 | 77.2% |
| 2003 | 6,902 | 5,344 | 77.4% |
| All | 63,155 | 49,860 | 78.9% |

The low proportion of Canadian residents claiming foreign priority (17 per cent) suggests that the majority of Canadian SE inventors are going directly to the USPTO to file. This may represent a feeling on the part of Canadian inventors that the US patent system is as convenient for them as the Canadian patent office and that it may afford a wider degree of protection in return for similar effort and expense. Alternatively it may reflect a closeness of relationship in cultural or investment terms between Canada and the US. Mexico, another OECD\* member nation which shares a border with the US, had 31 per cent of its Small Entity patents claiming priority; higher than Canada but still much lower than the European or Asian OECD\* countries. Mexico had, of course, quite a low patent count for this period relative to its population. Apart from Canada, Israel and Norway, the countries which show a proportion of foreign priority lower than 50 per cent in Table 2.1 are countries with a negligible SE patent count for the period in question. Canada has already been discussed. An explanation for Israel's low priority proportion may be that Israel has a high presence of US firms and the country's economic relationship with the US is generally regarded as very strong. The most unexpected exception is Norway, where only just over a quarter of the 657 SE patents had priority dates, meaning that almost three quarters of Norway's SE inventors went directly to the USPTO to file. It is not immediately apparent why such a large proportion of Norwegian SE patent applicants should disregard the benefits of the grace period provided by the Paris Convention. Along with Switzerland and Iceland, Norway is one of the three Western European nations not currently members of the EU (Norwegians having twice voted against joining, in referenda in 1972 and 1994) but, other than suggesting an innate reluctance to deal with European institutions like the EPO, this does not go very far towards an explanation.

For non-US residents, patent filings in the USPTO should represent the inventions for which they have the highest hopes. And that part which is Small Entity data represents the portion owned by nonprofit organisations (such as universities), firms with less than 500 employees, and individual inventors. But how large a portion do Small Entity patents represent of any nation's total USPTO patents? The distinction between the total patent count for any OECD* country and the proportion which is granted to inventors claiming Small Entity status is of great interest. As shown in Table 2.3, residents of the United States, between 1994 and 2003, the ten years of this study, were granted 746,359 Utility patents.[2] Out of this total 271,785, or 36.4 per cent, claimed Small Entity status. In the same period Japanese inventors were granted 287,219 USPTO patents of which a tiny 4.4 per cent claimed Small Entity status, by far the lowest proportion in the list. This leads to the conclusion that the great majority of the USPTO patents granted to Japanese inventors in the period were assigned to large corporate firms. To pursue this question for a moment, Table 2.4 shows that over half of the share of all Japanese Utility patents granted between 1994 and 2000 by the USPTO, Small Entity or otherwise, was accounted for by only 30 firms. The names are displayed as they appear in the 'Assignee' field of the USPTO records. In reality, Fuji Xerox is a consolidated subsidiary of Fuji Photo Film Co. which also appears in the list, and two other firms, Konica and Minolta, agreed to merge in January 2003. Although Japanese conglomerates have been perceived as strongly national in character, some evidence of internationalisation is provided by French car manufacturer Renault's acquisition of substantial equity in Nissan Motor in 1999. The large numbers of patents acquired by Japan's multinational firms puts the country's 4.4% proportion of Small Entity patents in context. In fact the actual count of Japanese Small Entity patents for the ten years, at 12,647, is higher than Germany's, the largest of the European nations. As might be expected, Japan's massive share of the global corporate firms, allied to an aggressive corporate

*Table 2.3  OECD\*; Small Entity patents as a proportion of all USPTO Utility patents, 1994 to 2003*

| Country | EU | OECD | All US patents | Small Entity | SE % |
|---|---|---|---|---|---|
| Slovakia | Y | Y | 30 | 18 | 60.0% |
| Greece | Y | Y | 178 | 106 | 59.6% |
| Portugal | Y | Y | 82 | 47 | 57.3% |
| Canada | N | Y | 28,805 | 15,196 | 52.8% |
| Israel | N | N | 7235 | 3791 | 52.4% |
| New Zealand | N | Y | 952 | 472 | 49.6% |
| Australia | N | Y | 6,641 | 3,262 | 49.1% |
| Mexico | N | Y | 636 | 311 | 48.9% |
| Spain | Y | Y | 2,244 | 1049 | 46.8% |
| Iceland | N | Y | 96 | 39 | 40.6% |
| Poland | Y | Y | 133 | 52 | 39.1% |
| US | N | Y | 746,359 | 271,785 | 36.4% |
| Italy | Y | Y | 14,704 | 4,926 | 33.5% |
| Norway | N | Y | 1,976 | 657 | 33.3% |
| Ireland | Y | Y | 984 | 305 | 31.0% |
| Turkey | N | Y | 75 | 23 | 30.7% |
| Czech Republic | Y | Y | 166 | 47 | 28.3% |
| Hungary | Y | Y | 469 | 129 | 27.5% |
| Austria | Y | Y | 4,446 | 1168 | 26.3% |
| Switzerland | N | Y | 12,399 | 2,539 | 20.5% |
| Sweden | Y | Y | 12,373 | 2,370 | 19.2% |
| UK | Y | Y | 31,975 | 6,098 | 19.1% |
| Denmark | Y | Y | 3,729 | 711 | 19.1% |
| Finland | Y | Y | 5,834 | 919 | 15.8% |
| Korea | N | Y | 26,891 | 3,864 | 14.4% |
| Germany | Y | Y | 89,807 | 11,880 | 13.2% |
| Netherlands | Y | Y | 11,018 | 1,447 | 13.1% |
| Belgium | Y | Y | 5,849 | 629 | 10.8% |
| France | Y | Y | 34,604 | 3,623 | 10.5% |
| Luxembourg | Y | Y | 273 | 26 | 9.5% |
| Japan | N | Y | 287,219 | 12,647 | 4.4% |
| OECD\* | | | 1,338,182 | 350,136 | 26.2% |
| OECD\* (excl. US) | | | 591,823 | 78,351 | 13.2% |

policy of patent portfolio building by those firms, has greatly reduced its proportion of Small Entity patents.[3] In fact we should expect that any country which is a base for large multinational corporations (MNCs) would have a lower proportion of SE patents than a country without such MNC activity. This is supported to some extent by Table 2.3 which shows that, in general, the smaller or less developed nations had the highest proportion of SE patents, while we see the large European industrial nations of Germany, France, the Netherlands and the UK with Small Entity proportions under 20 per cent.

The less developed countries, or those lacking MNC presence, display a higher proportion of Small Entity patents, which is in contrast to the US itself. We would expect US Small Entity inventors to represent a substantial proportion of all US patents, since the USPTO is the 'domestic' patent office for US inventors and this would offset the major presence of multi-national companies there. Year by year, Small Entity patents represent around one third of the total for Utility patents in the US. Canada is high on the list because, as suggested earlier, Canadian SE applicants behave like US ones. Naturally we would expect a lower proportion of SE patent applications from outside the US and Canada. In fact the proportion of SE patents for the entire OECD* group, when the US is omitted, is only 13.2 per cent. Among these countries the proportion fluctuates widely, from the Japanese low of 4.4% to the Slovakian high (admittedly on the basis of only 30 patents) of 60%. The pattern of invention indicated by this variation, from country to country within the OECD*, is of interest. It seems reasonable to expect that, in Germany, large corporate entities like Siemens and Bayer would raise the level of non-SE patenting activity; and the list of large Japanese MNCs (Table 2.4) explains that country's very small SE proportion. The total OECD* count for all USPTO patents, SE and non SE, between 1994 and 2003 was 1,338,182, with the US on its own accounting for 746,359 or about 56 per cent.

In order to make useful comparisons between the OECD* countries, in the analysis which follows they have been placed in one of two major groupings. The most obvious international grouping would be of the seven countries which comprise the group known to economists as G7: Canada, France, Germany, Italy, Japan, the UK and the US. This has been designated Group A in the analysis which follows (see Table 2.5).

The second group selected, Group B, consists of 14 countries: Australia, Austria, Belgium, Denmark, Finland, Israel (the only non-OECD country included), Ireland, Korea, the Netherlands, New Zealand, Norway, Spain, Sweden and Switzerland (Table 2.6). Israel has been included in the analysis because its share of USPTO Small Entity patents makes it impossible to ignore; Israel is close in size and general economy to a number of OECD countries (in Group B) but Israel's inventors have acquired, as we shall see, considerably more Small Entity patents, making their country an important point of comparison in

*Table 2.4 Japan; Top 30 firms; USPTO Utility patent counts, 1994 to 2000*

| Rank | Company | Count | % of Japanese USPTO patents | Cumulative Japanese % |
|------|---------|-------|------------------------------|------------------------|
| 1 | Canon | 11,015 | 5.7% | 5.7% |
| 2 | NEC | 9,584 | 5.0% | 10.7% |
| 3 | Toshiba | 7,474 | 3.9% | 14.6% |
| 4 | Sony | 7,394 | 3.9% | 18.5% |
| 5 | Mitsubishi | 6,991 | 3.6% | 22.1% |
| 6 | Hitachi | 6,918 | 3.6% | 25.7% |
| 7 | Matsushita | 6,704 | 3.5% | 29.2% |
| 8 | Fujitsu Ltd | 6,522 | 3.4% | 32.6% |
| 9 | Fuji Photo Film Co | 3,754 | 2.0% | 34.5% |
| 10 | Sharp | 3,366 | 1.8% | 36.3% |
| 11 | Honda | 2,488 | 1.3% | 39.2% |
| 12 | Nikon | 2,475 | 1.3% | 40.4% |
| 13 | Ricoh | 2,329 | 1.2% | 41.7% |
| 14 | Toyota | 1,789 | 0.9% | 42.6% |
| 15 | Olympus Optical | 1,684 | 0.9% | 43.5% |
| 16 | Seiko Epson | 1,670 | 0.9% | 44.3% |
| 17 | Minolta | 1,620 | 0.8% | 45.2% |
| 18 | Asahi Kogaku | 1,561 | 0.8% | 46.0% |
| 19 | Yazaki | 1,483 | 0.8% | 46.8% |
| 20 | Fuji Xerox | 1,446 | 0.8% | 47.5% |
| 21 | Nippondenso | 1,409 | 0.7% | 48.2% |
| 22 | Sanyo Electric | 1,355 | 0.7% | 49.0% |
| 23 | Murata | 1,309 | 0.7% | 49.6% |
| 24 | Sumitomo Electric | 1,301 | 0.7% | 50.3% |
| 25 | Brother | 1,284 | 0.7% | 51.0% |
| 26 | Konica | 1,191 | 0.6% | 51.6% |
| 27 | Yamaha | 1,153 | 0.6% | 52.2% |
| 28 | Nissan Motor | 1,122 | 0.6% | 52.8% |
| 29 | Sumitomo Chemical | 988 | 0.5% | 53.3% |
| 30 | Pioneer Electronic | 946 | 0.5% | 53.8% |

every category. Equally, although it is not an OECD member nation, Israel has a strong relationship with the US and good trading relationships with a number of European OECD countries. Using data from the year 2000, the countries with the smallest populations in Group B are Ireland and New Zealand with just under four million; Korea has the largest population with just over 47 million people. GDP per capita for Group B countries in 2000 ranged between Korea's $15,220 and Norway's $35,130. There is therefore quite a large degree of variation in the basic statistics for this group but, as will be shown, the corresponding variation in terms of Small Entity patents acquired is either more moderate or, on occasions, actually runs counter to what the economic statistics might lead us to expect.

*Table 2.5  Group A, with GDP per capita and population (year 2000)*

| Country | GDP per capita ($) | Population (m) |
| --- | --- | --- |
| Canada | 27,750 | 31.4 |
| France | 25,320 | 59.7 |
| Germany | 26,070 | 82 |
| Italy | 24,940 | 57.4 |
| Japan | 25,980 | 128 |
| UK | 24,690 | 58.8 |
| US | 34,160 | 289 |

*Table 2.6  Group B, with GDP per capita and population (year 2000)*

| Country | GDP per capita ($) | Population (m) |
| --- | --- | --- |
| Australia | 26,180 | 19.7 |
| Austria | 28,010 | 8.1 |
| Belgium | 26,430 | 10.3 |
| Denmark | 29,310 | 5.4 |
| Finland | 25,150 | 5.2 |
| Ireland | 30,100 | 3.9 |
| Israel | 20,600 | 6.6 |
| Korea, Rep. | 15,220 | 47.4 |
| Netherlands | 27,070 | 16.2 |
| New Zealand | 20,150 | 4 |
| Norway | 35,130 | 4.5 |
| Spain | 19,960 | 39.9 |
| Sweden | 24,530 | 8.8 |
| Switzerland | 28,130 | 7.2 |

There is a third group of OECD* countries, referred to as Group C, where the patent counts are negligible and which have not been included in the major lines of analysis throughout. This group comprises the Czech Republic,

Greece, Hungary, Iceland, Luxembourg, Mexico, Poland, Portugal, Slovakia, and Turkey. The non-OECD\* countries, dealt with in Chapter 6, are divided into two further groups. Group D consists of 32 countries and includes Taiwan, whose residents were granted more Small Entity patents than any other country other than the US itself, while Group E embraces the remaining 71 non OECD\* countries with SE patents counts largely in single figures. The reality highlighted by this study is that outside the Group A and Group B nations listed above, and with the singular exception of Taiwan in Group D, Small Entity patenting activity is at minimal levels.

Figure 2.1 displays the Small Entity patent count per million for the seven Group A countries, using the total counts for the ten years of the study. Omitting the US leaves us with an average for the other six countries combined of 130 patents per million. This figure throws into relief the high level of Canadian inventors' usage of Small Entity patents which, at 484 per million, is well over half the US figure; and confirms the manner in which Canadian inventors treat the USPTO as a 'local' office. Apart from Canada, the other country which exceeds the Group A average is Germany. By contrast the French figure of 61 SE patents per million is particularly low and deserves some explanation. It is either the case that, compared to other Group A countries, a much lower proportion of French inventors qualify for SE status, or else the qualifying proportion is similar but French inventors neglect to claim it. In the first case it would mean that France has a lower proportion of Individual inventors, Small Firm inventors or Nonprofits with globally marketable inventions than comparable countries. In the second case it might mean that

*Figure 2.1  Group A; SE patents per million population, 1994 to 2003*

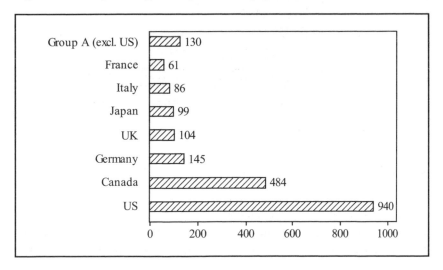

French small entities have particular reasons for not claiming SE status on the majority of their applications to the USPTO.

Figure 2.2, showing the Group B data, indicates the extent to which Israel surpasses comparable countries (in size and population) in its acquisition of SE patents. The remarkable disparity in the group is exemplified by the difference between the Spanish per million figure of 26 and Israel's figure of 574, a ratio of 23:1, that is, in relation to population, Israel's Small Entities were granted 22 times as many USPTO patents as their Spanish counterparts.

*Figure 2.2    Group B, SE patents per million population, 1994 to 2003*

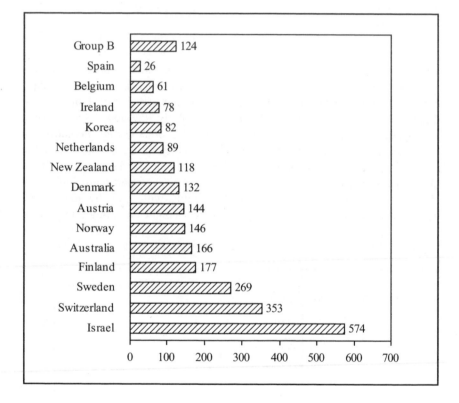

# CITATION OF SMALL ENTITY PATENTS

Given the very high per million figures for Canada in Group A and Israel, Switzerland and Sweden in Group B, it would be of interest to see whether the data for patent citations suggest any degree of variation in patent quality between these countries. It is an obvious question whether countries with fewer Small Entity patents are likely to have patents of a higher quality. If this is the case we might expect to see these countries with low patent counts have a higher rate of citation of patents. Table 2.7 shows that the proportion of Small Entity patents cited varies across the group from 51 per cent for Italy to 62.5 per cent for the US. The group average when the US is excluded from the data is 56 per cent. The average for Group B (Table 2.8) is 50.5 per cent and the lowest proportion here is Korea's 44 per cent.

*Table 2.7   Group A; SE patents cited at least once, 1994 to 2002*

| Country | Not cited | Cited>=1 | % cited | Total |
|---------|-----------|----------|---------|-------|
| Canada | 5,657 | 8,084 | 58.8% | 13,741 |
| Germany | 4,694 | 6,030 | 56.2% | 10,724 |
| Japan | 5,072 | 6,255 | 55.2% | 11,327 |
| France | 1,478 | 1,796 | 54.9% | 3,274 |
| UK | 2,589 | 2,838 | 52.3% | 5,427 |
| Italy | 2,145 | 2,267 | 51.4% | 4,412 |
| Group A (US excl.) | 21,635 | 27,270 | 55.8% | 48,905 |
| US | 91,800 | 153,143 | 62.5% | 244,943 |
| Group A | 113,435 | 180,413 | 61.4% | 293,848 |

*Table 2.8   Group B; SE patents cited at least once, 1994 to 2002*

| Country | Not cited | Cited>=1 | % cited | Total |
|---------|-----------|----------|---------|-------|
| Switzerland | 978 | 1,351 | 58.0% | 2,329 |
| Australia | 1,336 | 1,549 | 53.7% | 2,885 |
| Israel | 1,533 | 1,744 | 53.2% | 3,277 |
| Netherlands | 630 | 706 | 52.8% | 1,336 |
| Finland | 395 | 442 | 52.8% | 837 |
| Denmark | 313 | 318 | 50.4% | 631 |
| Ireland | 136 | 137 | 50.2% | 273 |
| Belgium | 290 | 285 | 49.6% | 575 |
| Austria | 532 | 510 | 48.9% | 1,042 |
| New Zealand | 218 | 203 | 48.2% | 421 |
| Spain | 510 | 436 | 46.1% | 946 |
| Sweden | 1,143 | 971 | 45.9% | 2,114 |
| Norway | 315 | 262 | 45.4% | 577 |
| Korea | 1,753 | 1,392 | 44.3% | 3,145 |
| Group B | 10,082 | 10,306 | 50.5% | 20,388 |

If these figures suggest anything, it is that the countries with higher SE patent counts are also those with the higher proportion of cited patents. One further refinement is important. On detailed examination a small proportion of the citations of SE patents turn out to be self-referential – the patent applicant is citing one or two of his own prior patents. Since by far the majority of patents include only a single self reference, or occasionally two, it is useful to see the tables revised to give the proportions of patents which have been cited a minimum of three times.[4] Table 2.9 and Table 2.10 show this information for the relevant Country Groups. It is notable that, while all percentages are lower when compared to those cited once or more, the rank order is largely unaltered. Perhaps the most dramatic change in ranking is Finland's in Group B, where 53 per cent of the SE patents were cited once and 18 per cent were cited three times or more, representing a fall from fifth to eleventh position.

*Table 2.9   Group A; SE patents cited at least three times, 1994 to 2002*

| Country | Cited < 3 | Cited >= 3 | % cited | Total |
|---|---|---|---|---|
| Canada | 9,677 | 4,064 | 29.6% | 13,741 |
| Japan | 8,430 | 2,897 | 25.6% | 11,327 |
| Germany | 7,990 | 2,734 | 25.5% | 10,724 |
| France | 2,442 | 832 | 25.4% | 3,274 |
| UK | 4,110 | 1,317 | 24.3% | 5,427 |
| Italy | 3,473 | 939 | 21.3% | 4,412 |
| Group A (US excl.) | 36,122 | 12,783 | 26.1% | 48,905 |
| US | 161,110 | 83,833 | 34.2% | 244,943 |
| Group A | 197,232 | 96,616 | 32.9% | 293,848 |

However, while the citation count may be a valuable indicator of patent quality, such counts may also be affected by other factors, such as a greater propensity to cite prior patents evident in some countries more than others. This may be attributable to patent agent practices or influenced by the scale of resources available to the patent applicant for researching and preparing the application. Equally the preponderant type of technology may be a factor, in so far as patent applicants from some areas of technology may tend to cite prior patents more assiduously than others. To complete this analysis the Small Entity patents were grouped under technology headings of Chemical, Electrical and Mechanical; the basis for this division is fully explained in the section following this one. From Table 2.11 it can be seen that, among the OECD* countries in general, there is a considerably greater likelihood (41 per cent) of an Electrical class SE patent being cited three times or more than a Chemical class patent (27 per cent).

*Table 2.10    Group B; SE patents cited at least three times, 1994 to 2002*

| Country | Cited < 3 | Cited >= 3 | % cited | Total |
|---|---|---|---|---|
| Israel | 2,396 | 881 | 26.9% | 3,277 |
| Switzerland | 1,734 | 595 | 25.5% | 2,329 |
| Australia | 2,153 | 732 | 25.4% | 2,885 |
| Netherlands | 1,006 | 330 | 24.7% | 1,336 |
| Ireland | 211 | 62 | 22.7% | 273 |
| Belgium | 446 | 129 | 22.4% | 575 |
| Austria | 827 | 215 | 20.6% | 1,042 |
| Denmark | 502 | 129 | 20.4% | 631 |
| New Zealand | 341 | 80 | 19.0% | 421 |
| Sweden | 1,716 | 398 | 18.8% | 2,114 |
| Finland | 684 | 153 | 18.3% | 837 |
| Korea | 2,572 | 573 | 18.2% | 3,145 |
| Spain | 776 | 170 | 18.0% | 946 |
| Norway | 475 | 102 | 17.7% | 577 |
| Group B | 15,839 | 4,549 | 22.3% | 20,388 |

*Table 2.11    OECD\*; Proportions of each Technology Class group cited three times or more, 1994 to 2002*

| Technology Class | Cited <3 | Cited >=3 | % cited | Total |
|---|---|---|---|---|
| Electrical | 32,019 | 22,284 | 41.0% | 54,303 |
| Mechanical | 132,174 | 60,885 | 31.5% | 193,059 |
| Chemical | 49,450 | 18,114 | 26.8% | 67,564 |
| OECD* | 213,643 | 101,283 | 32.2% | 314,926† |

† Over the ten years covered by the Small Entity database 24 patents, including 21 US patents, are missing a primary class number. The omission of these from any analysis of the Technology Class groups accounts for a very slight difference in totals.

Table 2.12 and Table 2.13 give the data for the US on its own and for Group A countries without the US. In both cases, although the US has a considerably higher proportion of citations than the other OECD* countries in Group A, the relative distribution between the three Technology Class groups remains the same. Table 2.14 shows that this distribution is preserved in the Group B data where Electrical class patents attracted over 50 per cent more citations than the Chemical class patents. We are left with the question whether the Electrical class SE patents are this much more valuable than Chemical ones. Since the Electrical patent classes include many of the 'high technology' classes, it is possible that the higher level of citations reflects an intensity of interest in high tech patents in an increasingly technology-centred world. High technology research topics attract attention.

The frequency of citation of an academic's work has been long accepted as a measure of the value of his contribution. However, some studies of the relationship between citations of articles from academic journals and the perceived quality of the research introduce an element of doubt. Researchers in one study on Psychology citations noted that 'only one-sixth of the total variance in predicting enduring worth was accounted for by citations' while going on to conclude that 'citations-by-others and research quality, at least when quality is measured in terms of enduring worth, are hardly interchangeable concepts.'[5] If it is possible for academics to be 'famous for being famous' perhaps a similar effect is at work with patents.

*Table 2.12   US; Proportions of each Technology Class group cited three times or more, 1994 to 2002*

| Technology Class | Cited <3 | Cited >=3 | % cited | Total |
|---|---|---|---|---|
| Electrical | 24,590 | 19,086 | 43.7% | 43,676 |
| Mechanical | 99,951 | 49,880 | 33.3% | 149,831 |
| Chemical | 36,560 | 14,866 | 28.9% | 51,426 |
| US | 161,101 | 83,832 | 34.2% | 244,933 |

*Table 2.13   Group A (US excl.); Proportions of each Technology Class group cited three times or more, 1994 to 2002*

| Technology Class | Cited <3 | Cited >=3 | % cited | Total |
|---|---|---|---|---|
| Electrical | 4,945 | 2,266 | 31.4% | 7,211 |
| Mechanical | 22,564 | 8,175 | 26.6% | 30,739 |
| Chemical | 8,613 | 2,342 | 21.4% | 10,955 |
| Group A (US excl.) | 36,122 | 12,783 | 26.1% | 48,905 |

*Table 2.14   Group B; Proportions of each Technology Class group cited three times or more, 1994 to 2002*

| Technology Class | Cited <3 | Cited >=3 | % cited | Total |
|---|---|---|---|---|
| Electrical | 2,419 | 920 | 27.6% | 3,339 |
| Mechanical | 9,334 | 2,760 | 22.8% | 12,094 |
| Chemical | 4,085 | 869 | 17.5% | 4,954 |
| Group B | 15,838 | 4,549 | 22.3% | 20,387 |

It is notable that, in every table, the Chemical class patents showed the lowest proportion of citations. One explanation for this may be that the Chemical class patents include patents for drugs which are subject to tight regulation and clinical testing programs which prevent their immediate introduction to the marketplace. This, in turn, is likely to produce an additional lag period between publication of the actual patent and its citation in following patents. We might expect, therefore, a lower proportion of citations for Chemical class patents within the nine year period examined. For exactly the same reason we should expect, when looking at the rate of maintenance, to see Chemical class patents better maintained in the early stages. A drug undergoing clinical trials will certainly have its patent maintenance fees paid at the four year renewal stage. The subject of patent maintenance is dealt with later in this chapter.

Not all of the Chemical class patents are patents for drug treatments, affected by the US Food and Drug Administration controls. This is likely to be even more true of Small Entity patents than for other kinds, since the resources available to small entities for development and prolonged testing of such treatments must present a barrier. In a random sample of 93 Small Entity Chemical patents taken from the nine years 1994 to 2002 (the years covered by the Small Entity citations data in the database) only about 15 per cent of the inventions appeared to have subject matter involving drug treatments.[6]

## TECHNOLOGY CLASS GROUPS

Technology Class groups were introduced in the previous section. They may be explained as follows: The USPTO attempts to define the nature of each invention described in a patent by assigning it to at least one 'class' of technology. Patent examiners must choose from over 400 major class numbers and many thousands of subclasses. The patent class numbering system is, therefore, a complex one and the assignment of inventions may be extremely difficult. A single invention, particularly if it spans a variety of technologies, may justifiably be assigned to a number of classes. Regardless of how many class numbers may apply, however, the examiner must determine a single major class number as the predominant one for each invention. These major class numbers have been grouped, by the USPTO and other agencies, to form Technology Class groups.[7] The Technology Class groups used in this study are those used by the USPTO in its own analysis. The full list of the USPTO class numbers and their corresponding Technology Class group, Chemical, Electrical or Mechanical, are provided in Appendix B. The advantage of using the Technology Class groups defined in this way is that they provide a useful, if broad, profile of invention for each of the countries and groups included in the study.

The previous section examined the distribution of citations for the different types of Technology Class. It is necessary to look at the distribution of these Technology Classes for each Country Group. Figure 2.3 gives the distribution for Country Group A including the US data and Figure 2.4 the distribution with the US data excluded. The proportions hardly vary, even when the dominating US data are set aside. The picture changes very little when we look at the Group B distribution shown in Figure 2.5; the proportion for Chemical class patents has slightly increased. No dramatic variation is observed and it appears the main areas of SE invention are relatively stable from group to group.

*Figure 2.3    Group A; SE patents, distribution of Technology Class groups, 1994 to 2003*

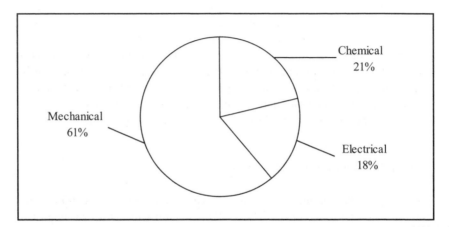

*Figure 2.4    Group A (excl. US); SE patents; distribution of Technology Class groups, 1994 to 2003*

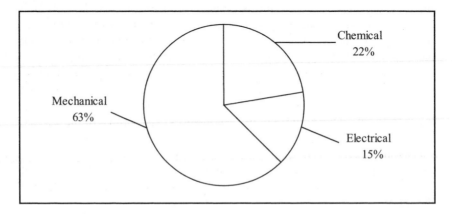

*Figure 2.5   Group B; SE patents, distribution of Technology Class groups*

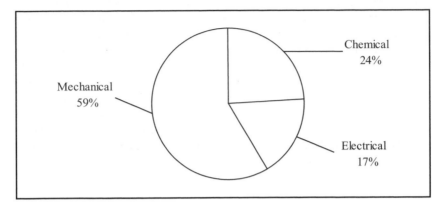

Given that there appears to be little difference in Technology Classes between our Country Groups, we can examine whether there is any large variation within the groups, from country to country. Figure 2.6 displays the profile of Technology Class distribution for Group A.

*Figure 2.6   Group A; Technology Class profile, 1994 to 2003*

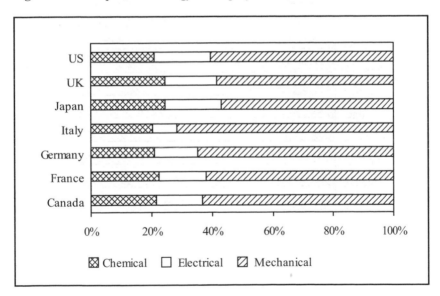

These figures suggest a reasonable degree of conformity within the group. The proportion of Chemical class patents varies a little between 20 and 25

per cent. The greatest variation between Group A countries occurs in the
Electrical and Mechanical categories. Eight per cent of Italy's SE patents were
in the Electrical classes against 72 per cent in the Mechanical classes; the
corresponding figures for Japan were 18 per cent Electrical and 58 per cent
Mechanical. The Technology Class profile for Group B (Figure 2.7) displays
far greater variation. The percentages for Group B are shown in Table 2.15. In
the Chemical classes we see a variation between Belgium's 37.2 per cent and
Ireland's 17.4 per cent. Almost 30 per cent of Israel's SE patents were in the
Electrical classes against 9 per cent of Austria's. Korea and Ireland were the
other two countries with a proportion of Electrical class patents greater than 20
per cent. In the Mechanical classes the proportion varies between a high of 71
per cent for Austria and Norway to a low of 43 per cent for Korea.

*Figure 2.7    Group B; Technology Class profile, 1994 to 2003*

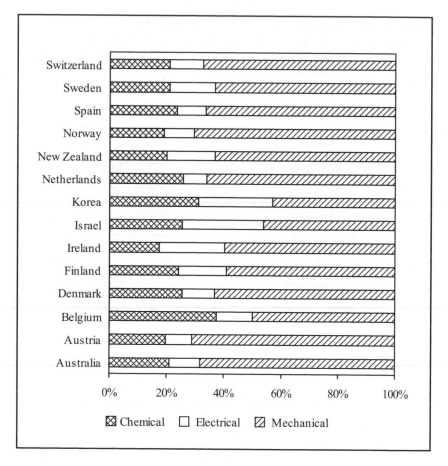

*Table 2.15   Group B; Technology Class data by country, 1994 to 2003*

| Country | Chemical | Electrical | Mechanical | Total |
|---|---|---|---|---|
| Australia | 20.8% | 10.9% | 68.2% | 3,262 |
| Austria | 19.8% | 9.1% | 71.1% | 1,168 |
| Belgium | 37.2% | 12.7% | 50.1% | 629 |
| Denmark | 25.2% | 11.5% | 63.3% | 711 |
| Finland | 24.0% | 16.8% | 59.2% | 919 |
| Ireland | 17.4% | 23.0% | 59.7% | 305 |
| Israel | 25.4% | 28.4% | 46.2% | 3,791 |
| Korea | 30.9% | 26.0% | 43.2% | 3,864 |
| Netherlands | 25.5% | 8.4% | 66.1% | 1,447 |
| New Zealand | 19.9% | 16.7% | 63.3% | 472 |
| Norway | 18.9% | 10.7% | 70.5% | 657 |
| Spain | 23.3% | 10.3% | 66.4% | 1,049 |
| Sweden | 20.8% | 15.8% | 63.4% | 2,370 |
| Switzerland | 20.8% | 11.7% | 67.5% | 2,539 |
| Total | 24.2% | 17.2% | 58.7% | 23,183 |

## SMALL ENTITY PATENT DECAY

A further filter for patent quality, as outlined in the Introduction, is the proportion of Small Entity patents which were allowed to lapse by the inventors or assignees at the various renewal stages. In this study the data were available in full for the first renewal stage, at four years, for those patents which were issued between 1994 and 1998 and for the second renewal stage, at eight years, for patents issued in 1994. A patent which was granted in December 1998 would require the payment of maintenance fees by the same date in December 2002. However, there are a number of reasons why the USPTO might not 'drop the axe' immediately, and all patent holders have an opportunity to seek reinstatement of their patent.[8] Therefore, the latest data in this study, from 2003, only permit a proper analysis of patents which lapsed up to the end of the year 1998.

When we look at the data for Small Entity patents which lapsed at the first (fourth year) renewal milestone, we find the proportion of lapsed patents for all countries in Group A, when the US is excluded, was 22.4 per cent (Table 2.16). The US figure was a little above that at 24.4 per cent. We might have expected the US proportion to be higher than the group's. Since the USPTO is the 'domestic' patent office for US residents, the filtering effect for non-US residents is not present and thus SE patents originating with US inventors ought to show a higher proportion lapsing at the maintenance milestones. As Table 2.16 shows, however, France had a similar proportion of lapsed patents as the US, and proportions for the UK and Canada were higher. The Japanese proportion was considerably below the average. The average for the Group B countries was 22.8 per cent (Table 2.17).

*Table 2.16   Group A; SE patents lapsing at the 4 year renewal stage*

| Country | Count (94 to 98) | Lapsed at 4 yrs | % Lapsed |
|---|---|---|---|
| Canada | 6,878 | 1,813 | 26.4% |
| UK | 2,515 | 631 | 25.1% |
| France | 1,731 | 401 | 23.2% |
| Germany | 5,213 | 1,175 | 22.5% |
| Italy | 2,276 | 495 | 21.7% |
| Japan | 5,593 | 898 | 16.1% |
| All (excl. US) | 24,206 | 5,413 | 22.4% |
| US | 124,044 | 30,239 | 24.4% |
| All | 148,250 | 35,652 | 24.0% |

*Table 2.17   Group B; SE patents lapsing at the 4 year renewal stage*

| Country | Count (94 to 98) | Lapsed at 4 yrs | % Lapsed |
|---|---|---|---|
| New Zealand | 180 | 49 | 27.2% |
| Spain | 478 | 130 | 27.2% |
| Ireland | 108 | 29 | 26.9% |
| Israel | 1,381 | 360 | 26.1% |
| Australia | 1,389 | 346 | 24.9% |
| Denmark | 310 | 75 | 24.2% |
| Austria | 477 | 109 | 22.9% |
| Switzerland | 1,266 | 279 | 22.0% |
| Korea | 1,082 | 234 | 21.6% |
| Norway | 263 | 56 | 21.3% |
| Netherlands | 654 | 137 | 20.9% |
| Belgium | 265 | 52 | 19.6% |
| Finland | 435 | 84 | 19.3% |
| Sweden | 922 | 160 | 17.4% |
| All | 9,210 | 2,100 | 22.8% |

New Zealand and Spain had the highest rate of lapsed SE patents with 27.2 per cent apiece, while the other southern hemisphere country, Australia, was well above the group average. Notably, in both groups of countries, the Asian members, Japan and Korea, had low proportions of lapsed SE patents. Also of note in Group B is the fact that the Scandinavian countries of Norway, Finland and Sweden are all below the group average with Finland and Sweden showing the lowest rate of lapsed SE patents.

The Canadian proportion of lapsed patents is sufficiently high to warrant a more detailed look at Canadian SE patents. In Table 2.18 we see that the rate of lapsed patents is largely due to the sizeable proportion of Individual inventors. This tends to support the idea that Individual inventors may be less likely to exhibit cold rationality in respect of their initial IP investment than a firm with shareholders and financial controls in place, or than a research institution with similar controls, a limited budget and a variety of investment opportunities to select from. Secondly, the high proportion of Individual inventors (well over half the Canadian total for these five years) lends credence to the idea that Canadian inventors have been treating the USPTO almost as a 'domestic' patent office.

*Table 2.18    Canada; SE patents lapsing at the first (4 year) renewal stage, 1994 to 1998*

| SE Type | Count (94 to 98) | Lapsed at 4 yrs | % Lapsed |
|---------|------------------|-----------------|----------|
| Individual | 3,735 | 1,248 | 33.4% |
| Small Firm | 2,689 | 490 | 18.2% |
| Nonprofit | 454 | 75 | 16.5% |

For a more complete picture of the rate of Small Entity patent decay it is necessary to examine the proportions of each of the Technology Class groups which are being allowed to lapse after four years. Table 2.19 makes it clear that the Chemical class patents were better maintained than either of the other two Technology Class groups; the proportion of lapsed patents in the Mechanical class group was almost twice that of the Chemical classes. A partial explanation for the lower rate of decay among Chemical class patents was suggested earlier in this chapter; it concerned the time lag, due to regulations, between the granting of a patent and its exploitation in the marketplace. In summary, the Chemical class Small Entity patents attracted the lowest proportion of citations and the lowest rate of decay among the OECD\* countries.

The Technology Class figures for the Group A countries, when the US data are excluded, show a slightly more even rate of decay, though Chemical class patents were still considerably more likely to be maintained. Finally, Table 2.21 reveals that the Country Group with the highest rate of patent decay, near 30 per cent, is Group C, containing those ten countries in the study with minimal patent counts. The rate for US inventors is well under that at 24.4 per cent. Bearing in mind that the measurement only applies to the first five years of the study, 1994 to 1998, this means that approaching one quarter of those patents originating with US inventors were not maintained beyond the first renewal stage. The other six Group A countries had the best rate of maintenance: 77.6 per cent were in force following the first renewal date.

*Table 2.19    OECD\*; Proportion of each Technology Class group lapsing at the first (4 year) renewal stage, 1994 to 1998*

| Technology Class | Count (94 to 98) | Lapse at 4 yrs | % Lapsed |
|---|---|---|---|
| Mechanical | 100,432 | 27,970 | 27.8% |
| Electrical | 25,377 | 4,930 | 19.4% |
| Chemical | 31,964 | 4,946 | 15.5% |
| Total | 157,775 | 37,846 | 24.0% |

*Table 2.20    Group A (US excl.); Proportion of each Technology Class group lapsing at the first (4 year) renewal stage, 1994 to 1998*

| Technology Class | Count (94 to 98) | Lapse at 4 yrs | % Lapsed |
|---|---|---|---|
| Mechanical | 15,688 | 3,889 | 24.8% |
| Electrical | 3,427 | 643 | 18.8% |
| Chemical | 5,091 | 881 | 17.3% |
| Group A (excl. US) | 24,206 | 5,413 | 22.4% |

*Table 2.21    OECD\*; Proportion of each Country Group lapsing at the first (4 year) renewal stage, 1994 to 1998*

| Country/Group | Count (94 to 98) | Lapse at 4 yrs | % Lapsed |
|---|---|---|---|
| Group C | 315 | 94 | 29.8% |
| US alone | 124,044 | 30,239 | 24.4% |
| Group B | 9,210 | 2,100 | 22.8% |
| Group A (excl. US) | 24,206 | 5,413 | 22.4% |

Unfortunately there are insufficient data available in the study to examine the rate of patents lapsing at the second (eight year) renewal stage. Because of the length of the span, it is only possible to do this safely for the first year, 1994, and this year may be exceptional. Nevertheless, it is instructive to see from Table 2.22 that over half of all the OECD* Small Entity patents acquired in 1994 had expired by December 2003 due to the patent owners' failure to pay the stipulated maintenance fees. Again we can observe that the rate of decay among the Mechanical class patents is substantially the highest of the three Technology Class groups.

*Table 2.22   OECD\*; Proportion of each Technology Class group lapsing at the second (8 year) renewal stage, 1994 only*

| Technology Class | 1994 count | Lapsed by 8 yrs | % Lapsed |
| --- | --- | --- | --- |
| Mechanical | 19,151 | 10,456 | 54.6% |
| Electrical | 4,020 | 1,789 | 44.5% |
| Chemical | 4,737 | 1,920 | 40.5% |
| OECD\* | 27,908 | 14,165 | 50.8% |

## SMALL ENTITY PATENT OWNERSHIP BY US ENTITIES

The Patents BIB database provides information on whether or not assignees (as opposed to inventors) of patents are US residents. On the face of it, our matching of this information with the Small Entity data should provide some indication of the extent to which inventive capacity in other countries is being exploited in the United States rather than in the inventor's own country – an aspect of what might represent a kind of 'brain drain'.

It does do this, but the results have to be treated with caution. This is not only because the number of instances for any country is small, but also because of the fuzziness of the distinctions between the three Small Entity categories, referred to in Chapter 1. Individual inventors may have their inventions assigned to a Company for tax or other purposes, and vice versa. It is also possible that patents which appear in the Small Firm category actually relate to inventions which were made in universities or research institutes. Still, if these reservations are borne in mind, differences between countries can be seen in the matched data (particularly for small businesses covered in Chapter 4) which do appear to be both real and interesting.

Table 2.23 and Table 2.24 show the proportion of all Small Entity patents originating in the Group A and Group B countries which were assigned to a US-owned Entity. As explained, this attribute is flagged in the USPTO database during the patent application and issuing process. Naturally, almost all of the SE patents originating with US resident inventors were assigned to US entities. The proportions for the other countries are probably as we should expect. In Group A the highest proportion outside the US was the United Kingdom's 7.4 per cent, which approaches twice the group average (when the US is omitted) and reflects the economic relationship between the two countries.

*Table 2.23   Group A; SE patents; % assigned to US entities, 1994 to 2003*

| Country | Total | US owned | % US owned |
|---|---|---|---|
| UK | 6,098 | 460 | 7.5% |
| Italy | 4,926 | 223 | 4.5% |
| Canada | 15,196 | 679 | 4.5% |
| France | 3,623 | 151 | 4.2% |
| Germany | 11,880 | 385 | 3.2% |
| Japan | 12,647 | 240 | 1.9% |
| All (excl. US) | 54,370 | 2,138 | 3.9% |
| US | 271,785 | 269,986 | 99.3% |
| All | 326,155 | 272,124 | 83.4% |

*Table 2.24   Group B; SE patents; % assigned to US entities, 1994 to 2003*

| Country | Total | US owned | % US owned |
|---|---|---|---|
| Belgium | 629 | 93 | 14.8% |
| Israel | 3,791 | 391 | 10.3% |
| Netherlands | 1,447 | 90 | 6.2% |
| Sweden | 2,370 | 145 | 6.1% |
| Austria | 1,168 | 59 | 5.1% |
| Switzerland | 2,539 | 105 | 4.1% |
| Australia | 3,262 | 124 | 3.8% |
| Ireland | 305 | 10 | 3.3% |
| New Zealand | 472 | 14 | 3.0% |
| Denmark | 711 | 17 | 2.4% |
| Norway | 657 | 15 | 2.3% |
| Korea | 3,864 | 87 | 2.3% |
| Spain | 1,049 | 17 | 1.6% |
| Finland | 919 | 9 | 1.0% |
| All | 23,183 | 1,176 | 5.1% |

Predictably, the Japanese proportion is the lowest, with under 2 per cent of US assignees. Similarly Korea, the Asian country in Group B, displays a very low proportion of US assignees with just over 2 per cent.

However, the most eye-catching figure in Group B is the Belgian proportion. At almost 15 per cent this is nearly three times the average for the group. This proportion is explained to a large extent in Chapter 3 on Nonprofit patents, since a sizeable number of Belgian-originating Small Entity patents were acquired by the Ludwig Institute for Cancer Research which appears in the USPTO records as a US Entity. The proportionately high count for the Ludwig Institute has a distorting effect on the figures for Belgium (and one or two other countries where the overall SE patent count is not high). It is not present in the Israeli proportion, which is still twice the group average. Nor is it present in the Netherlands figure, where the US-assigned proportion of 6 per cent appears to be attributable to a variety of Small Firm patents. In the following three chapters we analyse the distribution of USPTO patents between the three Small Entity types. Before doing so it is useful to know what proportions of Small Entity patents were acquired by each of our three SE categories and for each of our defined Country Groups. These data are presented in Table 2.25. The proportion of Nonprofit patents is small compared to the other two SE types, but it is highest in the Group B countries. Understandably, since it is their domestic patent office, Individual inventors take the largest share of US Small Entity patents. Individual patentees also represent the major portion of the Group C patents, a fact which is probably indicative of the low level of R&D by commercial firms in those countries.

*Table 2.25    OECD\*; Distribution of Small Entity patents for each Country Group, across the three SE categories, 1994 to 2003*

| Country Group | Individual | Small Firm | Nonprofit | Total |
|---|---|---|---|---|
| Group A (US excl.) | 35.6% | 58.9% | 5.5% | 100% |
| Group B | 35.3% | 54.9% | 9.8% | 100% |
| Group C | 58.3% | 33.5% | 8.3% | 100% |
| US | 47.5% | 43.5% | 9.1% | 100% |
| All | 44.8% | 46.6% | 8.6% | 100% |

## NOTES

1. The Paris Convention for the Protection of Industrial Property was signed on 20 March 1883 and revised six times between 1900 and 1967.
2. Utility patents (as opposed to Design or Plant patents) are the focus of this study. They form the vast majority of the patent total and their subject matter is invention. Future work will examine the other forms of patent.
3. The USPTO's list of 'Top Patenting Organizations' regularly shows several Japanese MNCs in the top ten. In 2003, for example, Canon, Matsushita and Hitachi occupied 2nd, 3rd and 4th positions on this list. See: http://www.uspto.gov/web/offices/ac/ido/oeip/taf/top03cos.htm

4. As noted later (page 55), a random sample of German small firm patents provides support for the view that that the number of self referential citations rarely exceeds three.
5. Keen, B. et al. (1998) *Publication Frequency, Citation Frequency, and Quality of Counseling Psychology Research*. Annual meeting of the American Psychological Association, San Francisco.
6. See Appendix C for the full list.
7. Derwent's classification system for example.
8. For example, under certain circumstances, the Director of the United States Patent and Trademark Office may accept a delayed payment with a surcharge. In these cases the patent is treated as not having expired. There is, therefore, a time lag between the final date for payment of a maintenance fee and the actual recording of a patent as lapsed.

# 3. Nonprofit patents (including universities)

The database of USPTO small entities does not contain a field which helps us to distinguish between Small Firms and Nonprofit organisations. The identification and separation of commercial firms from assignees whose central motivation is research for educational, charitable or humanitarian purposes can only be achieved by examination of the individual records. In the process, a distinction needs to be made about the precise conditions necessary for Nonprofit status. The US Office of Management and Budget provides a working definition[1] of the term 'Nonprofit'; it bestows this status on any organisation engaged in an activity 'primarily in the public interest'.

Of course, defining what is and what is not in the public interest is frequently complex. In this analysis, we have interpreted the definition broadly to mean that a 'not for profit' or 'Nonprofit' organisation is one where the primary beneficiary of the organisation's activities is not a private shareholder; it is not organised primarily for profit. A profit-making firm is expected to act in the financial interests of its shareholders or investors; and its research and development activities, while crucial to its own innovation and whose spillovers contribute to general economic growth, are directed towards that end. It is a feature of Nonprofit organisations that any returns from inventions are, in general, recycled to further the research activities of the organisation. This distinction has become complicated by the fact that many universities have hived off their technology transfer function to profit generating entities. This has been done for a variety of reasons: to attract private investment, to increase efficiency, to move the innovation process closer to the marketplace, or to change the management perspective to one of profit-orientation. The traditional management structures of a university, focused on academic excellence and long term social commitment, may not be easily applied to a short term goal of maximising returns on the exploitation of inventions and discoveries.

In preparing this analysis the guiding principle has been, where possible, to look beyond the overt corporate structure. If a 'for profit' corporation is a wholly owned subsidiary of a Nonprofit, publicly funded entity, or if the majority of the corporation's returns appear to go to a Nonprofit entity, then it is included within the Nonprofit frame of reference. By far the majority of the Nonprofit organisations are universities. There is currently some discussion concerning the extent to which it is important that universities retain ownership and control over the intellectual property they develop and the manner in which licensing should be managed. One view is that unless public research organisations actively defend the information commons, by retaining some ownership, they may find themselves excluded from whole areas of potential research, as these become progressively the subject of 'enclosure' by private interests.[2]

There is no requirement that a Nonprofit organisation should be publicly funded. Its funds may be from any source and are, on occasions, provided by an individual benefactor, a private trust or charitable foundation. The major consideration is the long term goal of the organisation, that the work is directed towards research in the public interest.

The first thing to be understood from the data in this analysis is that the proportion of Nonprofit patents is by far the smallest of the three Small Entity categories; it represents a mere 8.6 per cent of the Small Entity patents for the Group A and B countries, as shown in Table 3.1.

*Table 3.1   Groups A and B combined; distribution of Small Entity categories, 1994 to 2003*

| SE Type | Count | % |
|---|---|---|
| Individually owned | 156,550 | 44.8% |
| Small Firm | 162,899 | 46.6% |
| Nonprofit | 29,889 | 8.6% |
| Total | 349,338 | 100% |

Universally, but particularly outside the US, funding for public research institutions is difficult to raise and it is expended with caution. The OECD* numbers for Nonprofits are very low. Only ten of the 31 OECD* countries in this study acquired more than five Nonprofit patents per million of population over the entire ten years and there is considerable variance between them. A recent report by the OECD dealing with technology transfer offices and revenue from the licencing of intellectual property, concluded that there was

> enormous variation across OECD countries and even among PROs (public research organisations) within a country. In absolute terms, U.S. universities generated the largest amount of income from licences, over USD 1.2 billion followed by Germany at EUR 6.6 million (PROs only).[3]

It comes as no surprise to find the US Nonprofits so much in the lead on revenue generation through technology transfer, since the Bayh-Dole Act in 1980 was specifically introduced to enable universities and research organisations in the

United States to lay claim to the intellectual property arising from research supported by public funds. This has led to a great increase in patenting activity by US Nonprofit organisations, especially universities.[4] Soon after the introduction of Bayh-Dole, many US universities joined in the process, which had been led by MIT, of establishing offices of technology transfer, with professional staff from a business and marketing background, to actively promote their organisation's inventive activity and to encourage disclosure and licensing of inventions to the private sector.[5]

As noted, the numbers of Nonprofit patents per million population shows wide variance throughout the OECD* countries. In line with previous commentary we would expect the US, Canada and Israel to be the most active in this regard, although it comes as a surprise, nevertheless, to see that the differences are so large. Central to this research on Small Entity patents is the idea that Nonprofit patents are of higher than average quality. Considering this, it is surprising to see such disparity between the German and French Nonprofit patent counts (Figure 3.1). It is conceivable that French universities are more assiduous in transferring, to their non-SE partners in the R&D process, the responsibility for patenting the output of their research; however, as was apparent from Chapter 2, the low French SE patent count is not restricted to Nonprofits, but is general across the three SE categories.

*Figure 3.1    Group A; Nonprofit patents per million population, 1994 to 2003*

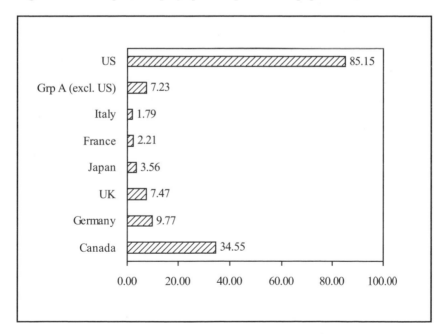

Even when we ignore the US data in Group A, the degree of difference between Canada and the European countries remains. We may make considerable allowance for Canada's proximity to the US as a driving mechanism here but still wonder how the historic university infrastructure and strong research tradition in Germany, United Kingdom, France and Italy can produce such a low number of SE patents in comparison to Canada. To emphasise the point, it is notable that, in Group B, South Korean Nonprofit organisations were granted 23 patents per million population in the same period (Figure 3.2). A question of interest is whether there is a substantial difference in the quality of the patents acquired by the European universities compared to other countries.

*Figure 3.2   Group B; Nonprofit patents per million population, 1994 to 2003*

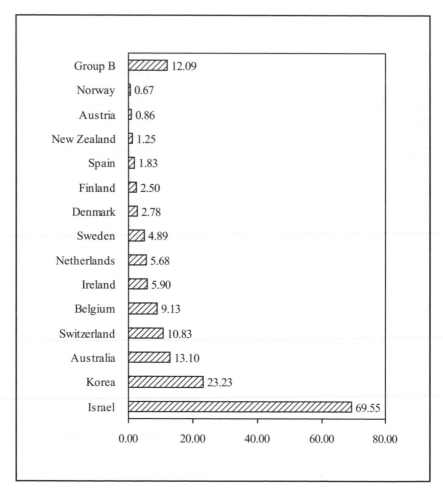

It is possible that a close relationship between Israeli and US institutions is at least partly responsible for the exceptional Israeli Nonprofit figure. Israeli universities have established a strong set of corporations to manage the technology transfer process, similar to the US model. The majority of the Israeli Nonprofit patents during the ten year period were contributed by two limited companies: the Yeda Research and Development Company established by the Weizman Institute of Science and the Yissum Research and Development Company of the Hebrew University of Jerusalem. In addition, there may be specific circumstances affecting research and development activity in Israel. Trajtenberg has suggested that in Israel 'the time path of patents seems to have been strongly influenced by major supply shocks such as the termination of the project to build a jet fighter which freed a large number of engineers and technicians, and the mass immigration from the former Soviet Union.'[6]

It seems likely that, more than patents from the other two categories of SE inventor, research carried on in the Nonprofit sector tends to focus on subject matter of global significance. Consequently if a university considers that its research is patentable at all, it must surely consider that it should be protected in the United States. The corollary of this was pointed out in Chapter 1; that Nonprofit small entities should not be researching in 'patentable' areas at all, if they do not intend to look for protection in the United States. For this reason, it is surprising to see such a small number of US Small Entity patents acquired by the Nonprofit sector in the European countries, including the Scandinavian countries like Finland and Denmark where technological research in the universities is strong. As with all the French data, the low per million figure for France (Figure 3.1) deserves particular attention.

Table 3.2 lists the top 35 Small Entity patent counts acquired by Nonprofit assignees in the period 1994 to 2003. The University of California was responsible for over 8.6 per cent of the Nonprofit patents acquired by the 31 OECD* countries. The first non-US entity, Korea's Institute of Science and Technology, appears in thirteenth position with 311 SE patents. Other non-US organisations in this top table include the University of British Columbia and Germany's Fraunhofer Gesellschaft in positions 34 and 35 respectively. In reality the Fraunhofer Gesellschaft is not a single entity but a network of about 80 research institutions located in different parts of Germany; as is the Max Planck Gesellschaft, which is well outside the top 35 with 70 patents. A third German Nonprofit, the Deutsche Forschungsanstalt fur Luft und Raumfahrt (German Aeronautic and Space Research Centre) acquired 119 SE patents.

Israel's major research institutions are shown separately in Table 3.3. The top three: Yissum Research and Development Company, Yeda Research and Development Company, which handles technology transfer from the Weizmann Institute of Science, and Ramot University Authority from Tel Aviv University are outside the top 35 and do not, therefore, appear in Table 3.2.

*Table 3.2   OECD\*; Top 35 Nonprofit assignees; SE patents, 1994 to 2003*

| Rank | Institution | Count |
|------|-------------|-------|
| 1  | University of California | 2,553 |
| 2  | Massachusetts Institute of Technology | 726 |
| 3  | University of Texas | 685 |
| 4  | California Institute of Technology | 657 |
| 5  | Johns Hopkins University | 430 |
| 6  | Cornell Research Foundation | 402 |
| 7  | Stanford University | 381 |
| 8  | University of Michigan | 358 |
| 9  | State University of New York | 353 |
| 10 | University of Pennsylvania | 339 |
| 11 | Michigan State University | 336 |
| 12 | Columbia University | 324 |
| 13 | Korea Institute of Science and Technology | 311 |
| 14 | Iowa State University | 281 |
| 15 | Battelle Memorial Institute | 270 |
| 16 | Wisconsin Alumni Research Foundation | 247 |
| 17 | University of Florida | 246 |
| 18 | Southwest Research Institute | 243 |
| 19 | University of Washington | 239 |
| 20 | Georgia Tech | 239 |
| 21 | Gas Research Institute | 229 |
| 22 | Duke University | 227 |
| 23 | ETRI (Korea) | 216 |
| 24 | Korea Advanced Institute of Science and Technology | 204 |
| 25 | University of North Carolina | 198 |
| 26 | Thomas Jefferson University | 184 |
| 27 | University of Chicago | 184 |
| 28 | University of Illinois | 182 |
| 29 | University of Utah | 181 |
| 30 | North Carolina State University | 176 |
| 31 | University of Pittsburgh | 175 |
| 32 | University of Minnesota | 172 |
| 33 | Yale University | 172 |
| 34 | University of British Columbia | 168 |
| 35 | Fraunhofer Gesellschaft | 163 |

Perhaps the most notable feature of Table 3.2 is the fact that the three highest non-US research organisations in the table are Korean; with the ETRI (Electronic and Telecommunications Research Institute) in 23rd position and the Korean Advanced Institute for Science and Technology in 24th. Equally noteworthy is the fact that of ETRI's 216 SE patents, 214 (or virtually 100 per cent) were granted in the years 2001 to 2003, the last three years in this study. So were 126 (or 62 per cent) of the 204 SE patents granted to the Korean Advanced Institute for Science and Technology, an organisation which has a strong relationship with the University of Michigan. So there has been, in effect, a substantial late upsurge of SE patenting activity by leading Korean research organisations, which has seen them overtake the major European (particularly German) research institutes in the acquisition of USPTO patents within a short period.

*Table 3.3   Israel; Top ten Nonprofit assignees, 1994 to 2003*

| Assignee Name | Count |
| --- | --- |
| Hebrew University of Jerusalem ( YISSUM) | 142 |
| Weizmann Institute (YEDA Research) | 126 |
| Tel Aviv University (RAMOT) | 98 |
| Technion Foundation Limited | 26 |
| Ben-Gurion University | 17 |
| Bar Ilan University | 12 |
| Massachusetts Institute of Technology | 6 |
| Cornell Research Foundation Inc. | 5 |
| Rappaport Family Institute for Research in the Medical Sciences | 4 |
| Children's Medical Center Corporation | 3 |

*Table 3.4   Nonprofit; Distribution between Country groups; 1994 to 2003*

| Country group | Count | % |
| --- | --- | --- |
| US | 24,609 | 82.2% |
| Group A (excl. US) | 3,016 | 10.1% |
| Group B | 2,264 | 7.6% |
| Group C | 66 | 0.2% |
| Total | 29,955 | 100% |

In fact, as Table 3.4 shows, US research organisations acquired over 82 per cent of the USPTO Nonprofit patents during the ten years of the study. The remaining six countries of Group A acquired 10 per cent. The ten countries identified earlier as having a negligible number of patents overall (Group C) were responsible for less than 0.2 per cent of the Nonprofit patents.

## CITATION OF NONPROFIT PATENTS

Table 3.5 shows that almost 50 per cent of Group A Nonprofit Small Entity patents were cited at least once in later patent documents. Nearly 57 per cent of US patents were cited, with Germany and Canada a little below this figure. The Japanese rate of citations was the lowest. In Group B (Table 3.6) 41 per cent of the patents were cited at least once. Finland has by far the highest proportion of cited patents (75 per cent) though, admittedly, this was based on a total of only nine. The apparently low Korean rate (of 35 per cent) may be discounted since, as pointed out earlier, the majority of the Korean Nonprofit patents were acquired in the years 2001 to 2003 and the patent citation data used was measured at the end of 2002.

*Table 3.5   Group A; Nonprofit patents cited at least once, 1994 to 2002*

| Country | Not cited | Cited>=1 | % cited | Total |
|---|---|---|---|---|
| Germany | 333 | 412 | 55.3% | 745 |
| Canada | 446 | 540 | 54.8% | 986 |
| Italy | 46 | 44 | 48.9% | 90 |
| France | 66 | 54 | 45.0% | 120 |
| UK | 233 | 162 | 41.0% | 395 |
| Japan | 241 | 128 | 34.7% | 369 |
| Group A (US excl.) | 1,365 | 1,340 | 49.5% | 2,705 |
| US | 9,480 | 12,470 | 56.8% | 21,950 |
| Group A | 10,845 | 13,810 | 56.0% | 24,655 |

When we move on to examine the corresponding tables for Nonprofit patents which were cited at least three times, we find the relative rankings stay more or less the same. In Group A (Table 3.7) the average (without the US data) is 23 per cent. The US is well above this with 31.5 per cent, but both Germany and Canada are also above it. The Japanese proportion has now fallen to under 10 per cent. When only patents cited three times or more are counted, the group B average falls to 17 per cent (Table 3.8). Sweden still performs strongly with almost 36 per cent of its Nonprofit patents. The most noticeable change is the fact that while close to 60 per cent of the Irish Nonprofit patents were cited once or more, only 9.5 per cent were cited three times or more. Again, the very

*Table 3.6   Group B; Nonprofit patents cited at least once, 1994 to 2002*

| Country | Not cited | Cited>=1 | % cited | Total |
|---|---|---|---|---|
| Finland | 3 | 9 | 75.0% | 12 |
| Sweden | 17 | 25 | 59.5% | 42 |
| Ireland | 9 | 12 | 57.1% | 21 |
| Switzerland | 30 | 32 | 51.6% | 62 |
| Israel | 212 | 190 | 47.3% | 402 |
| Belgium | 47 | 40 | 46.0% | 87 |
| Australia | 133 | 101 | 43.2% | 234 |
| Netherlands | 47 | 35 | 42.7% | 82 |
| Spain | 41 | 25 | 37.9% | 66 |
| Denmark | 9 | 5 | 35.7% | 14 |
| Korea | 568 | 302 | 34.7% | 870 |
| Austria | 4 | 2 | 33.3% | 6 |
| New Zealand | 5 | 0 | 0.0% | 5 |
| Norway | 1 | 0 | 0.0% | 1 |
| Group B | 1,126 | 778 | 40.9% | 1,904 |

*Table 3.7   Group A; Nonprofit patents cited at least three times, 1994 to 2002*

| Country | Cited < 3 | Cited >= 3 | % cited | Total |
|---|---|---|---|---|
| Canada | 706 | 280 | 28.4% | 986 |
| Germany | 557 | 188 | 25.2% | 745 |
| France | 95 | 25 | 20.8% | 120 |
| Italy | 72 | 18 | 20.0% | 90 |
| UK | 316 | 79 | 20.0% | 395 |
| Japan | 333 | 36 | 9.8% | 369 |
| Group A (US excl.) | 2,079 | 626 | 23.1% | 2,705 |
| US | 15,044 | 6,906 | 31.5% | 21,950 |
| Group A | 16,409 | 8,246 | 33.4% | 24,655 |

low total of Nonprofit patents for Ireland (21) makes it difficult to reach any useful conclusions.

The low citation rates for Japan in Group A and Korea in Group B are again striking. Some explanation, but certainly not all, is provided by the point when citations are measured. In Table 3.9 we see that, as one might expect, between 70 per cent and 80 per cent of all Nonprofit patents in our data were acquired

*Table 3.8   Group B; Nonprofit patents cited at least three times, 1994 to 2002*

| Country | Cited < 3 | Cited >= 3 | % cited | Total |
|---|---|---|---|---|
| Sweden | 27 | 15 | 35.7% | 42 |
| Finland | 8 | 4 | 33.3% | 12 |
| Denmark | 10 | 4 | 28.6% | 14 |
| Belgium | 66 | 21 | 24.1% | 87 |
| Israel | 313 | 89 | 22.1% | 402 |
| Australia | 185 | 49 | 20.9% | 234 |
| Spain | 53 | 13 | 19.7% | 66 |
| Switzerland | 50 | 12 | 19.4% | 62 |
| Netherlands | 67 | 15 | 18.3% | 82 |
| Austria | 5 | 1 | 16.7% | 6 |
| Korea | 767 | 103 | 11.8% | 870 |
| Ireland | 19 | 2 | 9.5% | 21 |
| New Zealand | 5 | 0 | 0.0% | 5 |
| Norway | 1 | 0 | 0.0% | 1 |
| Group B | 1,576 | 328 | 17.2% | 1,904 |

in the eight years between 1994 and 2001. The major exceptions to this are Japan and Korea. Thus the proportion cited for Japan and Korea will be affected by any measurement of citations which mainly focuses on those early years. As explained, there is a 'lag' period after a patent is granted before it begins to be cited, so there may well be some optimum period when it becomes 'recognised' as significant in its field.

There is some support in the data for the idea that, with some exceptions, there is a 'critical mass' effect with patent citations, and that the greater the number of patents in a technology or country, the larger is the proportion of cited ones. It would also be useful to investigate fully the extent to which the citations are 'self-referential'; in other words to what extent do the patents acquired by inventors from any country cite previous patents from the same country and to what extent do they cite patents originating abroad. Since it is a requirement of the patent office that applicants must cite any relevant prior patent known to them, it follows that inventors are very likely to cite previous patents of their own, or those of their colleagues. This would suggest that, compared to a country where patent applications are low, a very active patenting culture might be expected to generate a greater number of citations per patent, since the flow of information among members of the patenting community will be that much greater there.

Of course, the above has a bearing on citations as an indicator of patent value. During the preparation of this analysis a limited test was performed, using a random sample of German Small Firm patents that had been cited at least once. About 13 per cent of all the citations in the sample were citations by patentees of their own prior patents and in almost every case there was a maximum of two such self references. That sample, therefore, supports the idea that counting SE patents which were cited at least three times might exclude the bulk of self referential citations among the Small Entity patents.

*Table 3.9  Groups A and B; Proportion of Nonprofit patents acquired before and after 2001*

| Country | 94 to 01 | % 94 to 01 | 01 to 03 | % 02 to 03 | Total |
|---|---|---|---|---|---|
| Group A | 21,613 | 78.2% | 6,012 | 21.6% | 27,625 |
| Germany | 662 | 82.6% | 139 | 17.4% | 801 |
| France | 108 | 81.8% | 24 | 18.2% | 132 |
| Canada | 862 | 79.4% | 223 | 20.6% | 1,085 |
| US | 19,298 | 78.4% | 5,311 | 21.6% | 24,609 |
| Italy | 79 | 76.7% | 24 | 23.3% | 103 |
| UK | 329 | 74.9% | 110 | 25.1% | 439 |
| Japan | 275 | 60.3% | 181 | 39.7% | 456 |
| | | | | | |
| Group B | 1,584 | 70.0% | 680 | 30.0% | 2,264 |
| Denmark | 14 | 93.3% | 1 | 6.7% | 15 |
| Sweden | 37 | 86.0% | 6 | 14.0% | 43 |
| Austria | 6 | 85.7% | 1 | 14.3% | 7 |
| Finland | 11 | 84.6% | 2 | 15.4% | 13 |
| Ireland | 19 | 82.6% | 4 | 17.4% | 23 |
| Belgium | 76 | 80.9% | 18 | 19.1% | 94 |
| New Zealand | 4 | 80.0% | 1 | 20.0% | 5 |
| Australia | 206 | 79.8% | 52 | 20.2% | 258 |
| Netherlands | 73 | 79.3% | 19 | 20.7% | 92 |
| Israel | 356 | 77.6% | 103 | 22.4% | 459 |
| Switzerland | 57 | 73.1% | 21 | 26.9% | 78 |
| Spain | 52 | 71.2% | 21 | 28.8% | 73 |
| Korea | 672 | 61.0% | 429 | 39.0% | 1101 |
| Norway | 1 | 33.3% | 2 | 66.7% | 3 |

In Chapter 2 it was established that 41 per cent of all OECD* Small Entity patents in the Electrical classes had been cited a minimum of three times (Table 2.11), compared to 31.5 per cent in the Mechanical and 27 per cent in the Chemical classes. When the equivalent data for the Nonprofit category are examined (Table 3.10) we find the citation rate for Electrical classes marginally higher at 42 per cent, while the Chemical classes show a lower rate of 24 per cent. When the US Nonprofits are discounted the Group A proportions fall considerably (see Table 3.11), while the proportions for Group B Nonprofits cited three times or more are lower again, as shown in Table 3.12. It is to be expected that US universities would have the highest rate of citation compared to the other countries. It comes as something of a surprise, however, to discover that the proportion of SE patents cited three times or more is lower for the Nonprofit category than for Small Firms, as shown in the next chapter.

*Table 3.10   OECD*; Nonprofit patents, proportions of each Technology Class cited three times or more, 1994 to 2002*

| Technology Class | Cited < 3 | Cited >= 3 | % cited | Total |
|---|---|---|---|---|
| Electrical | 2,511 | 1,830 | 42.2% | 4,341 |
| Mechanical | 3,262 | 1,982 | 37.8% | 5,244 |
| Chemical | 12,969 | 4,062 | 23.9% | 17,031 |
| OECD* Nonprofit | 18,742 | 7,874 | 29.6% | 26,616 |

*Table 3.11      Group A (excl. US); Nonprofit patents, proportions of each Technology Class cited three times or more, 1994 to 2002*

| Technology Class | Cited < 3 | Cited >= 3 | % cited | Total |
|---|---|---|---|---|
| Electrical | 401 | 160 | 28.5% | 561 |
| Mechanical | 511 | 169 | 24.9% | 680 |
| Chemical | 1,478 | 297 | 16.7% | 1,775 |
| Group A | 2,390 | 626 | 20.8% | 3,016 |

*Table 3.12   Group B; Nonprofit patents, proportions of each Technology Class cited three times or more, 1994 to 2002*

| Technology Class | Cited < 3 | Cited >= 3 | % cited | Total |
|---|---|---|---|---|
| Mechanical | 250 | 75 | 23.1% | 325 |
| Electrical | 284 | 58 | 17.0% | 342 |
| Chemical | 1,042 | 195 | 15.8% | 1,237 |
| Group B | 1,576 | 328 | 17.2% | 1,904 |

For the Nonprofits, therefore, the Technology Class patents with the highest count, Chemical, were cited least often. Again, as discussed in Chapter 2, regulatory factors may affect citations for Chemical patents to some extent. It is worth noting that, for Group B, the Mechanical class patents showed the highest citation frequency.

As previously discussed, the Group C countries had very few Small Entity patents and only 57 Nonprofit patents between 1994 and 2002, as shown in Table 3.13. Nevertheless it is of interest to note that, for these few Nonprofit patents, the citation rate was higher than Group B, and higher than the Group A countries when the US data is omitted.

*Table 3.13  Group C; Nonprofit patents, proportions of each Technology Class cited three times or more, 1994 to 2002*

| Technology Class | Cited < 3 | Cited >= 3 | % cited | Total |
| --- | --- | --- | --- | --- |
| Electrical | 2 | 1 | 33.3% | 3 |
| Mechanical | 7 | 3 | 30.0% | 10 |
| Chemical | 34 | 10 | 22.7% | 44 |
| Group C | 43 | 14 | 24.6% | 57 |

## NONPROFIT TECHNOLOGY CLASS GROUPS

Looking further into the nature of inventive activity indicated by the Technology Class numbers we find in the Nonprofit patents, as perhaps we might expect, a predominance of inventions in the Chemical classes, which naturally include pharmaceutical patents. Figure 3.3 shows the broad distribution of Technology Classes in the Nonprofit patents for Group A.

*Figure 3.3  Group A (excl. US); Nonprofit patents, distribution of Technology Class Groups, 1994 to 2003*

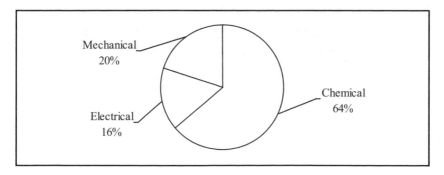

Mechanical 20%

Electrical 16%

Chemical 64%

*Figure 3.4    Group B; Nonprofit patents, distribution of Technology Class Groups, 1994 to 2003*

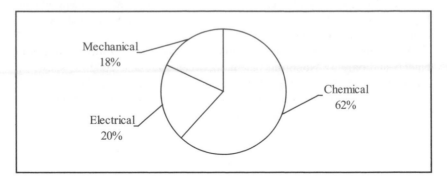

Almost two thirds of the Group A patents were in the Chemical classes, while the Electrical classes, which include software, computing and much high technology, represented 16 per cent. This chart omits the US data, but the inclusion of the US does not change the picture very much for the Nonprofit category. The corresponding chart for Group B (Figure 3.4) again shows a similar picture, although the share of Electrical patents has risen.

The country charts showing Technology Class distribution suggest some greater variation. In Group A (Figure 3.5) Italian Nonprofits acquired over 70 per cent of their SE patents in the Chemical classes, while in Germany and Japan this proportion is around 50 per cent.

*Figure 3.5    Group A; Nonprofit patents, Technology Class profile, 1994 to 2003*

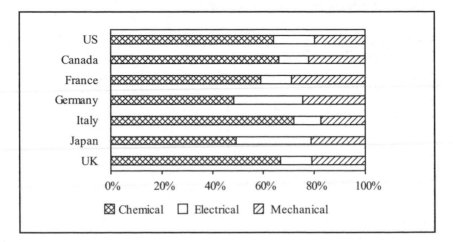

Group B distribution is even more varied (Figure 3.6) although this may be partly due to the fact that the overall patent counts are so low for our Nonprofits. Four countries, three of them the Scandinavian countries of Norway, Finland and Denmark, acquired no SE patents in the Electrical classes. Fourteen of Denmark's 15 Nonprofit patents were acquired in Chemical classes. The fourth Scandinavian country in our data, Sweden, acquired 34 out of its 43 Nonprofit patents – nearly 80 per cent – in the Chemical classes. Out of the very small Irish total of 23 Nonprofit patents for the ten years, the largest proportion was in the Chemical classes. However, Table IE.3 on page 139 provides the Technology Class data for Ireland for each year from 1994 to 2003 and demonstrates the extent to which Ireland's very low SE patent count has produced sharp fluctuations in the Technology Class proportions.

*Figure 3.6   Group B; Nonprofit patents, Technology Class profile, 1994 to 2003*

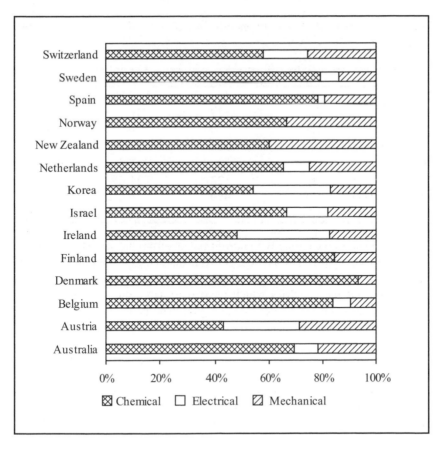

## NONPROFIT PATENT DECAY

Next, we examine the proportion of Nonprofit patents which were allowed to lapse at the first renewal stage. Table 3.14 shows the number of Small Entity patents of this type granted to the Group A countries between the start of 1994 and the end of 1998, and the proportion of those patents failing to be renewed, by payment of the appropriate maintenance fees, after four years (by the end of 2002 at latest). It is useful to restate that the proportion showing as lapsed is not a proportion of all the patents for the full ten years since, at the time of measurement, many of these were not yet subject to renewal fees. The group A average is 16 per cent (US excluded) and the US, with 11.4 per cent, was well below this figure. Only Japan shows a proportion comparable to the US. The country with the most notable proportion of lapsed patents is France, particularly given that French SE patenting is not high and Nonprofit patents might have been expected to be of higher than average quality.

*Table 3.14   Group A; Nonprofit patents lapsed at 4 year renewal stage, 1994 to 1998*

| Country | Lapse (4 yr) | Maintained | % Lapsed | Total |
|---------|-----------|------------|----------|-------|
| France | 11 | 42 | 20.8% | 53 |
| UK | 28 | 139 | 16.8% | 167 |
| Canada | 75 | 379 | 16.5% | 454 |
| Germany | 51 | 268 | 16.0% | 319 |
| Italy | 7 | 39 | 15.2% | 46 |
| Japan | 16 | 122 | 11.6% | 138 |
| All (excl. US) | 188 | 989 | 16.0% | 1,177 |
| US | 1,203 | 9,386 | 11.4% | 10,589 |

Table 3.15 shows the Group B Nonprofit patents from the same period, which were allowed to lapse. The average is lower than Group A but the very small number of Nonprofit patents for Group B makes it difficult to draw any conclusion. Of the countries which have reasonable numbers of Nonprofit patents, Israel's rate of 14.6 per cent is higher than the US rate but lower than the Group A average, and also lower than the 'lapsed' percentage for Canada, France, Germany and the United Kingdom individually. Of Finland's low count of eight Nonprofit SE patents for the period, five were allowed to lapse, nearly two thirds. In general, considering patent quality, and making allowance for the small numbers of Nonprofit SE patents in the study, it can be seen that the proportion of the Nonprofit patents being allowed to lapse after four years was substantially lower than the proportion for all SE categories combined,

discussed in Chapter 2. Chapter 4 reveals that Small Firm patents decay at at a higher rate than Nonprofits. So although the actual count of Nonprofit patents (outside the US) is very small, they would appear to be more robust, as indicated by their having a better chance of being maintained.

*Table 3.15   Group B; Nonprofit patents lapsed at 4 year stage, 1994 to 1998*

| Country | Lapse (4 yr) | Maintained | % Lapsed | Total |
|---|---|---|---|---|
| Finland | 5 | 3 | 62.5% | 8 |
| Ireland | 1 | 3 | 25.0% | 4 |
| Switzerland | 5 | 21 | 19.2% | 26 |
| Australia | 18 | 84 | 17.6% | 102 |
| Netherlands | 5 | 29 | 14.7% | 34 |
| Denmark | 1 | 6 | 14.3% | 7 |
| Israel | 26 | 159 | 14.1% | 185 |
| Belgium | 5 | 36 | 12.2% | 41 |
| Sweden | 2 | 21 | 8.7% | 23 |
| Spain | 1 | 25 | 3.8% | 26 |
| Korea | 6 | 263 | 2.2% | 269 |
| Austria | 0 | 3 | 0.0% | 3 |
| New Zealand | 0 | 1 | 0.0% | 1 |
| All | 75 | 654 | 10.3% | 729 |

As with the citation data it is necessary to see whether there is a difference in the rate of decay between the three broad technology groupings. Again, only the data from the years 1994 to 1998 is used. The proportion of each Technology Class group being allowed to lapse at the first renewal stage (after four years) is presented in Table 3.16. It is notable that the 12 per cent rate of decay for Nonprofits is half that for all OECD* small entities as shown in Chapter 2. Of equal note is the fact the Group A proportion of 16 per cent was considerably higher than the Group B one of 10.3 per cent. In all cases the Chemical classes showed the lowest rate of decay; remarkably only 8.5 per cent of the Group B Chemical class Nonprofits were allowed to lapse at the four year renewal stage.

It was also revealed in Chapter 2 that just over half of all the OECD* Small Entity patents had expired following the second renewal stage at eight years. Taking the 1994 patents as before, Table 3.19 reveals that considerably fewer of the Nonprofit patents had expired at this stage; in fact just under 40 per cent had done so. The Electrical and Mechanical patents had lapsed in about the same proportion, but only 35 per cent of the Chemical patents had lapsed. Of course both of these proportions reflect the US data; when the US data is removed from Group A figures the decay rate rises to 43 per cent. Once more the corresponding figure for Group B is markedly lower at 30 per cent. However, in Group B, it was the Chemical class patents which showed the highest rate of lapsing at the eight year stage.

*Table 3.16   OECD\*; Nonprofit patents, proportion of each Technology Class group lapsed at the 4 year renewal stage, 1994 to 1998*

| Technology Class | Lapse (4 yrs) | Maintained | % Lapsed | Total |
|---|---|---|---|---|
| Mechanical | 359 | 2,235 | 13.8% | 2,594 |
| Electrical | 281 | 1,907 | 12.8% | 2,188 |
| Chemical | 836 | 6,906 | 10.8% | 7,742 |
| OECD* Nonprofit | 1,476 | 11,048 | 11.8% | 12,524 |

*Table 3.17      Group A (US excl.); Nonprofit patents, proportion of each Technology Class group lapsed at the 4 year renewal stage, 1994 to 1998*

| Technology Class | Lapse (4 yrs) | Maintained | % Lapsed | Total |
|---|---|---|---|---|
| Mechanical | 58 | 232 | 20.0% | 290 |
| Electrical | 44 | 209 | 17.4% | 253 |
| Chemical | 86 | 548 | 13.6% | 634 |
| Group A | 188 | 989 | 16.0% | 1,177 |

*Table 3.18   Group B; Nonprofit patents, proportion of each Technology Class group lapsed at the 4 year renewal stage, 1994 to 1998*

| Technology Class | Lapse (4 yrs) | Maintained | % Lapsed | Total |
|---|---|---|---|---|
| Electrical | 16 | 80 | 16.7% | 96 |
| Mechanical | 16 | 112 | 12.5% | 128 |
| Chemical | 43 | 462 | 8.5% | 505 |
| Group B | 75 | 654 | 10.3% | 729 |

*Table 3.19   OECD\*; Nonprofit patents, proportion of each Technology Class group lapsed at the 8 year renewal stage, 1994 only*

| Technology Class | Lapse (8 yrs) | Maintained | % Lapsed | Total |
|---|---|---|---|---|
| Electrical | 158 | 187 | 45.8% | 345 |
| Mechanical | 217 | 274 | 44.2% | 491 |
| Chemical | 350 | 638 | 35.4% | 988 |
| OECD* Nonprofit | 725 | 1,099 | 39.7% | 1,824 |

*Table 3.20   Group A; Nonprofit patents, proportion of each Technology Class group lapsed at the 8 year renewal stage, 1994 only*

| Technology Class | Lapse (8 yrs) | Maintained | % Lapsed | Total |
|---|---|---|---|---|
| Electrical | 24 | 17 | 58.5% | 41 |
| Mechanical | 24 | 19 | 55.8% | 43 |
| Chemical | 22 | 56 | 28.2% | 78 |
| Group A | 70 | 92 | 43.2% | 162 |

*Table 3.21   Group B; Nonprofit patents, proportion of each Technology Class group lapsed at the 8 year renewal stage, 1994 only*

| Technology Class | Lapse (8 yrs) | Maintained | % Lapsed | Total |
|---|---|---|---|---|
| Chemical | 17 | 37 | 31.5% | 54 |
| Electrical | 2 | 5 | 28.6% | 7 |
| Mechanical | 6 | 16 | 27.3% | 22 |
| Group B | 25 | 58 | 30.1% | 83 |

## NONPROFIT PATENT OWNERSHIP BY US ENTITIES

We begin this section by noting that, of the 29,955 Nonprofit patents acquired by the 31 OECD* countries in our database, 24,609, or 82 per cent, were granted to US residents. With this in mind we consider the ownership of patents by examining the proportion from each country assigned to US entities, using the assignee type field in the USPTO database explained earlier. Table 3.22 gives the proportion of Group A Nonprofit Small Entity patents assigned to US entities of one kind or another. As expected, virtually 100 per cent of US originating patents were assigned to US entities. The average for Group A with US data omitted is 6.5 per cent and both Japan and Germany are close to this figure. It is intriguing to see that between one fifth and one quarter of the Nonprofit patents originating with Italian resident inventors were assigned to US entities. In this case it may be of interest to see the actual breakdown of assignee organisations and the full distribution of the 23 Italian Nonprofit patents is given in Table 3.23. Almost all the patents were in biochemical and medical research.

The average US ownership for Group B, as shown in Table 3.24, is 8 per cent. Spain is under the group average and Israel is well below at 6 per cent. The main feature of this table, however, is the remarkable set of proportions for Sweden, Belgium and Austria. Austria admittedly has only 7 Nonprofit patents for the period, so this may be unreliable, but Belgium, with 94 patents, had 57.4 per cent assigned to US entities and Sweden, with 43, had 72 per cent so assigned. However, a reasonable explanation is available since, on closer examination of the data, we discover that 49 of the 54 Belgian 'US owned' patents, and 19 of Sweden's 31, were assigned to the Ludwig Institute for Cancer Research. Although the USPTO database records these as US assigned patents, the Ludwig Institute is probably one of the most international of research organisations, with centres in the US and in many European countries. This is, perhaps, one of the most important features of Nonprofit patents in general. Unlike Small Firm patents, where firms and their range of contacts and partners tend to be localised, the Nonprofit research community is internationalised and appears to have a greater readiness to share information and results with research partners in other countries.

*Table 3.22   Group A; Proportion of Nonprofit patents assigned to US entities, 1994 to 2003*

| Country | Total | US owned | % US-owned |
| --- | --- | --- | --- |
| Italy | 103 | 23 | 22.3% |
| France | 132 | 14 | 10.6% |
| UK | 439 | 45 | 10.3% |
| Germany | 801 | 57 | 7.1% |
| Japan | 456 | 26 | 5.7% |
| Canada | 1,085 | 32 | 2.9% |
| Group A (excl. US) | 3,016 | 197 | 6.5% |
| US | 24,609 | 24,514 | 99.6% |
| Group A | 27,625 | 24,711 | 89.5% |

One other point of significance from the table is the relatively low rate of US assignment (3 per cent) of Nonprofit patents originating in neighbouring Canada, which may indicate the strength of the Canadian university programs for technology transfer. Like Israel (where less than six per cent of the Nonprofit patents were assigned to US entities) a number of the major Canadian universities have emulated the US approach and have been active in establishing profit-oriented corporations to manage the process and to maximise the returns from their research activities.

In conclusion, it is worth examining the proportions of each Technology Class group assigned to US entities over the ten years of the study (Tables 3.25 and 3.26). As noted before, the Group A and B proportions so assigned were 6.5 per cent and 8.2 per cent respectively. More significantly, the Nonprofit Technology Classes with by far the highest proportion of US ownership were the Chemical ones. In the case of the Group B countries 11.4 per cent of all Chemical class Nonprofit patents were assigned to US entities.

*Table 3.23   Italy; Nonprofit patents assigned to US entities, 1994 to 2003*

| Assignee | Count |
|---|---|
| Picower Institute for Medical Research | 9 |
| University of California | 4 |
| Neurosciences Research Foundation, Inc. | 2 |
| Thomas Jefferson University | 2 |
| Associated Universities Inc. | 1 |
| Baylor College of Medicine | 1 |
| Cedars Sinai Medical Center | 1 |
| Ludwig Institute for Cancer Research | 1 |
| Sloan-Kettering Institute for Cancer Research | 1 |
| University of Georgia | 1 |
| Total | 23 |

*Table 3.24   Group B; Proportion of Nonprofit patents assigned to US entities, 1994 to 2003*

| Country | Total | US owned | % US-owned |
|---|---|---|---|
| Sweden | 43 | 31 | 72.1% |
| Belgium | 94 | 54 | 57.4% |
| Austria | 7 | 4 | 57.1% |
| Norway | 3 | 1 | 33.3% |
| Switzerland | 78 | 18 | 23.1% |
| Finland | 13 | 3 | 23.1% |
| Australia | 258 | 26 | 10.1% |
| Spain | 73 | 5 | 6.8% |
| Israel | 459 | 26 | 5.7% |
| Netherlands | 92 | 5 | 5.4% |
| Ireland | 23 | 1 | 4.3% |
| Korea | 1,101 | 11 | 1.0% |
| New Zealand | 5 | 0 | 0.0% |
| Denmark | 15 | 0 | 0.0% |
| All | 2,264 | 185 | 8.2% |

*Table 3.25    Group A (US excl.) Nonprofit; proportions of each Technology Class group assigned to US entities, 1994 to 2003*

| Technology Class | Non-US | US owned | % US owned | Total |
|---|---|---|---|---|
| Chemical | 1,626 | 149 | 8.4% | 1,775 |
| Electrical | 539 | 22 | 3.9% | 561 |
| Mechanical | 654 | 26 | 3.8% | 680 |
| Group A (US excl.) | 2,819 | 197 | 6.5% | 3,016 |

*Table 3.26    Group B (US excl.) Nonprofit; proportions of each Technology Class group assigned to US entities, 1994 to 2003*

| Technology Class | Non-US | US owned | % US owned | Total |
|---|---|---|---|---|
| Chemical | 1,239 | 160 | 11.4% | 1,399 |
| Electrical | 440 | 15 | 3.3% | 455 |
| Mechanical | 400 | 10 | 2.4% | 410 |
| Group B | 2,079 | 185 | 8.2% | 2,264 |

## NOTES

1.  Office of Management and Budget, Executive Office of the President, Circular No. A-133, Audits of States, Local Governments, and Non-Profit Organizations, accessed 21 July 2003, available at http://www.whitehouse.gov/omb/circulars/a133/a133.html#a
2.  See Brown, J. R. (2001) 'Privatizing the University – The New Tragedy of the Commons.' *Science* 290: 1701.; Monotti, A. L. and S. Ricketson (2003). *Universities and intellectual property : ownership and exploitation.* Oxford, Oxford University Press.; Auril, Universities UK, UK Patent Office, A Guide to Managing Intellectual Property, Strategic Decision-Making in Universities, accessed April 2003, available at http://www.patent.gov.uk/about/notices/manip/overview.pdf
3.  OECD (2003) *Turning science into business; patenting and licencing at public research organisations.* Paris, OECD.
4.  Mowery, D. et al. (2001) 'The Growth of Patenting by American Universities: An Assessment of the Bayh-Dole Act of 1980.' *Research Policy* 30: 99–119.
5.  Argyres, N. S. and J. P. Liebeskind (1998) 'Privatizing the intellectual commons: Universities and the commercialization of biotechnology.' *Journal of Economic Behavior & Organization* 35: 427–454.
6.  Trajtenberg, M. (2001) 'Innovation in Israel 1968–1997: a comparative analysis using patent data.' *Research Policy* 30: 363–389.

# 4. Small Firm patents

Of the total number of utility patents (not merely Small Entity ones) granted by the USPTO to US resident inventors in any year, roughly 15 per cent are assigned to US firms qualifying as Small Entities under the regulations. As with the other two categories, a Small Firm is eligible for a remission of 50 per cent of certain fees.[1] The USPTO, along with other Federal agencies, applies the Small Business Size Standards established by the US Small Business Administration (SBA). The SBA definition of a Small Firm varies by industry but, broadly speaking, it depends either on the number of employees or on annual receipts averaged over three years. Where the number of employees is used as the criterion, the most common upper limit is 500, but some industries are allowed a higher limit; in computer manufacturing, for example, the limit is 1,000 employees and in aircraft manufacturing it is 1,500. On the other hand, firms in the wholesale trade are regarded as Small Firms only if their employee count is less than 100. The financial criteria are, predictably, more varied. The lowest limit is in agriculture where average annual receipts must not exceed three quarters of a million dollars, while the commercial banking sector is allowed an upper limit of $150 million in assets. The broad categories and bands are summarised in Table 4.1.

*Table 4.1   Abbreviated summary of SBA's Small Business Size Standards*

| Industry Group | No. employees | Annual receipts ($m) |
|---|---|---|
| Manufacturing | 500 | |
| Wholesale Trade | 100 | |
| Agriculture | | 0.75 |
| Retail Trade | | 6 |
| General & Heavy Construction | | 28.5 |
| Dredging | | 17 |
| Special Trade Contractors | | 12 |
| Travel Agencies | | 3 |
| Business and Personal Services | | 6 |

As noted earlier, in the majority of countries around the world a firm with 500 employees would be regarded as a very substantial enterprise. For example, the

Canadian Intellectual Property Office (CIPO) defines the term 'Small Entity' to mean: 'an entity that employs 50 or fewer employees'.[2] The European Union revised its definition of a SME in on 15 May 2003. The balance sheet threshold was increased to €43 million from €27 million, but the threshold for the number of employees was retained at 250.[3] The same document defines a subcategory of 'small' enterprise as one which has fewer than 50 employees and less than €10 million on its balance sheet.[4] We should therefore be aware, when looking at the analysis of the USPTO 'Small Firm' data, that for patents originating outside the US a firm may be a medium or large entity in its country of origin, while remaining within the size constraints laid down by the SBA.

Whatever their size, there is evidence for the value of Small Firms in the innovation process.[5] The European Commission's website makes it clear that SMEs are 'socially and economically important, since they represent 99% of all enterprises in the EU and provide around 65 million jobs and contribute to entrepreneurship and innovation'.[6] Small Firms retain a degree of flexibility in relation to their market; they often come into existence for the single purpose of delivering innovative new products or services and frequently the maintenance of a high level of innovation is their only means of continuing to thrive in a competitive environment. The importance of the innovative contribution from small to medium enterprises was recognised in the US by the establishment of the SBIR Program, under the Small Business Innovation Development Act of 1982. The purpose of this Act, as the US Environmental Protection Agency puts it, was 'to strengthen the role of small businesses in federally funded R&D and help develop a stronger national base for technical innovation'.[7] The unanimous view is that these objectives have been met and that the SBIR Program has succeeded beyond even the expectations of its creators. Some attempts have been made in the United Kingdom and in Europe to reproduce the effect of the SBIR, but the scale of funding available and the models chosen for the allocation and administration of the funds have not, so far, been on a par with the US scheme.[8]

The patent system has not necessarily produced great rewards for Small Firms. A recent EU-commissioned study found that 'use of the patent system often left SMEs worse off than if it had not existed at all – sometimes tragically so'.[9] In fact the European experience has been that firms are wary of the costs involved and the difficulties of securing and defending their intellectual property. Meanwhile these costs would appear to be rising. According to one report, litigation costs in the US are rising faster than investment in research and development.[10] Figure 4.1 shows the number of USPTO patents per million acquired by Small Firms from our Group A countries in the period. As with other Small Entity categories in this study, the French figure is the lowest by a considerable margin, being under half the patents per million figure for the group (with US data excluded). And again, as in all Small Entity categories, the Canadian figure is the highest of the six countries, being a little over half the US figure.

*Figure 4.1   Group A; Small Firm patents per million of population, 1994 to 2003*

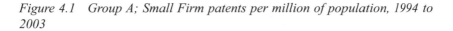
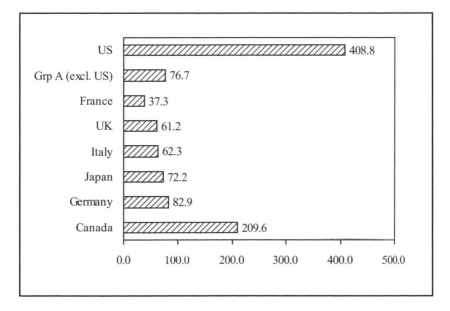

Figure 4.2 shows the data for Group B. As observed in other SE categories Israel's figure is the highest while the two Scandinavian countries of Finland and Sweden are reasonably close behind. Looking back at the equivalent Nonprofit table in Chapter 3 (Table 3.2) it is noticeable that the figure for patents per million for Small Firms, across the board, is far higher than the corresponding figure for Nonprofit patents, with the exception of Korea where the Nonprofit ratio of 23 patents per million is not far below the Small Firm ratio of 29 patents per million.

## CITATION OF SMALL FIRM PATENTS

How does the proportion of Small Firm citations compare with other categories of Small Entity? In Table 4.2 we may observe that, for the Group A countries other than the US, the proportion cited at least once varied between 52 and 58 per cent, the average being 55.6 per cent. The US proportion was 64.6 per cent. The variation in our Group B countries was between 44 and 57 per cent.

*Figure 4.2    Group B; Small Firm patents per million of population, 1994 to 2003*

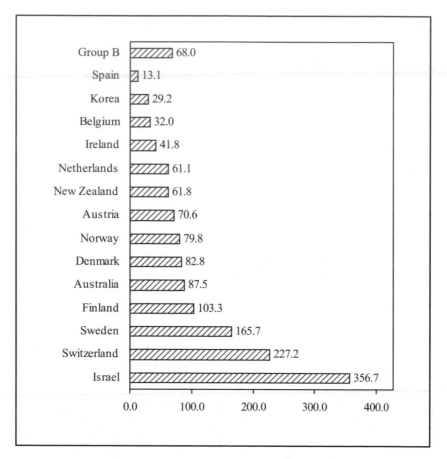

Do countries with lower patent counts for their Small Firms have relatively more valuable patents? This might arise where the lower patent count per million was due to the filtering mechanisms acting in a more efficient manner, leaving a smaller residual, but with patents of higher quality. There is, however, insufficient support in the data for this idea. While it is the case that 56.5 per cent of Ireland's 147 Small Firm patents were cited, Finland, a country close to Ireland in size, had 51 per cent cited from a much larger count of 480. In the same period 53 per cent of Israel's massive count of 1,991 Small Firm patents were cited and close to 57 per cent of Switzerland's 1,492. There is little evidence of a relationship between the patent count size and the proportion cited in any country.

*Table 4.2   Group A; Small Firm patents cited at least once, 1994 to 2002*

| Country | Not cited | Cited>=1 | % cited | Total |
|---|---|---|---|---|
| Canada | 2,426 | 3,420 | 58.5% | 5,846 |
| Japan | 3,614 | 4,668 | 56.4% | 8,282 |
| Germany | 2,717 | 3,361 | 55.3% | 6,078 |
| France | 891 | 1,088 | 55.0% | 1,979 |
| UK | 1,511 | 1,664 | 52.4% | 3,175 |
| Italy | 1,533 | 1,678 | 52.3% | 3,211 |
| Group A (US excl.) | 12,692 | 15,879 | 55.6% | 28,571 |
| US | 37,267 | 67,952 | 64.6% | 105,219 |
| Group A | 49,959 | 83,831 | 62.7% | 133,790 |

*Table 4.3   Group B; Small Firm patents cited at least once, 1994 to 2002*

| Country | Not cited | Cited>=1 | % cited | Total |
|---|---|---|---|---|
| Switzerland | 648 | 844 | 56.6% | 1,492 |
| Ireland | 64 | 83 | 56.5% | 147 |
| Israel | 929 | 1,062 | 53.3% | 1,991 |
| Australia | 703 | 797 | 53.1% | 1,500 |
| Netherlands | 444 | 469 | 51.4% | 913 |
| Finland | 235 | 245 | 51.0% | 480 |
| Korea | 564 | 560 | 49.8% | 1,124 |
| Belgium | 151 | 148 | 49.5% | 299 |
| Denmark | 201 | 185 | 47.9% | 386 |
| Austria | 266 | 240 | 47.4% | 506 |
| New Zealand | 115 | 102 | 47.0% | 217 |
| Norway | 171 | 140 | 45.0% | 311 |
| Spain | 260 | 211 | 44.8% | 471 |
| Sweden | 704 | 560 | 44.3% | 1,264 |
| All | 5,455 | 5,646 | 50.9% | 11,101 |

Next, we examine whether the proportions are significantly different for Small Firm patents cited three times or more. The data for Group A (Table 4.4) shows these proportions are naturally lower than for patents cited once or more, but in more or less the same degree; the rank order is virtually identical. Again, while the average for the six non-US countries is 26 per cent, the US average is substantially higher at close to 40 per cent.  Thus, if the number of citations of patents is any indication of patent quality, then the US, as well as having by far the major proportion of Small Firm USPTO patents, also appears to have the better quality ones.

*Table 4.4    Group A; Small Firm patents cited three times or more, 1994 to 2002*

| Country | Not cited | Cited>=1 | % cited | Total |
|---|---|---|---|---|
| Canada | 4,066 | 1,780 | 30.4% | 5,846 |
| Japan | 6,062 | 2,220 | 26.8% | 8,282 |
| France | 1,482 | 497 | 25.1% | 1,979 |
| Germany | 4,556 | 1,522 | 25.0% | 6,078 |
| UK | 2,398 | 777 | 24.5% | 3,175 |
| Italy | 2,516 | 695 | 21.6% | 3,211 |
| Group A (excl. US) | 21,080 | 7,491 | 26.2% | 28,571 |
| US | 65,392 | 39,827 | 37.9% | 105,219 |
| Group A | 86,472 | 47,318 | 35.4% | 133,790 |

*Table 4.5    Group B; Small Firm patents cited three times or more, 1994 to 2002*

| Country | Not cited | Cited>=1 | % cited | Total |
|---|---|---|---|---|
| Ireland | 106 | 41 | 27.9% | 147 |
| Israel | 1,456 | 535 | 26.9% | 1,991 |
| Australia | 1,114 | 386 | 25.7% | 1,500 |
| Switzerland | 1,118 | 374 | 25.1% | 1,492 |
| Netherlands | 688 | 225 | 24.6% | 913 |
| Belgium | 228 | 71 | 23.7% | 299 |
| Korea | 884 | 240 | 21.4% | 1,124 |
| Austria | 398 | 108 | 21.3% | 506 |
| New Zealand | 176 | 41 | 18.9% | 217 |
| Finland | 393 | 87 | 18.1% | 480 |
| Denmark | 317 | 69 | 17.9% | 386 |
| Norway | 256 | 55 | 17.7% | 311 |
| Sweden | 1,046 | 218 | 17.2% | 1,264 |
| Spain | 391 | 80 | 17.0% | 471 |
| Group B | 8,571 | 2,530 | 22.8% | 11,101 |

To the extent that citations may *not* be an indicator of patent quality then perhaps other factors cause the patents of one country to be cited to a higher degree than another. One reason suggested earlier was that patent applicants and patent agents from a given region may, through habit or custom, simply cite more prior patents than applicants from another region. Any particular patent is cited because it is necessary to distinguish it from one's own invention; and the patents most likely to be cited are the ones about which an inventor is most aware or most concerned. The reasons why any patent applicant might be aware of any particular patent, or group of patents, might extend beyond the inherent quality of the patents themselves and include the resources of the patent's owner, his capability in economic and legal terms and the perceived capability of the owner of the patent being cited.[11]

*Table 4.6   OECD\*; Small Firm patents, proportions of each Technology Class group cited three times or more, 1994 to 2002*

| Technology Class | Cited<3 | Cited>=3 | % cited | Total |
| --- | --- | --- | --- | --- |
| Electrical | 18,069 | 13,477 | 42.7% | 31,546 |
| Mechanical | 52,738 | 26,588 | 33.5% | 79,326 |
| Chemical | 24,418 | 9,823 | 28.7% | 34,241 |
| OECD* Small Firms | 95,225 | 49,888 | 34.4% | 145,113 |

*Table 4.7   Group A (US excl.); Small Firm patents, proportions of each Technology Class group cited three times or more, 1994 to 2002*

| Technology Class | Cited<3 | Cited>=3 | % cited | Total |
| --- | --- | --- | --- | --- |
| Electrical | 3,071 | 1,410 | 31.5% | 4,481 |
| Mechanical | 12,792 | 4,651 | 26.7% | 17,443 |
| Chemical | 5,217 | 1,430 | 21.5% | 6,647 |
| Group A (US excl.) | 21,080 | 7,491 | 26.2% | 28,571 |

*Table 4.8   Group B; Small Firm patents, proportions of each Technology Class group cited three times or more, 1994 to 2002*

| Technology Class | Cited<3 | Cited>=3 | % cited | Total |
| --- | --- | --- | --- | --- |
| Electrical | 1,495 | 605 | 28.8% | 2,100 |
| Mechanical | 4,962 | 1,450 | 22.6% | 6,412 |
| Chemical | 2,113 | 475 | 18.4% | 2,588 |
| Group B | 8,570 | 2,530 | 22.8% | 11,100 |

We continue by looking at the proportions of Small Firm patents cited three times or more in each of the defined technology groups. The proportions for the OECD* countries are shown in Table 4.6 where we see that 43 per cent of the Electrical class patents were cited. Bearing in mind that US firms acquired 72 per cent of the OECD* Small Firm patents we note that, when the US data is excluded, the Group A average (Table 4.7) falls to 26 per cent and the proportion of Electrical class patents cited was 31.5 per cent. Despite the overall drop the relative distribution remains the same: the proportion of Electrical class patents cited three times or more was considerably higher than the Chemical class proportion. The cited proportions are even lower for the Group B countries (Table 4.8) but the same distribution persists. Thus the pattern appears to be consistent across each Country Group: Electrical class patents are cited (three times or more) about half as much again as Chemical class patents. Mechanical class citations hover around the group average.

## SMALL FIRM TECHNOLOGY CLASS GROUPS

As Figure 4.3 shows, just over half of the US Small Firm patents in the ten years of the study were in the Mechanical classes, while the Chemical and Electrical classes were equally divided. The distributions for the other six countries in Group A (Figure 4.4) revealed more activity in Mechanical and considerably less in the Electrical classes. Group B (Figure 4.5) is closer to the distribution for the US. Interestingly, the proportion of Chemical classes hardly varies, remaining steady at 23 or 24 per cent.

*Figure 4.3   US alone; Small Firm patents, distribution of Technology Classes, 1994 to 2003*

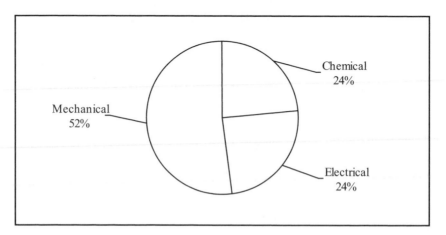

The detailed profile of Group A (Table 4.6) does not show great variation between the six non-US countries. The very small proportion of Electrical class patents in Italy is notable, where Small Firms appear to have concentrated on the Mechanical classes. The Electrical classes include computer patents and much of the high technology invention. In Group B (Figure 4.7) we can see that the largest proportions of Electrical class patents were acquired by Korean and Israeli Small Firms.

*Figure 4.4  Group A (excl. US); Small Firm patents, distribution of Technology Classes, 1994 to 2003*

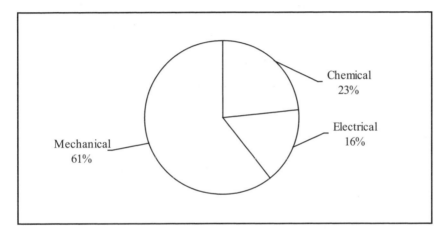

*Figure 4.5  Group B; Small Firm patents, distribution of Technology Classes, 1994 to 2003*

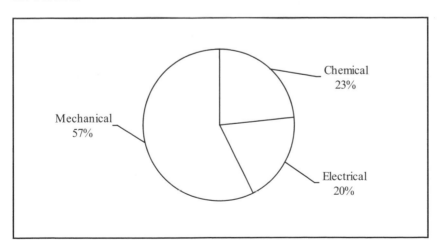

*Figure 4.6   Group A; Small Firms, Technology Class profile, 1994 to 2003*

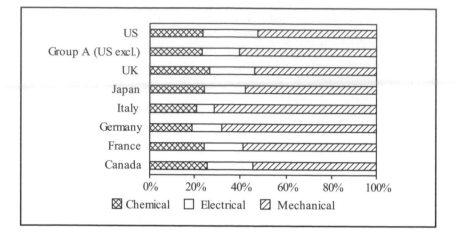

*Figure 4.7   Group B; Small Firms, Technology Class profile, 1994 to 2003*

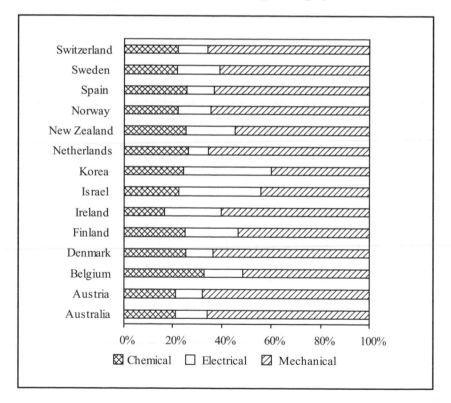

## SMALL FIRM RATE OF PATENT DECAY

Table 4.9 shows the Group A data for Small Firm patents which were not maintained after four years, the first renewal stage. We note that the average rate of decay for the Group A countries rises substantially – from 16 per cent to over 18 per cent – when the US data is discounted; and Table 4.10 reveals that the rate is over 20 per cent for the Group B countries. It is also notable, when looking at Table 4.9, that the Group A proportion lapsed is larger for Small Firms than for Nonprofits (as shown previously in Table 3.14). Excluding the US data the average for the Group A Nonprofits was 16 per cent, while for Group A Small Firms it was 18.4 per cent.

The second point of interest is that the rate of decay for Japanese Small Firm patents is lower than those originating in the US (that is, Japanese Small Firms maintained their patents at a higher rate). The Group B data (Table 4.10) shows a further three countries with a rate of decay lower than the US. New Zealand and Sweden are just below at 15.9 and 15.2 per cent respectively, but the rate for Korean Small Firms is considerably lower at 11 per cent. Thus the Small Firms from the the two Asian countries, Japan and Korea, were more assiduous at paying the required maintenance fees during the period under observation.

A further useful comparison lies in the behaviour of Finland's Small Firms, which maintained their patents at the same rate as the US Small Firms, in contrast to Finnish Nonprofits which, as we saw, acquired only eight SE patents between 1994 and 1998 and allowed five of those to lapse. We are accustomed to the idea that large multi-national corporates are careful to maintain their acquired portfolio of patents; it is instructive to see that, in some countries, small to medium enterprises appear to adopt the same approach.

*Table 4.9   Group A; Small Firm patents lapsed at 4 year renewal stage, 1994 to 1998*

| Country | Lapse (4 yr) | Maintained | % Lapsed | Total |
|---|---|---|---|---|
| UK | 311 | 1,133 | 21.5% | 1,444 |
| Germany | 609 | 2,282 | 21.1% | 2,891 |
| Italy | 327 | 1,307 | 20.0% | 1,634 |
| France | 200 | 806 | 19.9% | 1,006 |
| Canada | 490 | 2,199 | 18.2% | 2,689 |
| Japan | 591 | 3,487 | 14.5% | 4,078 |
| All (excl. US) | 2,528 | 11,214 | 18.4% | 13,742 |
| US | 8,174 | 42,999t | 16.0% | 51,173 |

*Table 4.10   Group B; Small Firm patents lapsed at 4 year renewal stage, 1994 to 1998*

| Country | Lapse (4 yr) | Maintained | % Lapsed | Total |
| --- | --- | --- | --- | --- |
| Spain | 65 | 178 | 26.7% | 243 |
| Denmark | 43 | 132 | 24.6% | 175 |
| Ireland | 16 | 50 | 24.2% | 66 |
| Israel | 179 | 561 | 24.2% | 740 |
| Australia | 151 | 529 | 22.2% | 680 |
| Switzerland | 169 | 603 | 21.9% | 772 |
| Netherlands | 89 | 335 | 21.0% | 424 |
| Austria | 38 | 167 | 18.5% | 205 |
| Norway | 23 | 105 | 18.0% | 128 |
| Belgium | 22 | 108 | 16.9% | 130 |
| Finland | 36 | 189 | 16.0% | 225 |
| New Zealand | 13 | 69 | 15.9% | 82 |
| Sweden | 76 | 425 | 15.2% | 501 |
| Korea | 39 | 316 | 11.0% | 355 |
| All | 959 | 3,767 | 20.3% | 4,726 |

We next look at the proportion of Small Entity patents in each Technology Class group which were allowed to lapse after four years. It is clear from the OECD* data in Table 4.11 and the Group A data in Table 4.12 that Chemical class patents were maintained at a higher rate than the other two Technology Classes, even if only marginally more so in Group A. However, in Table 4.13, we see that, for the Group B countries, the Electrical classes showed the lowest rate of decay.

Looking back at the corresponding tables for Nonprofits (Tables 3.16 to 3.18) we note that, at the four year renewal stage, the rate of decay for Small Firms was substantially higher for the countries in Group B and Group C. However, in Group A, when the US data was discounted, we see that the Small Firm proportion lapsing at four years, 15.3 per cent, was a little below the Nonprofit proportion of 16 per cent. At the second – eight year – renewal stage the OECD* proportions are very similar: 39.7 per cent of Nonprofits lapsed against 39.4 per cent of Small Firm patents. On this limited evidence – based exclusively on the 1994 patents – commercial firms appear more reluctant to terminate the patent at the later stage. As further data becomes available to allow better analysis of the second stage renewals, it will be possible to see if this behaviour is the norm.

*Table 4.11   OECD\*; Small Firms, proportion of each Technology Class group lapsed at the first (4 year) renewal stage, 1994 to 1998*

| Technology Class | Lapse (4 yr) | Maintained | % Lapsed | Total |
|---|---|---|---|---|
| Mechanical | 7,523 | 32,176 | 19.0% | 39,699 |
| Electrical | 2,038 | 12,054 | 14.5% | 14,092 |
| Chemical | 2,118 | 13,826 | 13.3% | 15,944 |
| OECD* Small Firms | 11,679 | 58,057 | 16.7% | 69,736 |

*Table 4.12   Group A (US excl.): Small Firms; proportion of each Technology Class group lapsed at the first (4 year) renewal stage, 1994 to 1998*

| Technology Class | Lapse (4 yr) | Maintained | % Lapsed | Total |
|---|---|---|---|---|
| Mechanical | 1,743 | 6,892 | 20.2% | 8,635 |
| Electrical | 318 | 1,730 | 15.5% | 2,048 |
| Chemical | 467 | 2,592 | 15.3% | 3,059 |
| Group A (US excl.) | 2,528 | 11,214 | 18.4% | 13,742 |

*Table 4.13   Group B; Small Firms, proportion of each Technology Class group lapsed at the first (4 year) renewal stage, 1994 to 1998*

| Technology Class | Lapse (4 yr) | Maintained | % Lapsed | Total |
|---|---|---|---|---|
| Mechanical | 632 | 2,267 | 21.8% | 2,899 |
| Chemical | 200 | 870 | 18.7% | 1,070 |
| Electrical | 127 | 630 | 16.8% | 757 |
| Group B | 959 | 3,767 | 20.3% | 4,726 |

Table 4.14 displays the OECD* data for the 1994 Small Firm patents which were allowed to lapse after eight years. The average, at just under 40 per cent, is more than double the proportion lapsing at four years (Table 4.11). In general the proportion lapsing at the eight year renewal stage is more than twice the proportion lapsing at the four year stage. It should be noted, however, that the order does not change. Chemical class patents show the lowest rate of decay at eight years in Group A (Table 4.15) and Group B (Table 4.16), while the Mechanical class patents showed the highest rate, approaching 47 per cent in the Group B countries. As a rule of thumb it is possible to say that one in five of the OECD* Small Firm patents had lapsed at the first stage and at least two in five at the second stage.

*Table 4.14   OECD\*; Small Firms, proportion of each Technology Class group lapsed at the second (8 year) renewal stage, 1994 only*

| Technology Class | Lapse (8yr) | Maintained | % Lapsed | Total |
|---|---|---|---|---|
| Mechanical | 3,098 | 4,288 | 41.9% | 7,386 |
| Electrical | 775 | 1,420 | 35.3% | 2,195 |
| Chemical | 807 | 1,497 | 35.0% | 2,304 |
| OECD* | 4,680 | 7,205 | 39.4% | 11,885 |

*Table 4.15   Group A (US excl.); Small Firms, proportion of each Technology Class group lapsed at the second (8 year) renewal stage, 1994 only*

| Technology Class | Lapse (8yr) | Maintained | % Lapsed | Total |
|---|---|---|---|---|
| Mechanical | 714 | 867 | 45.2% | 1,581 |
| Electrical | 142 | 220 | 39.2% | 362 |
| Chemical | 156 | 280 | 35.8% | 436 |
| Group A (US excl.) | 1,012 | 1,367 | 42.5% | 2,379 |

*Table 4.16   Group B; Small Firms, proportion of each Technology Class group lapsed at the second (8 year) renewal stage, 1994 only*

| Technology Class | Lapse (8yr) | Maintained | % Lapsed | Total |
|---|---|---|---|---|
| Mechanical | 237 | 270 | 46.7% | 507 |
| Electrical | 38 | 56 | 40.4% | 94 |
| Chemical | 68 | 104 | 39.5% | 172 |
| Group B | 343 | 430 | 44.4% | 773 |

## SMALL FIRM PATENTS ASSIGNED TO US ENTITIES

Historians and economists generally recognise and comment on the existence of a 'special relationship' between the US and the UK, perhaps due to a shared culture dating back to the former colonial foundations. This study's main focus is on the Small Entity data but examination of the main USPTO BIB database will confirm that a significant proportion of the non-SE patents, originating with UK resident inventors, have subsequently been assigned to US entities.

Similarly, we can observe in the data for US ownership of Small Firm patents in Group A (Table 4.17), that the UK heads the table with 11.2 per cent. We might expect Canada (due to its geographic proximity to the US) to have a high proportion of assignment to US entities, and it is, in fact, second in the list with 9.6 per cent. In contrast we saw that Canadian Nonprofits (see Chapter 3) had the lowest proportion of US ownership in Group A. The Japanese Small Firm proportion is the lowest for Group A, at 2.2 per cent.

*Table 4.17    Group A; Small Firms; % assigned to US entities, 1994 to 2003*

| Country | Total | US owned | % US-owned |
|---------|-------|----------|------------|
| UK | 3,601 | 404 | 11.2% |
| Canada | 6,582 | 631 | 9.6% |
| France | 2,227 | 132 | 5.9% |
| Italy | 3,576 | 194 | 5.4% |
| Germany | 6,797 | 320 | 4.7% |
| Japan | 9,242 | 199 | 2.2% |
| Grp A (excl. US) | 32,025 | 1,880 | 5.9% |

*Table 4.18    Group B; Small Firms; % assigned to US entities, 1994 to 2003*

| Country | Total | US owned | % US-owned |
|---------|-------|----------|------------|
| Israel | 2,354 | 355 | 15.1% |
| Belgium | 330 | 39 | 11.8% |
| Austria | 572 | 53 | 9.3% |
| Netherlands | 990 | 85 | 8.6% |
| Sweden | 1,458 | 114 | 7.8% |
| New Zealand | 247 | 14 | 5.7% |
| Australia | 1,724 | 96 | 5.6% |
| Switzerland | 1,636 | 86 | 5.3% |
| Ireland | 163 | 8 | 4.9% |
| Korea | 1,386 | 68 | 4.9% |
| Norway | 359 | 14 | 3.9% |
| Denmark | 447 | 16 | 3.6% |
| Spain | 523 | 10 | 1.9% |
| Finland | 537 | 6 | 1.1% |
| Group B | 12,726 | 964 | 7.6% |

Presumably due to close commercial cooperation and shared research initiatives, the Group B country with the highest proportion of US ownership is Israel with 15 per cent (Table 4.18). Korea had about 5 per cent of its Small Firm patents assigned to US entities, but was not, as one might expect, the lowest. This place is occupied largely by a block of Scandinavian countries:

Norway and Denmark with 3.9 and 3.6 per cent respectively and Finland which had a mere 1 per cent of its Small Firm patents assigned to US entities. This is a good illustration, if one were required, of Finland's focus on indigenous development of technology.

Table 4.19 displays the Technology Class distribution for the Group A countries without the US data. The proportions of Group A Small Firm patents assigned to US entities is 6 per cent and for Group B (Table 4.20) it is 7.6 per cent. In both Country Groups the lowest proportion of Small Firm patents assigned to US entities was in the Mechanical class patents. Eleven per cent of the Chemical class patents acquired by inventors in the Group B countries were assigned to US entities. Although the actual counts for the Group C countries were very low, it is important to note (see Table 4.21) that the proportion assigned to US entities was substantial; one fifth of the Electrical class patents was so assigned, and 14 per cent overall.

*Table 4.19   Group A (excl. US); Small Firms; % assigned to US entities, 1994 to 2003*

| Technology Class | Total | US owned | % US owned |
|---|---|---|---|
| Electrical | 5,214 | 413 | 7.9% |
| Chemical | 7,452 | 498 | 6.7% |
| Mechanical | 19,358 | 969 | 5.0% |
| Group A (US excl.) | 32,025 | 1,880 | 5.9% |

*Table 4.20   Group B; Small Firms; % assigned to US entities, 1994 to 2003*

| Technology Class | Total | US owned | % US owned |
|---|---|---|---|
| Chemical | 2,952 | 324 | 11.0% |
| Electrical | 2,506 | 222 | 8.9% |
| Mechanical | 7,267 | 418 | 5.8% |
| Group B | 12,726 | 964 | 7.6% |

*Table 4.21   Group C; Small Firms; % assigned to US entities, 1994 to 2003*

| Technology Class | Total | US owned | % US owned |
|---|---|---|---|
| Electrical | 39 | 8 | 20.5% |
| Chemical | 109 | 17 | 15.6% |
| Mechanical | 119 | 13 | 10.9% |
| Group C | 267 | 38 | 14.2% |

# NOTES

1. The US Department of Commerce, Manual of Patent Examining Procedure (6th ed. rev. 1997) outlines the fees that are reduced: patent application fees, 37 C.F.R. § 1.16 (1997), extension of time, revival, and appeal fees, 37 C.F.R. § 1.17 (1997), patent issue fees, 37 C.F.R. § 1.18 (1997), statutory disclaimer fee, 37 C.F.R. § 1.20(d) (1997), and maintenance fees on patents, 37 C.F.R. § 1.20 (1997).
2. Canadian Intellectual Property Office at http://strategis.ic.gc.ca/sc_mrksv/cipo/patents/e-filing/gloss.htm#S
3. Equivalent to about $57 million in March 2005.
4. Accessed at http://europa.eu.int/comm/enterprise/enterprise_policy/sme_definition/index_en.htm
5. Scherer, F. M. (1965). 'Firm size, market structure, opportunity, and the output of patented inventions.' *American Economic Review* 55: 1097–1125. and Schmookler, J. (1972) 'The size of firm and the growth of knowledge' in *Patents, Invention, and Economic Change* Schmookler, edited by Zvi Griliches and Leonid Hurwicz. Cambridge, MA, Harvard University Press.
6. Accessed at http://europa.eu.int/comm/enterprise/enterprise_policy/sme_definition/index_en.htm
7. Accessed at http://es.epa.gov/ncer/sbir
8. The UK Department of Trade and Industry scheme and the EU Framework Programme are examples.
9. Kingston, W. (2001) *Enforcing Small Firms' patents rights* Luxembourg, Office for Official Publications of the European Communities.
10. Barton, J. H. (2000) 'Intellectual Property Rights: Reforming the Patent System.' *Science* 287 5460: 1933–1934.
11. Verspagen, B. (2004) Review of A.B. Jaffe and M. Trajtenberg (eds) 'Patents, Citations & Innovations: A Window on the Knowledge Economy' MIT Press (2002), *Research Policy* 33 10: 1709 1711.

# 5. Individual patents

The stereotypical image in literature and cinema represents the individual inventor as an eccentric male, strong willed, obsessed and passionate. He is usually little concerned with the mundane details of daily existence like dress or sustenance, but is driven by the need to change the world, or to achieve immortality through some quirky application of imperfectly grasped science. If we base our presumptions on the stereotype, we might expect from our Individual inventors many whimsical and incongruous machines, perhaps only a little less bizarre than those depicted by Rube Goldberg or William Heath Robinson. Perhaps unfairly influenced by the image of the stereotypical inventor, Individual patents are often perceived as the poor relations of the invention and innovation system. Living examples of the stereotype may exist, but the majority of Individual inventor patents in the USPTO database appear to be pragmatic, business-oriented ones. Of course, this also reflects the filtering process, discussed in Chapter 1, for all countries other than the US. A random sample from the database of 30 non-US Individual patents, taken from across the full ten years (Table 5.1), suggests a wide variety of patent subject matter and a high level of technological sophistication. At the same time the data on comparative rates of decay in this study do suggest that, even after filtering, expenditure on patents by the Individual inventors may be affected by personal vanity or ego, to a greater extent than the other Small Entity categories.

Because of the cost-saving which claiming Small Entity status brings, it seems probable that the Small Entity patent database contains a high proportion of the Individual patents granted by the USPTO. The few exceptions arise for reasons which have been indicated before: where an individual applying for a patent already has an agreement in place with a firm that would not qualify for SE fees; or where a patent has been applied for by a firm which does not qualify, which has then been assigned to individuals, perhaps directors in the firm. Such an assignment might happen under the terms of a contract, or for taxation or other financial reasons. As mentioned in Chapter 1, the interface between Individual and Small Firm patents is permeable in both directions.

For the most part, inventions and discoveries which are genuinely made by individuals working alone, or with a few colleagues, will not tend to be in areas demanding extensive cooperative research and the resources of a large laboratory or research facility. This is most likely to be true for the non-US

*Table 5.1    Individual inventors (US excl.); a random sample taken from the OECD\* countries; 1994 to 2003*

| Patent no. | Patent title | Country |
|---|---|---|
| 5311411 | Fog lighting system for a motor vehicle | Italy |
| 5333981 | Bale loading, transporting and unloading trailer | Canada |
| 5372423 | Device for mixing pulverulent material into a liquid | Spain |
| 5375632 | Compressed air aerosol bombs and refilling apparatus | Italy |
| 5413183 | Spherical reaming bit | Canada |
| 5514346 | Dryer for deodorization and sterilization | Japan |
| 5557053 | Snare strainer for a drum | Canada |
| 5597345 | Apparatus for making an aperture in a tile | UK |
| 5599152 | Multicomponent attachment for moveable device | Germany |
| 5610516 | Device for checking presence of metal | Germany |
| 5673865 | Waste debarker | Canada |
| 5717579 | Power supply unit for electric vehicles | Germany |
| 5775862 | Threaded device for externally threaded screw | Australia |
| 5876202 | Stagger cut teeth | Switz. |
| 5930867 | Door hinge | Germany |
| 5934584 | Base frame for paper comminuting devices | Germany |
| 5986231 | Production method for deburring die for castings | Japan |
| 6022211 | Lighter | Canada |
| 6135683 | Parallel mechanism for machining center | Korea |
| 6161936 | Portable lighting device | Japan |
| 6165105 | Apparatus and method for training respiratory muscles | Switz. |
| 6186876 | Apparatus for grinding welding electrodes | Denmark |
| 6295666 | Method for changing patient posture | Japan |
| 6318498 | Collapsible ladder | Canada |
| 6331569 | Preparation for improving hair growth | Switz. |
| 6386068 | Apparatus for sharpening/bevelling of ski edges | Canada |
| 6523265 | Clasp knife | Germany |
| 6571747 | Method and device for producing energy or methanol | Germany |
| 6619623 | Chain pulling device | Canada |
| 6648316 | Device for centering and clamping sheet metal | France |

countries in the OECD* group; in the US, because the SBIR programs specifically allow large proportions of their awards to be spent on 'consultancy', a greater number of individual inventors have access to laboratory expertise. We should not expect, therefore, to see the major proportion of Individual patents resulting from pharmaceutical research, nor indeed many in the development of high technology projects on the grand scale. If we expect the bulk of Individual patents to be in any particular category of Technology Class it would be the Mechanical classes, since these embrace many of the types of invention most suitable for individuals working alone and with minimal resources; generating prototypes with basic workshops and inexpensive technology. This point is well illustrated by the sample shown in Table 5.1.

It seems likely that, lacking the finance and infrastructure for continuous research and development, the invention process for individual inventors will be more likely to begin with the moment of inspiration than it will for firms or research organisations with the budget to pursue a market-driven, incremental 'step by step' approach. Pharmaceutical research, in particular, is an arduous, resource intensive process of systematic exploration; but even high technology firms are under pressure to follow an incremental path to innovation, often for competitive and economic reasons. The incremental approach to innovation is perceived as less risky for commercial firms, since they can invest progressively; they can extend or build upon already established products or services and look for synergy and convergence within their existing product range or build around their core technological expertise. The apparent reliability of such an approach is more attractive to the commercial firm (and to potential investors) but also makes it more difficult to maintain a balance between predictable incremental R&D paths on one hand and so-called 'blue sky' research on the other. The history of many 'breakthrough' discoveries teaches us that the process can often include much that is accidental or unpredictable. Here, individual inventors can be of benefit to the innovation process in an economy, since, at least in some areas of technology, they may be better positioned to explore territory that is removed from the well worn paths of commercial research. They are less encumbered (at least initially) by external stakeholders and more free to follow, like Robert Frost, the 'road less travelled'. Of equal significance is the fact that the number of potential individual inventors is vast, since it should approximately equal the world's adult population. Even a small proportion of patents of quality arising from a pool of such a size must be regarded as important to the innovation process. Thus the US-based United Inventors Association can reasonably advance its claim to be 'the voice of one of the largest 'Think Tanks' in the World'.[1] At present, unfortunately, the 'think tank' is being filled only to about half of its potential capacity, since there are very few women inventors. A random sample of one hundred patents taken from the Individual inventor category contained *only five* female inventors.

Given the scale of resources required for pursuing patents internationally we should expect that inventors patenting 'locally' like US and Canadian inventors would contain a higher proportion of Individuals than those coming from abroad. It was shown at the end of Chapter 2 (Table 2.25) that the count of US Individual patents represents 47.5 per cent of all US resident Small Entities for the ten years covered by our database. This is as expected. Similarly, the Canadian figure was 49.5 per cent. In comparison, the German Individual proportion, which is the highest of the Group A countries, was 36 per cent, and the majority of the non-US Group A patents was in the Small Firm category.

Figure 5.1 shows the Individual patent count per million of population for the Group A countries. As with the other Small Entity inventor categories, France has the lowest figure. In Group B (Figure 5.2) we see that the three countries which had the lowest count per million of Nonprofit patents, Austria, New Zealand and Norway, move well up the table of Individual patents. In particular, about half of Austria's SE patents were acquired by Individuals, 47 per cent of New Zealand's and 45 per cent of Norway's. It is worth noting, however, that Austria's SE patents were evenly divided between Individual and Small Firm patents; Nonprofit patents in Austria were virtually non-existent. Although Israel had the highest count of Individual patents, as it did in all Group B categories, these represented only a quarter of Israel's SE patents for the period; for whatever reason, by far the majority of Israel's SE patents, 62 per cent, were Small Firm patents.

*Figure 5.1   Group A; Individual patents per million, 1994 to 2003*

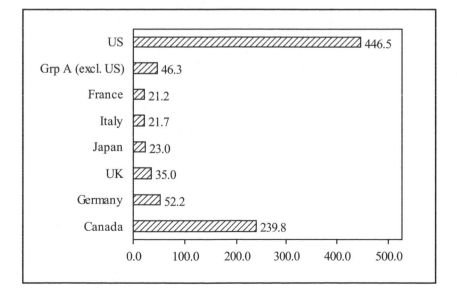

*Figure 5.2    Group B; Individual patents per million population, 1994 to 2003*

## CITATION OF INDIVIDUAL PATENTS

We next consider the potential value of the patents based on the citations data. Table 5.2 shows us that 57 per cent of the Individual patents for the Group A countries (without the US data) were cited at least once, compared to the figures we saw earlier of 56 per cent of Small Firm patents (Table 4.2) and 50 per cent of Nonprofit patents (Table 3.5). Thus, on the assumption that forward citations are a good measure of value for patents, Individual patents would appear to be the most valuable among our three categories of inventor. This order is repeated in the table for Group B countries (Table 5.3) where 53 per cent of Individual patents for the group were cited, against 51 per cent for Small Firms (Table 4.3) and 41 per cent for Nonprofits (Table 3.6).

*Table 5.2 Group A; Individual patents cited at least once, 1994 to 2002*

| Country | Not cited | Cited>=1 | % cited | Total |
|---|---|---|---|---|
| Canada | 2,785 | 4,124 | 59.7% | 6,909 |
| Germany | 1,644 | 2,257 | 57.9% | 3,901 |
| France | 521 | 654 | 55.7% | 1,175 |
| Japan | 1,217 | 1,459 | 54.5% | 2,676 |
| UK | 845 | 1,012 | 54.5% | 1,857 |
| Italy | 566 | 545 | 49.1% | 1,111 |
| Group A (US excl.) | 7,578 | 10,051 | 57.0% | 17,629 |
| US | 45,053 | 72,721 | 61.7% | 117,774 |
| Group A | 52,631 | 82,772 | 61.1% | 135,403 |

*Table 5.3 Group B; Individual patents cited at least once, 1994 to 2002*

| Country | Not cited | Cited>=1 | % cited | Total |
|---|---|---|---|---|
| Switzerland | 300 | 475 | 61.3% | 775 |
| Netherlands | 139 | 202 | 59.2% | 341 |
| Australia | 500 | 651 | 56.6% | 1,151 |
| Israel | 392 | 492 | 55.7% | 884 |
| Denmark | 103 | 128 | 55.4% | 231 |
| Finland | 157 | 188 | 54.5% | 345 |
| Belgium | 92 | 97 | 51.3% | 189 |
| New Zealand | 98 | 101 | 50.8% | 199 |
| Austria | 262 | 268 | 50.6% | 530 |
| Spain | 209 | 200 | 48.9% | 409 |
| Sweden | 422 | 386 | 47.8% | 808 |
| Korea | 621 | 530 | 46.0% | 1,151 |
| Norway | 143 | 122 | 46.0% | 265 |
| Ireland | 63 | 42 | 40.0% | 105 |
| Group B | 3,501 | 3,882 | 52.6% | 7,383 |

Looking back over the three inventor categories in Group B, Swiss inventors were at the top of the citations table for Small Firms (56.6 per cent were cited at least once) and also top the Individual inventor table (61.3 per cent cited). The largest change in these inventor categories is for Irish inventors who had 57 per cent of Small Firm patents cited once, but only 40 per cent of Individual patents. Also, as noted before, the proportion of US patents cited is comfortably above the average for Group A. This returns us to the argument presented earlier: that the 'filtering' mechanism of the USPTO applies equally to all nations other than the US itself. Since a filter for patent quality is not in operation on US patents (since virtually all US inventors go to the USPTO first) it becomes more difficult to explain – as a measure of value – the high US proportion of citations compared to other nations.

We can confirm from Table 5.4 showing Individual patents cited at least three times that the relative positions remain the same. The US proportion is 31.5 per cent; the figure for all other countries in the group is 26.5 per cent (and this figure includes Canada, which raises the average). The only change in rank order between Table 5.2 (cited once) and Table 5.4 (cited three times) is that Germany and France exchange 2nd and 3rd positions. For the Group B countries (Table 5.5) 23 per cent of the Individual patents were cited three times or more, which was almost identical to the proportion for Small Firm citations and well above the 17 per cent for Nonprofit patents.

*Table 5.4    Group A; Individual patents cited at least three times, 1994 to 2002*

| Country | Cited<3 | Cited>=3 | % cited | Total |
|---|---|---|---|---|
| Canada | 4,905 | 2,004 | 29.0% | 6,909 |
| France | 865 | 310 | 26.4% | 1,175 |
| Germany | 2,877 | 1,024 | 26.2% | 3,901 |
| UK | 1,396 | 461 | 24.8% | 1,857 |
| Japan | 2,035 | 641 | 24.0% | 2,676 |
| Italy | 885 | 226 | 20.3% | 1,111 |
| Group A (US excl.) | 12,963 | 4,666 | 26.5% | 17,629 |
| US | 80,674 | 37,100 | 31.5% | 117,774 |

Table 5.6 shows the distribution, for Group A, of Individual patents cited three times or more, distributed according to the three Technology Class groupings of Chemical, Electrical and Mechanical. The most cited classes were in the Electrical group with almost 26.5 per cent. The distribution for the US alone (Table 5.7) is similar but, as noted earlier, the proportion of citations

is substantially higher: almost 40 per cent of the Electrical class patents were cited. The Group B data is shown in Table 5.8, where we see lower citation proportions than Group A, but the same rank order. The pattern thus revealed is one where US Individual patents attracted a higher number of citations than Individual patents from any of the other Group A countries. Individual Group A patents, in turn, were cited more frequently than Group B patents. In every case the Electrical class patents were most frequently cited, and Chemical classes the least.

*Table 5.5    Group B; Individual patents cited three times or more, 1994 to 2002*

| Country | Cited<3 | Cited>=3 | % cited | Total |
|---|---|---|---|---|
| Israel | 627 | 257 | 29.1% | 884 |
| Switzerland | 566 | 209 | 27.0% | 775 |
| Netherlands | 251 | 90 | 26.4% | 341 |
| Australia | 854 | 297 | 25.8% | 1,151 |
| Denmark | 175 | 56 | 24.2% | 231 |
| Sweden | 643 | 165 | 20.4% | 808 |
| Austria | 424 | 106 | 20.0% | 530 |
| Korea | 921 | 230 | 20.0% | 1,151 |
| New Zealand | 160 | 39 | 19.6% | 199 |
| Belgium | 152 | 37 | 19.6% | 189 |
| Spain | 332 | 77 | 18.8% | 409 |
| Ireland | 86 | 19 | 18.1% | 105 |
| Finland | 283 | 62 | 18.0% | 345 |
| Norway | 218 | 47 | 17.7% | 265 |
| Group B | 5,692 | 1,691 | 22.9% | 7,383 |

*Table 5.6   Group A (US excl.); Individual patents cited three times or more by Technology Class, 1994 to 2002*

| Technology Class | Cited < 3 | Cited >= 3 | % cited | Total |
|---|---|---|---|---|
| Electrical | 1,532 | 696 | 31.2% | 2,228 |
| Mechanical | 9,325 | 3,355 | 26.5% | 12,680 |
| Chemical | 2,106 | 615 | 22.6% | 2,721 |
| Group A (US excl.) | 12,963 | 4,666 | 26.5% | 17,629 |

*Table 5.7    US; Individual patents cited three times or more by Technology Class, 1994 to 2002*

| Technology Class | Not Cited | Cited>=3 | % cited | Total |
|---|---|---|---|---|
| Electrical | 9,226 | 6,020 | 39.5% | 15,246 |
| Mechanical | 62,495 | 27,679 | 30.7% | 90,174 |
| Chemical | 8,949 | 3,401 | 27.5% | 12,350 |
| US | 80,670 | 37,100 | 31.5% | 117,770 |

*Table 5.8    Group B; Individual patents cited three times or more by Technology Class, 1994 to 2002*

| Technology Class | Not Cited | Cited>=3 | % cited | Total |
|---|---|---|---|---|
| Electrical | 640 | 257 | 28.7% | 897 |
| Mechanical | 4,122 | 1,235 | 23.1% | 5,357 |
| Chemical | 930 | 199 | 17.6% | 1,129 |
| Group B | 5,692 | 1,691 | 22.9% | 7,383 |

## INDIVIDUAL TECHNOLOGY CLASS GROUPS

It is appropriate to consider the previous data in the context of the distribution of class categories in each group. To begin we should examine the distribution of the class categories for Individual US inventors, presented in Figure 5.3. Over three quarters of all US Individual patents were acquired in the Mechanical classes, while Chemical and Electrical classes were evenly divided. When we look at the remaining Group A countries we see a similar picture, with 72 per cent of the Individual patents acquired in the Mechanical classes. The 15 Group B countries show a pattern almost identical to the non-US Group A countries, with 73 per cent in the Mechanical classes. It is safe to conclude that approaching three quarters of the USPTO patents acquired by Individual inventors from OECD* countries were in the Mechanical classes, perhaps an even higher proportion than might have been expected.

Figure 5.6 provides profile for each country in Group A. Across the group we can see that the proportion of Electrical class patents is relatively stable while the other two Technology Class groups fluctuate. The Japanese proportion of Chemical class patents was over 20 per cent. In Group B the proportion of Electrical class patents is more variable; we can observe the substantial difference between Austria and Israel as one example. Note that over 80 per cent of Australia's Individual patents were acquired in the Mechanical classes. Overall it is of interest that the Class category profile for Individual inventors, with a preponderance of Mechanical patents, is almost the inverse of the profile for Nonprofit inventors, where, as we saw in Chapter 3, Chemical patents take the lion's share.

*Figure 5.3   US alone; Individuals; Technology Classes, 1994 to 2003*

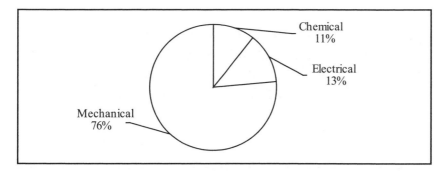

*Figure 5.4   Group A (excl. US); Individuals; Technology Classes, 1994 to 2003*

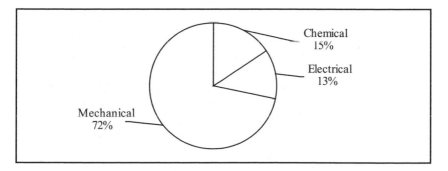

*Figure 5.5   Group B; Individuals; Technology Classes, 1994 to 2003*

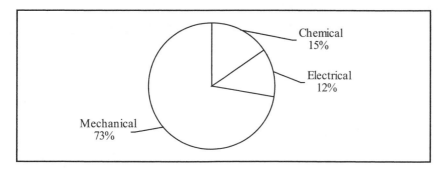

*Figure 5.6   Group A; Individuals, Technology Class Profile, 1994 to 2003*

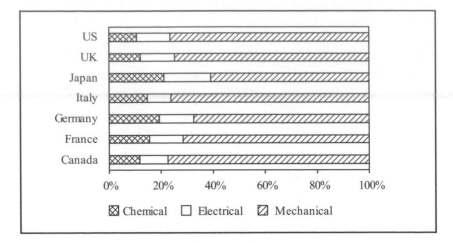

*Figure 5.7   Group B; Individuals,  Technology Class Profile, 1994 to 2003*

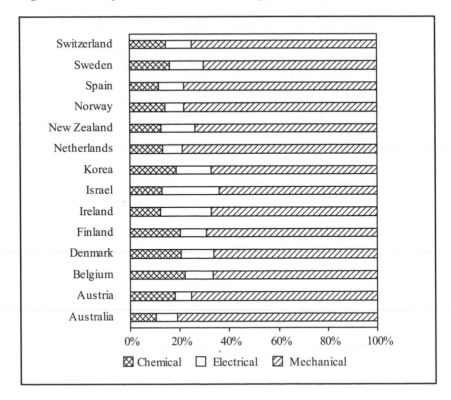

## INDIVIDUAL RATE OF DECAY

We drew attention at the outset of this study to assumptions that both citation counts and payment of renewal fees are measurements of patent value. However, the evidence so far from the database has raised a question about these two measures. We can compare the proportions of patents cited to the proportions which were permitted to lapse through non payment of the maintenance fees. In Table 5.4 the proportion of US inventor patents cited three times or more was 31.5 per cent, the highest citation rate for Individual patents. Table 5.9 shows the proportions of Individual patents from Group A countries which were allowed to lapse at four years. Here it is notable that the proportion of patents allowed to lapse by US inventors, at 33.5 per cent, is actually the highest of the group and substantially above the group average of 29 per cent. This is perhaps what we should expect. Since the USPTO does not provide the same filtering mechanism for US inventors as it does for foreign ones (except to some extent for Canadians), it seems natural to expect a larger proportion of US patents, particularly those acquired by Individual inventors, would not be maintained. However, as we have already seen, in the other two categories of inventor, Nonprofit (Chapter 3) and Small Firm (Chapter 4), the US rate for lapsed patents was actually below the average for the other six countries; in the case of Nonprofits it was well below. In summary, when we look at the citations data and the maintenance data side by side, we see that Individual US inventors have the highest proportion of patents cited, which would seem to suggest they are of greater value, but also the highest proportion of lapsed patents, meaning individual inventors lack the confidence, or the resources, to continue investment. Since the resources would be available if the patents were seen to have potential value, this contrast is puzzling.

*Table 5.9   Group A; Individual patents lapsing at 4 year renewal stage, 1994 to 1998*

| Country | Lapse (4 yr) | Maintained | % Lapsed | Total |
|---|---|---|---|---|
| Canada | 1,248 | 2,487 | 33.4% | 3,735 |
| UK | 292 | 612 | 32.3% | 904 |
| France | 190 | 482 | 28.3% | 672 |
| Italy | 161 | 435 | 27.0% | 596 |
| Germany | 515 | 1,488 | 25.7% | 2,003 |
| Japan | 291 | 1,086 | 21.1% | 1,377 |
| All (excl. US) | 2,697 | 6,590 | 29.0% | 9,287 |
| US | 20,862 | 41,420 | 33.5% | 62,282 |

We see in the Group B data (Table 5.10) an average patent decay rate just half a point below the average for the six non-US Group A countries. Of interest here is the rather high rate for Korea. It needs to borne in mind that the lapse data can only be safely measured for the years up to 1998 (since maintenance fees on the 1998 patents were due in 2002) and the bulk of Korea's SE patents were acquired in the later years of our ten year window. It is also important to point out that, during the same period, Korean Small Firms had the highest rate of patent maintenance (only 11 per cent lapsed) and 98 per cent of Korean Nonprofit patents were maintained at the four year stage. Nevertheless, 41 per cent of Korea's Individual inventors chose not to invest beyond that point.

*Table 5.10   Group B; Individual patents lapsing at 4 year renewal stage, 1994 to 1998*

| Country | Lapse (4 yr) | Maintained | % Lapsed | Total |
|---------|-------------|------------|----------|-------|
| Korea | 189 | 269 | 41.3% | 458 |
| New Zealand | 36 | 61 | 37.1% | 97 |
| Israel | 155 | 301 | 34.0% | 456 |
| Ireland | 12 | 26 | 31.6% | 38 |
| Spain | 64 | 145 | 30.6% | 209 |
| Australia | 177 | 430 | 29.2% | 607 |
| Belgium | 25 | 69 | 26.6% | 94 |
| Austria | 71 | 198 | 26.4% | 269 |
| Norway | 33 | 102 | 24.4% | 135 |
| Denmark | 31 | 97 | 24.2% | 128 |
| Switzerland | 105 | 363 | 22.4% | 468 |
| Netherlands | 43 | 153 | 21.9% | 196 |
| Finland | 43 | 159 | 21.3% | 202 |
| Sweden | 82 | 316 | 20.6% | 398 |
| All | 1,066 | 2,689 | 28.4% | 3,755 |

It is useful to see the proportion of lapsed patents in each group distributed according to the Technology Class categories. Table 5.11 gives this information for the Group A countries. Since we have established that Individual inventors are more likely to patent in the Mechanical classes and that those inventors may, in general, have less resources available for patent maintenance, it is perhaps not surprising to see the rate of decay at four years is highest (31 per cent) for Mechanical class patents. Individual patents in the Mechanical classes were allowed to expire at a substantially higher rate than those in the Chemical classes. We can confirm that the distribution of Class categories for Group B is much the same by referring to Table 5.13. We previously noted that the US rate of decay for Individual inventors is higher than the Group A or B countries. In Table 5.13 we see that, as we would expect, Mechanical class patents showed the highest rate of decay of all, at 35 per cent.

*Table 5.11   Group A (US excl.); Proportion of lapsed Individual patent by patent class category, 1994 to 1998*

| Technology Class | Lapse (4 yr) | Maintained | % Lapsed | Total |
|---|---|---|---|---|
| Mechanical | 2,088 | 4,675 | 30.9% | 6,763 |
| Electrical | 281 | 845 | 25.0% | 1,126 |
| Chemical | 328 | 1,070 | 23.5% | 1,398 |
| Group A | 2,697 | 6,590 | 29.0% | 9,287 |

*Table 5.12   US; Proportion of lapsed Individual patent by patent class category, 1994 to 1998*

| Technology Class | Lapse (4 yr) | Maintained | % Lapsed | Total |
|---|---|---|---|---|
| Mechanical | 17,095 | 31,369 | 35.3% | 48,464 |
| Electrical | 2,221 | 5,300 | 29.5% | 7,521 |
| Chemical | 1,546 | 4,750 | 24.6% | 6,296 |
| US Individual | 20,862 | 41,420 | 33.5% | 62,282 |

*Table 5.13   Group B; Proportion of lapsed Individual patent by patent class category, 1994 to 1998*

| Technology Class | Lapse (4 yr) | Maintained | % Lapsed | Total |
|---|---|---|---|---|
| Mechanical | 862 | 1,922 | 31.0% | 2,784 |
| Electrical | 103 | 329 | 23.8% | 432 |
| Chemical | 101 | 438 | 18.7% | 539 |
| Group B | 1,066 | 2,689 | 28.4% | 3,755 |

*Table 5.14   Group A; Proportion of Individual patent lapsing at 8 years, by patent class category, 1994 only*

| Technology Class | Lapse (8yr) | Maintained | % Lapsed | Total |
|---|---|---|---|---|
| Chemical | 138 | 119 | 46.3% | 257 |
| Electrical | 96 | 81 | 45.8% | 177 |
| Mechanical | 778 | 544 | 41.1% | 1,322 |
| Group A (US excl.) | 1,012 | 744 | 42.4% | 1,756 |

It is particularly interesting to look back now at the analysis for Group A citations shown in Table 5.6 and Group B citations in Table 5.8. In both cases the Technology Class group with the highest rate of citations was the Electrical one, but Electrical class patents were allowed to lapse at a higher rate than Chemical class patents. And while Individual Chemical class patents were better maintained than the other two Technology Class groups they also received the lowest number of citations. Again the contrast is puzzling.

It may or may not be significant that the limited data for Individual patents lapsing at the eight year renewal stage shows the decay of the Technology Class groups in exactly the reverse order. In Table 5.14 the Mechanical class showed the lowest rate of decay and Chemical classes the highest. Unfortunately, since the analysis for maintenance at the eight year renewal stage is based entirely on a single year of our data, 1994, only an accumulation of later data will reveal whether this pattern is consistent for the second renewal stage.

## INDIVIDUAL PATENT OWNERSHIP BY US ENTITIES

From the point of view of each member of the OECD* group (other than the US) it is of interest, but perhaps entirely predictable, that the proportion of Individual patents assigned to US entities should be virtually zero. Table 5.15 shows the Group A figures for the Individual category and here, for example, only 11 patents, about a half of one per cent of the patents where a UK resident was the first named inventor, were assigned to US Individuals (some of whom may well represent firms). These negligible percentages may represent US citizens working and living, at the time of the patent application, in the UK and this factor may apply equally to the other nations. In at least two of the UK patents, the inventor and the assignee were the same person, giving a UK address as inventor and a US address as assignee.

*Table 5.15   Group A; Individual patents; % assigned to US entities, 1994 to 2003*

| Country | Non-US | US owned | % US-owned | Total |
|---|---|---|---|---|
| UK | 2,047 | 11 | 0.5% | 2,058 |
| Japan | 2,934 | 15 | 0.5% | 2,949 |
| Italy | 1,241 | 6 | 0.5% | 1,247 |
| France | 1,259 | 5 | 0.4% | 1,264 |
| Canada | 7,513 | 16 | 0.2% | 7,529 |
| Germany | 4,274 | 8 | 0.2% | 4,282 |
| All (excl. US) | 19,268 | 61 | 0.3% | 19,329 |

In the Group B data in Table 5.16 we see the US-owned proportion climb above 1 per cent in Israel; which is again what we might expect. Ireland, which has a high degree of direct investment from the US and a significant presence of US corporate firms, has a relatively high proportion of Individual patents assigned to US Individuals. Looking back at Figure 5.7 we note that Israel and Ireland are also the two countries with the highest proportion of Electrical class patents, those classes which include the majority of the 'high technology' electronic inventions. So it is conceivable that this effect could be ascribed to the presence of high technology US firms in both countries and the consequent residence there, temporary or otherwise, of US engineers.

Finally, in this section we examine the distribution of Individual patents assigned to US entities according to the Technology Class groupings. We note that the highest proportion of US assignment for the Group A countries (Table 5.17) was among the Chemical class patents with half of one per cent. The Group B distribution (Table 5.18) is identical. In summary, the average assignment of Individual patents to US entities (discounting the US itself) was around 0.3 per cent.

*Table 5.16  Group B; Proportion of Individually owned patents assigned to US entities, 1994 to 2003*

| Country | Non-US | US owned | % US-owned | Total |
|---|---|---|---|---|
| Israel | 968 | 10 | 1.0% | 978 |
| Ireland | 118 | 1 | 0.8% | 119 |
| Korea | 1,369 | 8 | 0.6% | 1,377 |
| Spain | 451 | 2 | 0.4% | 453 |
| Denmark | 248 | 1 | 0.4% | 249 |
| Austria | 587 | 2 | 0.3% | 589 |
| Australia | 1,278 | 2 | 0.2% | 1,280 |
| Switzerland | 824 | 1 | 0.1% | 825 |
| Belgium | 205 | 0 | 0.0% | 205 |
| Finland | 369 | 0 | 0.0% | 369 |
| Netherlands | 365 | 0 | 0.0% | 365 |
| New Zealand | 220 | 0 | 0.0% | 220 |
| Norway | 295 | 0 | 0.0% | 295 |
| Sweden | 869 | 0 | 0.0% | 869 |
| All | 8,166 | 27 | 0.3% | 8,193 |

*Table 5.17    Group A (US excl.); Individual patents assigned to US entities, distributed by Technology Class group, 1994 to 2003*

| Technology Class | Non-US | US owned | % US-owned |
|---|---|---|---|
| Chemical | 2,964 | 16 | 0.5% |
| Electrical | 2,467 | 8 | 0.3% |
| Mechanical | 13,836 | 37 | 0.3% |
| Group A (US excl.) | 19,268 | 61 | 0.3% |

*Table 5.18    Group B; Individual patents assigned to US entities, distributed by Technology Class group, 1994 to 2003*

| Technology Class | Non-US | US owned | % US-owned |
|---|---|---|---|
| Chemical | 1,246 | 6 | 0.5% |
| Electrical | 1,016 | 3 | 0.3% |
| Mechanical | 5,904 | 18 | 0.3% |
| Group B | 8,166 | 27 | 0.3% |

## NOTE

1.  Accessed at http://www.uiausa.org

# 6. The non-OECD* countries

In the ten year period covered by this study 134 countries acquired at least a single USPTO Small Entity patent.[1] The previous three chapters have presented the data for 31 of these – the OECD* countries – in some detail. This chapter examines the balance of 103 countries. To facilitate analysis, since for most countries the actual USPTO patent count is negligible, two further groups were created. The first group, Group D, was established using a cut-off point of the total count of Small Entity patents held by the lowest of the OECD* countries, Slovakia. Thus any country in the 103 whose resident inventors acquired 18 Small Entity patents or more was included in Group D. This amounted to 32 countries, and Figure 6.1 below shows the patents per million data for this group. The final group of 71 countries becomes Group E. Over the full ten years of the study, these 71 countries accumulated 365 Small Entity patents, roughly averaging five SE patents per country or one Small Entity patent every two years. A full table for Group E is given as Appendix D.

As with previous chapters, it is helpful to see the proportions for each country in Group D where the inventor claimed priority under the Paris Convention (Table 6.1) and to compare them with the equivalent proportions for the OECD* countries. Table 2.1 showed that inventors from the OECD* countries claimed priority in almost 80 per cent of the cases. By contrast, the equivalent overall proportion for our Group D non-OECD* countries was 19 per cent. A major factor here is the high count for Taiwan and the fact that only 8 per cent of Taiwan's inventors claimed priority, meaning that 92 per cent of Taiwanese Small Entity patents were filed first with the USPTO.[2]

Taiwan is an exceptional case in this Group, nor is there a comparable country within the OECD* groups.[3] Between 1994 and 2003 Taiwanese residents acquired 19,159 Small Entity patents; a count larger than any other country in the world beside the US itself. It represents 80 per cent of the 23,993 Small Entity patents acquired by all the Group D countries combined. It is higher than Canada (15,196) and dramatically higher than Japan (12,647) or Germany (11,880). The scale of SE patenting activity by Taiwanese residents is remarkable, but even more remarkable when we find that SE patents represented 56 per cent of all Taiwan's USPTO patents for the period. This SE proportion is higher than Canada, the US's next door neighbour.

Returning to Figure 6.1, the extremely high per-million counts for Monaco,

*Figure 6.1   Group D; SE patents per million population, 1994 to 2003*

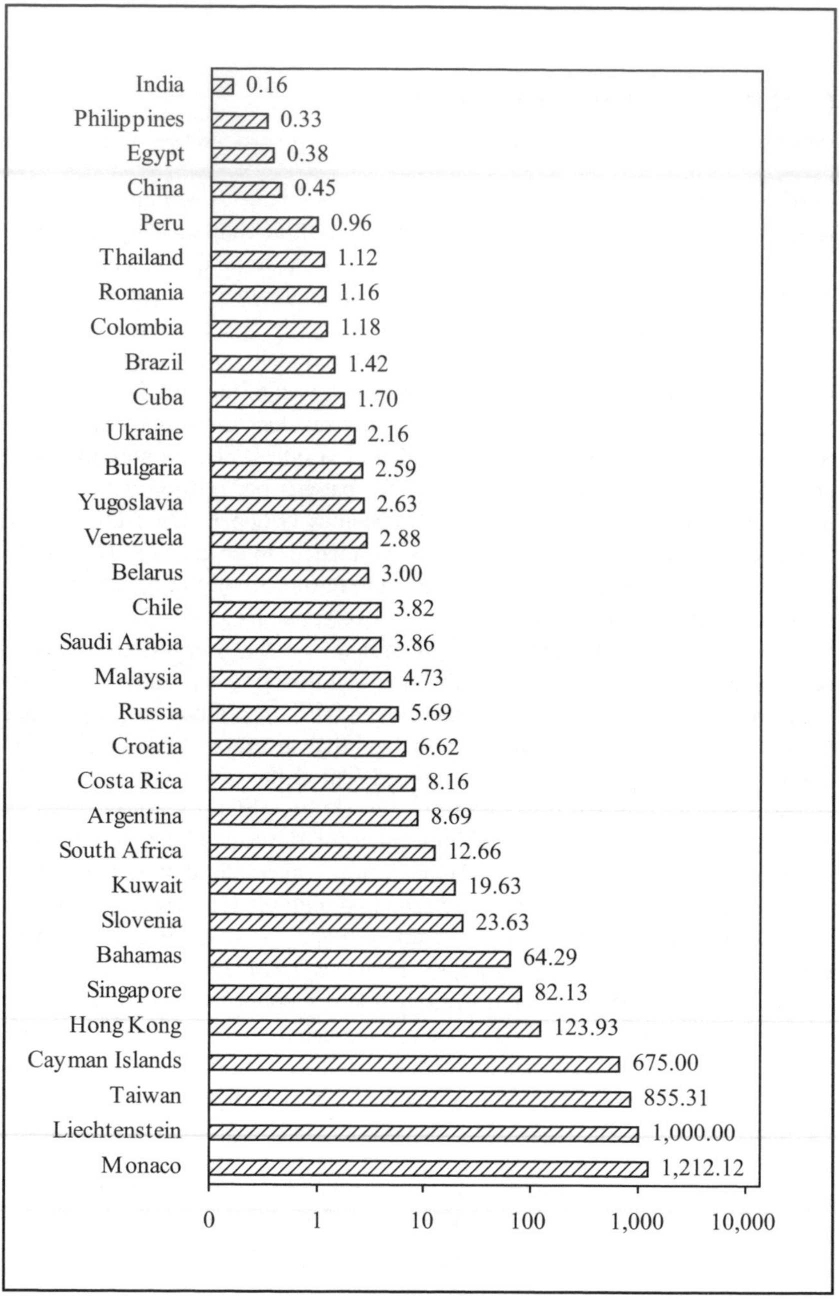

India          0.16
Philippines    0.33
Egypt          0.38
China          0.45
Peru           0.96
Thailand       1.12
Romania        1.16
Colombia       1.18
Brazil         1.42
Cuba           1.70
Ukraine        2.16
Bulgaria       2.59
Yugoslavia     2.63
Venezuela      2.88
Belarus        3.00
Chile          3.82
Saudi Arabia   3.86
Malaysia       4.73
Russia         5.69
Croatia        6.62
Costa Rica     8.16
Argentina      8.69
South Africa   12.66
Kuwait         19.63
Slovenia       23.63
Bahamas        64.29
Singapore      82.13
Hong Kong      123.93
Cayman Islands 675.00
Taiwan         855.31
Liechtenstein  1,000.00
Monaco         1,212.12

0     1     10     100     1,000     10,000

*Table 6.1  Group D; proportion of SE patents where priority was claimed under the Paris Convention, 1994 to 2003*

| Country | SE total | Priority claim | % Priority |
|---|---|---|---|
| Cuba | 19 | 19 | 100.0% |
| Liechtenstein | 34 | 30 | 88.2% |
| Monaco | 40 | 34 | 85.0% |
| Slovenia | 47 | 39 | 83.0% |
| Yugoslavia | 28 | 22 | 78.6% |
| South Africa | 557 | 416 | 74.7% |
| Bulgaria | 21 | 15 | 71.4% |
| Croatia | 29 | 20 | 69.0% |
| China | 562 | 358 | 63.7% |
| Brazil | 241 | 138 | 57.3% |
| Argentina | 313 | 174 | 55.6% |
| Romania | 26 | 14 | 53.8% |
| Ukraine | 107 | 50 | 46.7% |
| Russia | 828 | 382 | 46.1% |
| Malaysia | 110 | 44 | 40.0% |
| Singapore | 330 | 129 | 39.1% |
| India | 158 | 60 | 38.0% |
| Belarus | 30 | 11 | 36.7% |
| Chile | 58 | 21 | 36.2% |
| Thailand | 68 | 17 | 25.0% |
| Philippines | 25 | 6 | 24.0% |
| Bahamas | 27 | 6 | 22.2% |
| Hong Kong | 826 | 172 | 20.8% |
| Colombia | 50 | 9 | 18.0% |
| Egypt | 24 | 4 | 16.7% |
| Kuwait | 43 | 7 | 16.3% |
| Costa Rica | 31 | 5 | 16.1% |
| Venezuela | 70 | 8 | 11.4% |
| Taiwan | 19,159 | 1,566 | 8.2% |
| Saudi Arabia | 80 | 6 | 7.5% |
| Cayman Islands | 27 | 2 | 7.4% |
| Peru | 25 | 1 | 4.0% |
| Group D | 23,993 | 3,785 | 18.7% |

Liechtenstein and the Cayman Islands are notable. The distribution of SE patent ownership for these countries was divided between Small Firms and Individuals, and there were no Nonprofit patents. However, the absolute ten year counts are small: 40 for Monaco, 34 for Liechtenstein and 27 for the Caymans. It is the tiny population in each case which inflates the per-million proportion. It is also probably necessary to bear in mind potential benefits of owning USPTO patents as a resident of some of the smaller nations and principalities around the world and to allow for favourable tax regimes and regulations governing residency. Thus there is a difficulty in reading very much, in terms of national innovative activity, into the data for many of the countries with low SE counts.

A good illustration of the difficulty may be seen by looking in detail at the data for the Cayman Islands, whose residents acquired 27 Small Entity patents in the ten years. Nineteen of these (or 70 per cent) showed either Jens or Soren Sorensen (or both together) as the inventors. The assignees for the Sorensen patents included a variety of small firms such as 'Universal Ventures', 'Gillian Holdings Ltd', 'GB Electrical Inc' and 'Sorensen Research & Development Trust'.

## CITATION OF GROUP D SMALL ENTITY PATENTS

The proportion of Group D Small Entity patents cited at least once, at 55 per cent, is similar to that for the OECD* countries. Again, the countries with very small counts often show extreme figures. In Table 6.2 the top seven countries shared 214 SE patents. Taiwan, however, which acquired 80 per cent of Group D's Small Entity patents, saw 56 per cent of them cited. Of the other countries which had SE counts of any size, South Africa had the same proportion as Taiwan while the Russian Federation and Hong Kong were both above 50 per cent cited. The proportions cited three or more times, again largely due to Taiwan, are very close to the equivalent proportions for the Group A countries (Table 2.13) when the US data are omitted.

The proportions of each Technology Class group cited at least three times (Table 6.4) are similar to Group B of the OECD* countries; the Electrical classes were cited most frequently, though the Mechanical classes were cited almost as often. This is due to the fact that Group D is mainly about Taiwan, and Taiwan, as will be seen, had a huge preponderance of Mechanical class inventions during the period.

The distribution of citations for the Small Entity types is given in Table 6.5. Unlike the Groups A and B countries, where the proportions of Individual and Small Firm patents cited three times are almost the same, 28 per cent of the Individual inventors from the Group D countries were cited three or more

*Table 6.2   Group D; SE patents cited at least once, 1994 to 2002*

| Country | Not Cited | Cited>=1 | % cited | Total |
|---|---|---|---|---|
| Peru | 6 | 15 | 71.4% | 21 |
| Cayman Islands | 7 | 17 | 70.8% | 24 |
| Romania | 7 | 14 | 66.7% | 21 |
| Saudi Arabia | 27 | 50 | 64.9% | 77 |
| Thailand | 22 | 36 | 62.1% | 58 |
| Belarus | 11 | 16 | 59.3% | 27 |
| Yugoslavia | 11 | 16 | 59.3% | 27 |
| Taiwan | 7,314 | 9,315 | 56.0% | 16,629 |
| South Africa | 224 | 284 | 55.9% | 508 |
| Ukraine | 43 | 54 | 55.7% | 97 |
| Monaco | 17 | 21 | 55.3% | 38 |
| Venezuela | 30 | 35 | 53.8% | 65 |
| Bulgaria | 7 | 8 | 53.3% | 15 |
| India | 61 | 67 | 52.3% | 128 |
| Liechtenstein | 15 | 16 | 51.6% | 31 |
| Hong Kong | 336 | 355 | 51.4% | 691 |
| Brazil | 104 | 108 | 50.9% | 212 |
| Russia | 354 | 364 | 50.7% | 718 |
| Bahamas | 12 | 12 | 50.0% | 24 |
| Singapore | 120 | 116 | 49.2% | 236 |
| Argentina | 137 | 130 | 48.7% | 267 |
| Malaysia | 49 | 46 | 48.4% | 95 |
| Slovenia | 24 | 22 | 47.8% | 46 |
| Philippines | 12 | 10 | 45.5% | 22 |
| China | 252 | 207 | 45.1% | 459 |
| Chile | 30 | 22 | 42.3% | 52 |
| Costa Rica | 16 | 11 | 40.7% | 27 |
| Colombia | 25 | 17 | 40.5% | 42 |
| Egypt | 12 | 8 | 40.0% | 20 |
| Kuwait | 22 | 14 | 38.9% | 36 |
| Croatia | 17 | 8 | 32.0% | 25 |
| Cuba | 11 | 3 | 21.4% | 14 |
| Group D | 9,335 | 11,417 | 55.0% | 20,752 |

Table 6.3   Group D, SE patents cited three times or more, 1994 to 2002

| Country | Cited < 3 | Cited >= 3 | % cited | Total |
|---|---|---|---|---|
| Peru | 12 | 9 | 42.9% | 21 |
| Bahamas | 14 | 10 | 41.7% | 24 |
| Thailand | 36 | 22 | 37.9% | 58 |
| Belarus | 17 | 10 | 37.0% | 27 |
| Yugoslavia | 18 | 9 | 33.3% | 27 |
| Liechtenstein | 22 | 9 | 29.0% | 31 |
| Romania | 15 | 6 | 28.6% | 21 |
| Taiwan | 12,053 | 4,576 | 27.5% | 16,629 |
| Saudi Arabia | 56 | 21 | 27.3% | 77 |
| Malaysia | 70 | 25 | 26.3% | 95 |
| India | 96 | 32 | 25.0% | 128 |
| Cayman Islands | 18 | 6 | 25.0% | 24 |
| South Africa | 382 | 126 | 24.8% | 508 |
| Colombia | 32 | 10 | 23.8% | 42 |
| Singapore | 180 | 56 | 23.7% | 236 |
| Monaco | 29 | 9 | 23.7% | 38 |
| Hong Kong | 532 | 159 | 23.0% | 691 |
| Argentina | 210 | 57 | 21.3% | 267 |
| Venezuela | 52 | 13 | 20.0% | 65 |
| Russia | 580 | 138 | 19.2% | 718 |
| Costa Rica | 22 | 5 | 18.5% | 27 |
| Brazil | 173 | 39 | 18.4% | 212 |
| Philippines | 18 | 4 | 18.2% | 22 |
| Slovenia | 38 | 8 | 17.4% | 46 |
| China | 381 | 78 | 17.0% | 459 |
| Egypt | 17 | 3 | 15.0% | 20 |
| Ukraine | 83 | 14 | 14.4% | 97 |
| Croatia | 22 | 3 | 12.0% | 25 |
| Chile | 47 | 5 | 9.6% | 52 |
| Kuwait | 35 | 1 | 2.8% | 36 |
| Bulgaria | 15 | 0 | 0.0% | 15 |
| Cuba | 14 | 0 | 0.0% | 14 |
| Group D | 15,289 | 5,463 | 26.3% | 20,752 |

times, well ahead of the 23 per cent for Small Firm inventors. Perhaps more significantly, since Taiwan represents the major part of the non OECD\* Small Entity patents, Table 6.6 shows that almost 29 per cent of Taiwan's Individual inventors were cited three times or more against 23.6 per cent for Small Firms.

*Table 6.4   Group D; Proportions for each Technology Class group of patents cited three times or more, 1994 to 2002*

| Technology Class | Cited <3 | Cited >=3 | % cited | Total |
|---|---|---|---|---|
| Electrical | 2,985 | 1,136 | 27.6% | 4,121 |
| Mechanical | 10,499 | 3,962 | 27.4% | 14,461 |
| Chemical | 1,800 | 365 | 16.9% | 2,165 |
| Group D | 15,289 | 5,463 | 26.3% | 20,752 |

*Table 6.5   Group D; Proportions for each Small Entity type of patents cited three times or more, 1994 to 2002*

| SE Category | Cited <3 | Cited >=3 | % cited | Total |
|---|---|---|---|---|
| Individual | 10,582 | 4,070 | 27.8% | 14,652 |
| Small Firm | 4,160 | 1,243 | 23.0% | 5,403 |
| Nonprofit | 547 | 150 | 21.5% | 697 |
| Group D | 15,289 | 5,463 | 26.3% | 20,752 |

*Table 6.6   Taiwan; Proportions for each Small Entity type of patents cited three times or more, 1994 to 2002*

| SE Category | Cited < 3 | Cited >= 3 | % cited | Total |
|---|---|---|---|---|
| Individual | 8,970 | 3,622 | 28.8% | 12,592 |
| Nonprofit | 256 | 83 | 24.5% | 339 |
| Small Firm | 2,827 | 871 | 23.6% | 3,698 |
| Taiwan | 12,053 | 4,576 | 27.5% | 16,629 |

## GROUP D TECHNOLOGY CLASS GROUPS

The predominant type of invention in Group D was in the Mechanical classes, with almost 70 per cent (Figure 6.2). In effect this is the proportion for Taiwan which dominates the group. This can be better seen in the Technology Class profile in Figure 6.4. A few countries, mainly Eastern European ones like Belarus, Romania, Russia and Ukraine, have a balanced distribution. An extreme case is Cuba, whose 19 SE patents were all in the Chemical classes, and Peru, where 23 of the 25 SE patents were in the Mechanical classes. Over half of India's tiny SE total was in the Chemical classes, which may be a reflection of that country's strong indigenous pharmaceutical industry.

The distribution of the Technology Classes across the three Small Entity categories is shown for Taiwan in Figure 6.3. It is clear that the predominant invention among Taiwan's Nonprofits was in the Chemical classes, and in the Mechanical classes for the other two SE categories; in fact Mechanical class invention represented almost 80 per cent of Taiwan's Individual USPTO patents.

*Figure 6.2   Group D; SE patents – distribution of Technology Class groups*

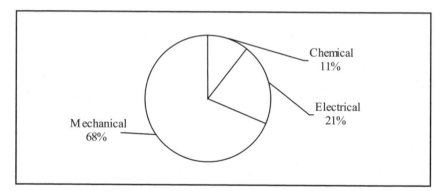

*Figure 6.3     Taiwan; Technology Class profile according to Small Entity category, 1994 to 2003*

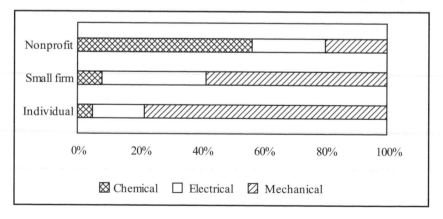

*Figure 6.4   Group D; Technology Class profile, 1994 to 2003*

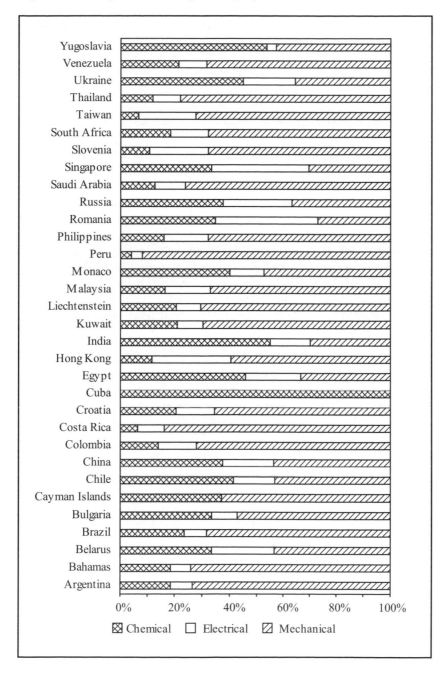

## GROUP D PATENT DECAY

The rate of decay for the Small Entity patents in Group D (Table 6.9) was high, particularly when compared to the equivalent figures for the OECD* countries (Tables 2.16 and 2.17). In general the OECD* countries showed a decay rate of around 20 to 25 per cent, or even less, whereas Taiwan's 50 per cent rate raised the rate for Group D to 46.4 per cent. In this respect Taiwan's Small Entity inventors behaved quite differently from Japanese and Korean inventors – the two other strong Asian economies in our data – which had decay rates of 16 per cent and 22 per cent respectively.

Although, as mentioned before, there is insufficient data in ten years for a useful study of the eight year maintenance point, it is remarkable to see in Table 6.10 that three quarters of the Small Entity patents acquired by the Group D countries in 1994 had lapsed by 1999, at the eight year stage. The figure for Taiwan was 78 per cent. The equivalent proportion for the OECD* countries was 51 per cent (see Table 2.22).

Table 6.7 and Table 6.8 show the proportions lapsing for each of the Technology Class groups. The figures are high across all Technology Classes, but the effect of the high Taiwanese decay rate affects the Mechanical class patents in particular. Chemical class patents were considerably more likely to be maintained and showed a rate of decay somewhat closer to that of the OECD* countries.

*Table 6.7   Group D; Proportion of each Technology Class group lapsing at the first (4 year) renewal stage, 1994 to 1998*

| Technology Class | Count (94 to 98) | Lapse at 4 yrs | % Lapsed |
| --- | --- | --- | --- |
| Mechanical | 4,740 | 2,381 | 50.2% |
| Electrical | 1,072 | 418 | 39.0% |
| Chemical | 611 | 184 | 30.1% |
| Group D | 6,423 | 2,983 | 46.4% |

*Table 6.8   Group D; Proportion of each Technology Class group lapsing at the second (8 year) renewal stage, 1994 only*

| Technology Class | 1994 count | Lapsed at 8 yrs | % Lapsed |
| --- | --- | --- | --- |
| Mechanical | 1,121 | 904 | 80.6% |
| Electrical | 220 | 136 | 61.8% |
| Chemical | 137 | 74 | 54.0% |
| Group D | 1,478 | 1,114 | 75.4% |

*Table 6.9   Group D; SE patents lapsing at the first (4 year) renewal stage*

| Country | Count (94 to 98) | Lapsed at 4 yrs | % Lapsed |
|---|---|---|---|
| Taiwan | 5,134 | 2,578 | 50.2% |
| Colombia | 18 | 9 | 50.0% |
| Egypt | 6 | 3 | 50.0% |
| Thailand | 20 | 9 | 45.0% |
| Ukraine | 29 | 13 | 44.8% |
| Monaco | 12 | 5 | 41.7% |
| Philippines | 5 | 2 | 40.0% |
| Romania | 5 | 2 | 40.0% |
| Singapore | 55 | 19 | 34.5% |
| Brazil | 93 | 31 | 33.3% |
| Saudi Arabia | 36 | 12 | 33.3% |
| Costa Rica | 12 | 4 | 33.3% |
| Slovenia | 12 | 4 | 33.3% |
| Russia | 196 | 65 | 33.2% |
| South Africa | 221 | 72 | 32.6% |
| Argentina | 87 | 28 | 32.2% |
| Chile | 13 | 4 | 30.8% |
| Hong Kong | 170 | 52 | 30.6% |
| Bulgaria | 7 | 2 | 28.6% |
| China | 134 | 37 | 27.6% |
| Malaysia | 29 | 8 | 27.6% |
| India | 27 | 7 | 25.9% |
| Venezuela | 31 | 7 | 22.6% |
| Cayman Islands | 9 | 2 | 22.2% |
| Belarus | 10 | 2 | 20.0% |
| Bahamas | 5 | 1 | 20.0% |
| Croatia | 5 | 1 | 20.0% |
| Liechtenstein | 13 | 2 | 15.4% |
| Peru | 8 | 1 | 12.5% |
| Yugoslavia | 16 | 1 | 6.3% |
| Kuwait | 4 | 0 | 0.0% |
| Cuba | 1 | 0 | 0.0% |
| Group D | 6,423 | 2,983 | 46.4% |

*Table 6.10   Group D; SE patents lapsing at the second (8 year) renewal stage, 1994 only*

| Country | Count 1994 | Lapsed at 8 yrs | % Lapsed |
|---|---|---|---|
| Monaco | 3 | 3 | 100.0% |
| Bulgaria | 2 | 2 | 100.0% |
| Colombia | 2 | 2 | 100.0% |
| Thailand | 2 | 2 | 100.0% |
| Peru | 1 | 1 | 100.0% |
| Saudi Arabia | 8 | 7 | 87.5% |
| India | 7 | 6 | 85.7% |
| Ukraine | 6 | 5 | 83.3% |
| Venezuela | 6 | 5 | 83.3% |
| Taiwan | 1,220 | 955 | 78.3% |
| Argentina | 24 | 18 | 75.0% |
| Russia | 16 | 10 | 62.5% |
| China | 29 | 18 | 62.1% |
| Malaysia | 5 | 3 | 60.0% |
| Brazil | 22 | 13 | 59.1% |
| South Africa | 58 | 34 | 58.6% |
| Hong Kong | 26 | 15 | 57.7% |
| Singapore | 14 | 7 | 50.0% |
| Costa Rica | 2 | 1 | 50.0% |
| Egypt | 2 | 1 | 50.0% |
| Slovenia | 2 | 1 | 50.0% |
| Yugoslavia | 8 | 3 | 37.5% |
| Liechtenstein | 8 | 2 | 25.0% |
| Belarus | 2 | 0 | 0.0% |
| Chile | 2 | 0 | 0.0% |
| Kuwait | 1 | 0 | 0.0% |
| Group D | 1,478 | 1,114 | 75.4% |

When Taiwan is examined on its own (Table 6.11) we see that the Individual inventor patents are chiefly responsible for the high rate of decay. Although, in relation to the country's overall total, the number of Nonprofit patents from Taiwan was small, the level of maintenance for the 1994 to 1998 Nonprofits was high, at over 93 per cent.

*Table 6.11   Taiwan; Proportion of each Small Entity category lapsing at the first (4 year) renewal stage, 1994 to 1998*

| SE Category | Lapsed 4 yrs | Maintained | % lapsed | Total |
|---|---|---|---|---|
| Individual | 3,040 | 2,716 | 52.8% | 5,756 |
| Small Firm | 430 | 689 | 38.4% | 1,119 |
| Nonprofit | 12 | 165 | 6.8% | 177 |
| Taiwan | 3,482 | 3,570 | 49.4% | 7,052 |

## GROUP D PATENT OWNERSHIP BY US ENTITIES

Table 6.13 displays the proportions assigned to US entities for Group D. When compared to the figures for the OECD\* countries the proportions assigned to US entities are high although the actual patent counts are minimal in most cases. It is particularly intriguing to observe the high proportion of assignment to US entities of SE patents from the Russian Federation (38.4%) and the former USSR states of Belarus (40%) and the Ukraine (25%). Taiwan, on the other hand, with the majority share of the SE patents for Group D, had only 1 per cent of them assigned to US entities, one of the lowest proportions in the world and lower even than Japan. The Group D average is 4 per cent, mainly because of Taiwan.

Table 6.12 reveals a substantial disparity between the proportion of Chemical class patents assigned to US entities (12%) and the other two class groups. The Mechanical class is the favoured class for Individual invention, and Individual inventors generally have the lowest level of assignment to US entities. Table 6.14 examines the proportion of US assignment for each of Taiwan's SE categories. Predictably, the Individual inventor category, the most prolific, has virtually zero US assignment, while the rate for Small Firms is about 4 per cent, well below the equivalent rate for the OECD\* countries shown in Tables 4.17 and 4.18.

*Table 6.12   Group D; proportions of each Technology Class group assigned to US entities, 1994 to 2003*

| Technology Class | Total | US owned | % US owned |
|---|---|---|---|
| Chemical | 2,545 | 297 | 11.7% |
| Electrical | 4,987 | 223 | 4.5% |
| Mechanical | 16,456 | 436 | 2.6% |
| Group D | 23,993 | 956 | 4.0% |

*Table 6.13  Group D; % assigned to US entities, 1994 to 2003*

| Country | Total | US owned | % US owned |
|---|---|---|---|
| Egypt | 24 | 13 | 54.2% |
| Cayman Islands | 27 | 12 | 44.4% |
| Belarus | 30 | 12 | 40.0% |
| Russia | 828 | 318 | 38.4% |
| Malaysia | 110 | 37 | 33.6% |
| Bahamas | 27 | 8 | 29.6% |
| Ukraine | 107 | 27 | 25.2% |
| Yugoslavia | 28 | 7 | 25.0% |
| Romania | 26 | 5 | 19.2% |
| India | 158 | 25 | 15.8% |
| Venezuela | 70 | 11 | 15.7% |
| China | 562 | 81 | 14.4% |
| Chile | 58 | 8 | 13.8% |
| Slovenia | 47 | 6 | 12.8% |
| Peru | 25 | 3 | 12.0% |
| Thailand | 68 | 6 | 8.8% |
| Hong Kong | 826 | 71 | 8.6% |
| Brazil | 241 | 18 | 7.5% |
| Croatia | 29 | 2 | 6.9% |
| Costa Rica | 31 | 2 | 6.5% |
| Saudi Arabia | 80 | 5 | 6.3% |
| Argentina | 313 | 17 | 5.4% |
| South Africa | 557 | 29 | 5.2% |
| Monaco | 40 | 2 | 5.0% |
| Bulgaria | 21 | 1 | 4.8% |
| Colombia | 50 | 2 | 4.0% |
| Philippines | 25 | 1 | 4.0% |
| Singapore | 330 | 9 | 2.7% |
| Kuwait | 43 | 1 | 2.3% |
| Taiwan | 19,159 | 217 | 1.1% |
| Liechtenstein | 34 | 0 | 0.0% |
| Cuba | 19 | 0 | 0.0% |
| Group D | 23,993 | 956 | 4.0% |

*Table 6.14   Taiwan; proportions of each Small Entity category assigned to US entities, 1994 to 2003*

| SE Category | Total | US owned | % US owned |
|---|---|---|---|
| Small Firm | 4,592 | 193 | 4.2% |
| Nonprofit | 381 | 5 | 1.3% |
| Individual | 14,186 | 19 | 0.1% |
| Taiwan | 19,159 | 217 | 1.1% |

# NOTES

1. Small Entity data for the USSR and Czechoslovakia appear in the original USPTO database but these have been omitted from this study.
2. Although Taiwan is not a signatory to the Paris Convention or the Patent Cooperation Treaty, the country has been party to a number of bilateral agreements governing mutual patent priority arrangements. These include an agreement between Taiwan and the United States allowing priority claims by US applicants to Taiwan and by Taiwanese applicants to the USPTO on patents originally filed after 10 April 1996. It may be supposed that, over time, Taiwan's inventors will make even more use of the the 12 month priority 'window'.
3. The rapid growth of the Asian Tiger economies (including Taiwan) has been well documented by other writers, often with reference to the USPTO patent data (see, for example, Mahmood, Ishtiaq P. and Jasjit Singh (2003) 'Technological dynamism in Asia' *Research Policy* 32 6: 1031 or Hu, Mei-Chih, and John A. Mathews (2005) 'National innovative capacity in East Asia' *Research Policy* 34 9:1322–1349). What does not emerge from previous studies is that Small Entity patents represent over half of all Taiwan's USPTO patents and, more crucially, three quarters of those SE patents were assigned to Individuals, as opposed to Small Firms.

# 7. Summary and conclusions

The general difficulties inherent in using patent counts to explore a country's technological performance were discussed at the beginning of the book. The database prepared for this study avoids a number of these inherent problems through careful filtering of the data. In the first instance, the database contains only Utility patents granted by the United States Patent and Trademark Office (USPTO), the world's largest and most active patent granting organisation. Further, it was based only on the Small Entity data supplied by that office (records of patent applicants who had claimed related patent fee remissions) for the period 1994 to 2003. This basic dataset was further refined by adding data concerning the payment of patent maintenance fees, assignee types, patent citations and Technology Class codes.

The study is mainly focused on the OECD countries with the addition of Israel, together designated the 'OECD*' countries. Small Entity patent applications to the USPTO from countries outside this group of countries have been extremely low, with the major exception of Taiwan. For the purpose of useful comparison, the OECD* countries were arranged in three groups according to GDP, population and general economic standing. The non-OECD* countries were arranged in two further groups: Group D which is largely to do with Taiwan, and Group E. At all times it must be borne in mind that the first filtering criterion – application to a patent office outside the inventor's jurisdiction – does not apply to the United States itself and also appears to have a limited application to Canadian inventors.

## THE PROPORTION OF SMALL ENTITY PATENTS

Of the total USPTO* patents acquired by the inventors of any country, the proportion which was Small Entity patents varied between 4.4 per cent for Japan and 60 per cent for Slovakia. This proportion depends on a nation's economic capability and the presence of MNCs, since prolific MNC patenting will clearly reduce the proportion of SE patents. Just over a quarter of the OECD* patents granted by the USPTO were Small Entity patents, although when the large US patent count was removed the proportion fell to 13 per cent. A contributory factor here is the small proportion of Japanese SE inventors (who represent a good proportion of the non-US OECD* figure) claiming Small Entity status. Japan is, of course, home to the largest group of MNCs outside the US. A potential subject for research would lie in the differences in Small Entity proportion between comparable nations, such as the UK, where 19 per cent of the USPTO patents were Small Entity, and France, where the equivalent proportion was 10.5 per cent, the lowest proportion of Small Entity patents among the nations with traditionally strong economies.

It was noted in the case of France that a number of institutions which had the character of Nonprofit institutions, entitled to the 50% reduction in fees, had not claimed Small Entity status on a substantial proportion of their USPTO patents. Typical examples would be the Université Joseph Fourier which acquired 12 US patents between 1994 and 2003, only 6 of which appeared in the SE records, and the Université Pierre et Marie Curie which acquired 13 US patents and claimed SE status on 8. A much more extreme example is the Commissariat a l'Energie Atomique which claimed SE status on only 2 patents from a ten year total of 727. A number of possible reasons for this suggest themselves, one being the existence of contractual arrangements with another party which was not a Small Entity. This is a topic which is deserving of further investigation, especially if a similar pattern is found in other countries.

## ON PATENT PRIORITY

The Small Entity patent database includes data about 'priority' claims. Specifically it provides the date of an original filing in a country, other than the US, which is a signatory to the Paris Convention. Close to 80 per cent of all non-US Small Entity patents in the database had been the subject of a priority claim. We should, of course, expect such a proportion. It does, however, leave a question for further investigation: why did 20 per cent of patent applicants, coming from patent jurisdictions outside the United States, choose to make their first filing with the USPTO?

In looking at the priority data it was noted that Canadian inventors made little use of the Paris Convention; only 17 per cent of Canadian inventors applying to the USPTO had filed first in Canada. Canadian inventors appear to treat the USPTO as a 'domestic' patent office. Supporting this view, it was found that Canadian inventors had acquired almost 500 USPTO patents per million of population, far ahead of any comparable OECD* country. More surprising was the discovery that Israeli and Taiwanese inventors had acquired Small Entity patents at an even higher rate, approaching 600 patents per million in the case of Israel and 855 patents per million for Taiwan, over the ten years. The proportion of Taiwanese inventors claiming priority was about 8 per cent; however, this proportion must be seen in the light of the fact that the agreement on patent priority between the US and Taiwan dates only from April 1996 and the behaviour of Taiwan's inventors may adjust with time.

## CITATIONS

If, as has been argued, a simple count of the number of citations of a patent is some guide to its value, it was apparent from the data that US resident inventors have acquired the most valuable patents, since in all three categories of inventor the US proportion cited was substantially higher than the other OECD* countries. This difference became even more marked when the filter was set to count only patents cited three times or more. Since virtually all US inventors make use of the USPTO, and no filter for quality can therefore be in place, this result is surprising.

In general, the inventions in the Electrical class group were more frequently cited than those in Mechanical, with Chemical class patents being cited least often. However it was pointed out that Chemical class patents include a proportion of patents involving human or animal treatments, or food additives which are subject to statutory trial periods. There may be, therefore, an additional time lag before the first citations of some Chemical patents begin. Further research will illuminate this point. Among Nonprofit patents the citation rate for the Scandinavian countries put them at the top of the table while two Asian countries, Japan and Korea, were near the bottom. However, Taiwan's Nonprofits exceeded the rate for the OECD* Group A and her rate for Individual inventors was at the upper end of the OECD* scale.

The low numbers of Nonprofit USPTO patents (for most countries) make comparison unreliable. The much greater numbers of Small Firm and Individual inventor patents in the database put comparisons on a sounder footing. In a reversal of the Nonprofit position, the Japanese citation rate was near the top of the Group A table for Small Firms. Among the Group B countries, Ireland and Israel, two countries in receipt of considerable investment from US firms, were at the top; only Switzerland had a higher rate.

## TECHNOLOGY CLASS GROUPS

When measured according to the defined Technology Class groups, the Mechanical class is the predominant category of invention and accounts for over 60 per cent of the inventions in the Small Entity patent database. One logical explanation for this is that the Mechanical classes embrace the kinds of inventive activity most suited to Individuals and to Small Firms in light industry. Chemical and particularly pharmaceutical research is an expensive activity.

The Electrical class group embraces a substantial part of the high technology invention likely to demand an advanced level of training, expensive facilities and R&D resources. In the Nonprofit category, where laboratory facilities are most likely to be found, the Chemical class patents accounted for over 60 per cent (although Germany and Japan both have a Chemical class proportion just under 50 per cent).

## RATE OF DECAY

The data for patents lapsing at the four year renewal stage, through failure to pay the required maintenance fees, supports the view that a filter for quality is in operation on all patent applications to the USPTO, other than the US itself. In the Group A countries the US rate (and the Canadian rate) is higher than all other group members apart from the UK. The geographic proximity of Canada and the cultural affinity of the UK with the US were referred to previously as possibly helping to explain a weaker filtering effect. The important point here is that it is the failure of Individual inventors to maintain their patents, compared to Nonprofits and Small Firms, which raises the US and Canadian rates. Over a third of US and Canadian Individual inventors allowed their patents to lapse at the first stage. US Small Firms maintained their patents more assiduously than the majority of other OECD* countries; the few exceptions included Japan and Korea. It was notable that Taiwan, which had the highest rate of SE acquisition, also had a very high rate of decay; in the case of Individual patents over 50 per cent of the 1994 to 1998 SE patents had lapsed after four years. In addition, over three quarters of Taiwan's 1994 SE patents had lapsed after eight years. This merits attentions as, perhaps, suggesting a different attitude to the use of the patent system than in other countries.

Of particular note is the fact that, in the Individual inventor category, US Individuals had the highest rate of citations while, at the same time, having the lowest rate of patent maintenance. Since both maintenance data and renewals data are conventionally used to support patent analysis (as additional means of assessing patent value) this apparent conflict between the two accepted measures invites further examination.

The predominant Technology Class group for the OECD* patents, the Mechanical class, was also the Technology Class showing the highest rate of decay at four years – well over one quarter had lapsed. The only exception to this was among the Group B Nonprofit patents where Electrical patents showed the highest decay rate, moving ahead of Mechanical. Overall, Nonprofit patents showed the lowest rate of decay among the three inventor categories, though it was noted that the French Nonprofit decay proportion was well above the average for the Group B countries.

## US OWNERSHIP

In general, the data on assignment of patents to US entities supports the view that countries with a traditionally close relationship with the US, like the UK or Israel, will tend to have a higher proportion of SE patents assigned to US entities. Overall 7.5 per cent of UK SE patents were US assigned and 10 per cent of Israel's.

Almost one quarter of Italy's Nonprofit patents was US assigned and, unexpectedly, 10.6 per cent of French ones. At the same time, despite geographic proximity, only 3 per cent of Canadian SE patents were so assigned. The high US Nonprofit proportion of 72 per cent in Sweden and 57 per cent for Belgium was explained by the presence of the Ludwig Institute of Cancer Research. More difficult to understand is the fact that 12 per cent of Belgium's Small Firms were assigned to US firms. This figure is second only to Israel's proportion of 15 per cent. The equivalent UK figure was 11 per cent.

The Chemical class patents showed the highest proportion assigned to US entities; the OECD* figure (US excluded) was 6.5 per cent for Chemical and 5.6 per cent for Electrical class patents. A substantial 11 per cent of the Chemical class patents for the Group B countries were assigned to US firms. Very few of the Individual inventor patents were US assigned; the two highest were Israel's 1 per cent and Ireland's 0.8 per cent.

A related phenomenon was the proportion of SE patents where the first named inventor was a US resident (meaning the patent origin was given as US) but the balance of named inventors, sometimes three or four, were residents of another country and, typically, employees of a US firm. This issue was identified during the analysis but a full investigation has been left for a later publication.

# PART TWO

# Small Entity data for selected countries

# Australia

*Table AU.1   Small Entity patent counts by year, 1994 to 2003*

| Year | Individual | Small Firm | Nonprofit | Total |
|------|-----------|------------|-----------|-------|
| 1994 | 119 | 116 | 14 | 249 |
| 1995 | 119 | 113 | 17 | 249 |
| 1996 | 97 | 134 | 16 | 247 |
| 1997 | 119 | 128 | 18 | 265 |
| 1998 | 153 | 189 | 37 | 379 |
| 1999 | 142 | 177 | 33 | 352 |
| 2000 | 121 | 216 | 30 | 367 |
| 2001 | 140 | 196 | 41 | 377 |
| 2002 | 141 | 231 | 28 | 400 |
| 2003 | 129 | 224 | 24 | 377 |
| 10 yrs | 1,280 | 1,724 | 258 | 3,262 |

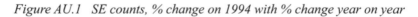

*Figure AU.1   SE counts, % change on 1994 with % change year on year*

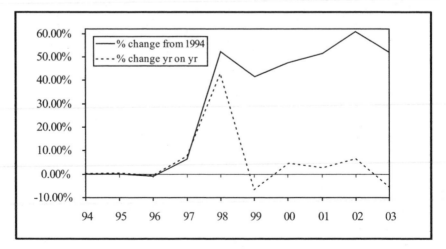

*Table AU.2   Cited Small Entity patents, 1994 to 2002*

| Year | Cited>=1 | % >=1 | Cited >= 3 | % >= 3 | Total |
|------|----------|-------|------------|--------|-------|
| 1994 | 216 | 86.7% | 136 | 54.6% | 249 |
| 1995 | 214 | 85.9% | 138 | 55.4% | 249 |
| 1996 | 210 | 85.0% | 124 | 50.2% | 247 |
| 1997 | 212 | 80.0% | 121 | 45.7% | 265 |
| 1998 | 259 | 68.3% | 107 | 28.2% | 379 |
| 1999 | 208 | 59.1% | 68 | 19.3% | 352 |
| 2000 | 143 | 39.0% | 33 | 9.0% | 367 |
| 2001 | 81 | 21.5% | 5 | 1.3% | 377 |
| 2002 | 6 | 1.5% | 0 | 0.0% | 400 |

*Table AU.3   Distribution of SE patents by Technology Class, 1994 to 2003*

| Year | Chem. | % Chem. | Elec. | % Elec. | Mech. | % Mech. |
|------|-------|---------|-------|---------|-------|---------|
| 1994 | 41 | 16.5% | 21 | 8.4% | 187 | 75.1% |
| 1995 | 50 | 20.1% | 23 | 9.2% | 176 | 70.7% |
| 1996 | 40 | 16.2% | 17 | 6.9% | 190 | 76.9% |
| 1997 | 66 | 24.9% | 24 | 9.1% | 175 | 66.0% |
| 1998 | 87 | 23.0% | 35 | 9.2% | 257 | 67.8% |
| 1999 | 77 | 21.9% | 31 | 8.8% | 244 | 69.3% |
| 2000 | 78 | 21.3% | 40 | 10.9% | 249 | 67.8% |
| 2001 | 86 | 22.8% | 38 | 10.1% | 253 | 67.1% |
| 2002 | 89 | 22.3% | 65 | 16.3% | 246 | 61.5% |
| 2003 | 66 | 17.5% | 62 | 16.4% | 249 | 66.0% |

*Table AU.4   Small Entity patents lapsing at 4 yr and 8 yr stages*

| Year | Lapsed 4 | % Lapsed 4 | Lapsed 8 | % Lapsed 8 | Total |
|------|----------|------------|----------|------------|-------|
| 1994 | 67 | 26.9% | 131 | 52.6% | 249 |
| 1995 | 60 | 24.1% | - | - | 249 |
| 1996 | 51 | 20.6% | - | - | 247 |
| 1997 | 68 | 25.7% | - | - | 265 |
| 1998 | 100 | 26.4% | - | - | 379 |

# Austria

*Table AT.1   Small Entity patent counts by year, 1994 to 2003*

| Year | Individual | Small Firm | Nonprofit | Total |
|------|-----------|-----------|-----------|-------|
| 1994 | 40 | 33 | 0 | 73 |
| 1995 | 55 | 43 | 0 | 98 |
| 1996 | 52 | 34 | 0 | 86 |
| 1997 | 63 | 39 | 0 | 102 |
| 1998 | 59 | 56 | 3 | 118 |
| 1999 | 70 | 76 | 1 | 147 |
| 2000 | 67 | 73 | 2 | 142 |
| 2001 | 79 | 85 | 0 | 164 |
| 2002 | 45 | 67 | 0 | 112 |
| 2003 | 59 | 66 | 1 | 126 |
| 10 yrs | 589 | 572 | 7 | 1,168 |

*Figure AT.1   SE counts, % change on 1994 with % change year on year*

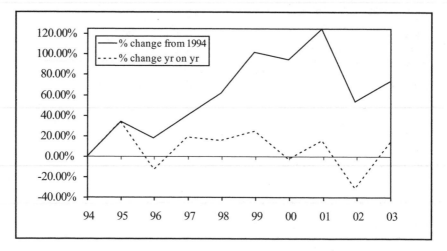

*Table AT.2   Cited Small Entity patents, 1994 to 2002*

| Year | Cited>=1 | % >=1 | Cited >= 3 | % >= 3 | Total |
|------|----------|-------|------------|--------|-------|
| 1994 | 56 | 76.7% | 25 | 34.2% | 73 |
| 1995 | 77 | 78.6% | 51 | 52.0% | 98 |
| 1996 | 68 | 79.1% | 34 | 39.5% | 86 |
| 1997 | 72 | 70.6% | 39 | 38.2% | 102 |
| 1998 | 70 | 59.3% | 27 | 22.9% | 118 |
| 1999 | 90 | 61.2% | 27 | 18.4% | 147 |
| 2000 | 49 | 34.5% | 9 | 6.3% | 142 |
| 2001 | 28 | 17.1% | 3 | 1.8% | 164 |
| 2002 | 0 | 0.0% | 0 | 0.0% | 112 |

*Table AT.3   Distribution of SE patents by Technology Class, 1994 to 2003*

| Year | Chem. | % Chem. | Elec. | % Elec. | Mech. | % Mech. |
|------|-------|---------|-------|---------|-------|---------|
| 1994 | 13 | 17.8% | 14 | 19.2% | 46 | 63.0% |
| 1995 | 20 | 20.4% | 5 | 5.1% | 73 | 74.5% |
| 1996 | 13 | 15.1% | 5 | 5.8% | 68 | 79.1% |
| 1997 | 27 | 26.5% | 10 | 9.8% | 65 | 63.7% |
| 1998 | 28 | 23.7% | 6 | 5.1% | 84 | 71.2% |
| 1999 | 27 | 18.4% | 15 | 10.2% | 105 | 71.4% |
| 2000 | 18 | 12.7% | 14 | 9.9% | 110 | 77.5% |
| 2001 | 35 | 21.3% | 13 | 7.9% | 116 | 70.7% |
| 2002 | 26 | 23.2% | 12 | 10.7% | 74 | 66.1% |
| 2003 | 24 | 19.0% | 12 | 9.5% | 90 | 71.4% |

*Table AT.4   Small Entity patents lapsing at 4 yr and 8 yr stages*

| Year | Lapsed 4 | % Lapsed 4 | Lapsed 8 | % Lapsed 8 | Total |
|------|----------|------------|----------|------------|-------|
| 1994 | 19 | 26.0% | 36 | 49.3% | 73 |
| 1995 | 23 | 23.5% | - | - | 98 |
| 1996 | 13 | 15.1% | - | - | 86 |
| 1997 | 36 | 35.3% | - | - | 102 |
| 1998 | 18 | 15.3% | - | - | 118 |

# Belgium

*Table BE.1  Small Entity patent counts by year, 1994 to 2003*

| Year | Individual | Small Firm | Nonprofit | Total |
|------|-----------|-----------|-----------|-------|
| 1994 | 21 | 19 | 1 | 41 |
| 1995 | 12 | 15 | 3 | 30 |
| 1996 | 19 | 21 | 9 | 49 |
| 1997 | 16 | 25 | 10 | 51 |
| 1998 | 26 | 50 | 18 | 94 |
| 1999 | 28 | 47 | 16 | 91 |
| 2000 | 18 | 42 | 10 | 70 |
| 2001 | 32 | 38 | 9 | 79 |
| 2002 | 17 | 42 | 11 | 70 |
| 2003 | 16 | 31 | 7 | 54 |
| 10 yrs | 205 | 330 | 94 | 629 |

*Figure BE.1  SE counts, % change on 1994 with % change year on year*

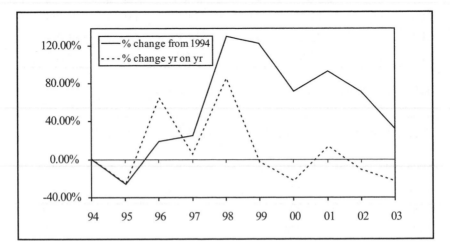

*Table BE.2   Cited Small Entity patents, 1994 to 2002*

| Year | Cited>=1 | % >=1 | Cited >= 3 | % >= 3 | Total |
|------|----------|-------|------------|--------|-------|
| 1994 | 33 | 80.5% | 21 | 51.2% | 41 |
| 1995 | 23 | 76.7% | 10 | 33.3% | 30 |
| 1996 | 44 | 89.8% | 25 | 51.0% | 49 |
| 1997 | 41 | 80.4% | 27 | 52.9% | 51 |
| 1998 | 55 | 58.5% | 25 | 26.6% | 94 |
| 1999 | 50 | 54.9% | 14 | 15.4% | 91 |
| 2000 | 28 | 40.0% | 7 | 10.0% | 70 |
| 2001 | 7 | 8.9% | 0 | 0.0% | 79 |
| 2002 | 4 | 5.7% | 0 | 0.0% | 70 |

*Table BE.3   Distribution of SE patents by Technology Class, 1994 to 2003*

| Year | Chem. | % Chem. | Elec. | % Elec. | Mech. | % Mech. |
|------|-------|---------|-------|---------|-------|---------|
| 1994 | 7 | 17.1% | 3 | 7.3% | 31 | 75.6% |
| 1995 | 10 | 33.3% | 3 | 10.0% | 17 | 56.7% |
| 1996 | 22 | 44.9% | 6 | 12.2% | 21 | 42.9% |
| 1997 | 22 | 43.1% | 9 | 17.6% | 20 | 39.2% |
| 1998 | 38 | 40.4% | 8 | 8.5% | 48 | 51.1% |
| 1999 | 40 | 44.0% | 16 | 17.6% | 35 | 38.5% |
| 2000 | 29 | 41.4% | 9 | 12.9% | 32 | 45.7% |
| 2001 | 30 | 38.0% | 5 | 6.3% | 44 | 55.7% |
| 2002 | 24 | 34.3% | 10 | 14.3% | 36 | 51.4% |
| 2003 | 12 | 22.2% | 11 | 20.4% | 31 | 57.4% |

*Table BE.4   Small Entity patents lapsing at 4 yr and 8 yr stages*

| Year | Lapsed 4 | % Lapsed 4 | Lapsed 8 | % Lapsed 8 | Total |
|------|----------|------------|----------|------------|-------|
| 1994 | 9 | 22.0% | 22 | 53.7% | 41 |
| 1995 | 6 | 20.0% | - | - | 30 |
| 1996 | 11 | 22.4% | - | - | 49 |
| 1997 | 12 | 23.5% | - | - | 51 |
| 1998 | 14 | 14.9% | - | - | 94 |

# Canada

*Table CA.1   Small Entity patent counts by year, 1994 to 2003*

| Year | Individual | Small Firm | Nonprofit | Total |
|------|-----------|-----------|-----------|-------|
| 1994 | 717 | 436 | 54 | 1,207 |
| 1995 | 720 | 472 | 77 | 1,269 |
| 1996 | 662 | 484 | 100 | 1,246 |
| 1997 | 771 | 563 | 98 | 1,432 |
| 1998 | 865 | 734 | 125 | 1,724 |
| 1999 | 831 | 706 | 155 | 1,692 |
| 2000 | 841 | 831 | 116 | 1,788 |
| 2001 | 820 | 833 | 137 | 1,790 |
| 2002 | 682 | 787 | 124 | 1,593 |
| 2003 | 620 | 736 | 99 | 1,455 |
| 10 yrs | 7,529 | 6,582 | 1,085 | 15,196 |

*Figure CA.1   SE counts, % change on 1994 with % change year on year*

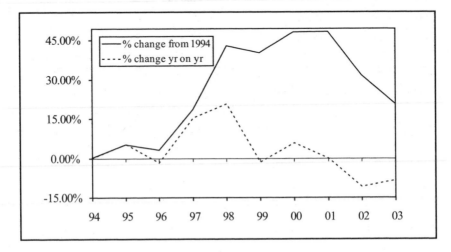

*Table CA.2   Cited Small Entity patents, 1994 to 2002*

| Year | Cited>=1 | % >=1 | Cited >= 3 | % >= 3 | Total |
|------|----------|-------|------------|--------|-------|
| 1994 | 1,097 | 90.9% | 789 | 65.4% | 1,207 |
| 1995 | 1,103 | 86.9% | 765 | 60.3% | 1,269 |
| 1996 | 1,073 | 86.1% | 657 | 52.7% | 1,246 |
| 1997 | 1,156 | 80.7% | 645 | 45.0% | 1,432 |
| 1998 | 1,269 | 73.6% | 601 | 34.9% | 1,724 |
| 1999 | 1,054 | 62.3% | 371 | 21.9% | 1,692 |
| 2000 | 843 | 47.1% | 179 | 10.0% | 1,788 |
| 2001 | 436 | 24.4% | 56 | 3.1% | 1,790 |
| 2002 | 53 | 3.3% | 1 | 0.1% | 1,593 |

*Table CA.3   Distribution of SE patents by Technology Class, 1994 to 2003*

| Year | Chem. | % Chem. | Elec. | % Elec. | Mech. | % Mech. |
|------|-------|---------|-------|---------|-------|---------|
| 1994 | 181 | 15.0% | 141 | 11.7% | 885 | 73.3% |
| 1995 | 228 | 18.0% | 163 | 12.8% | 878 | 69.2% |
| 1996 | 244 | 19.6% | 206 | 16.5% | 796 | 63.9% |
| 1997 | 289 | 20.2% | 190 | 13.3% | 953 | 66.6% |
| 1998 | 362 | 21.0% | 280 | 16.2% | 1,082 | 62.8% |
| 1999 | 422 | 24.9% | 246 | 14.5% | 1,024 | 60.5% |
| 2000 | 421 | 23.5% | 260 | 14.5% | 1,107 | 61.9% |
| 2001 | 429 | 24.0% | 263 | 14.7% | 1,098 | 61.3% |
| 2002 | 388 | 24.4% | 271 | 17.0% | 934 | 58.6% |
| 2003 | 323 | 22.2% | 246 | 16.9% | 886 | 60.9% |

*Table CA.4   Small Entity patents lapsing at 4 yr and 8 yr stages*

| Year | Lapsed 4 | % Lapsed 4 | Lapsed 8 | % Lapsed 8 | Total |
|------|----------|------------|----------|------------|-------|
| 1994 | 351 | 29.1% | 623 | 51.6% | 1,207 |
| 1995 | 330 | 26.0% | - | - | 1,269 |
| 1996 | 309 | 24.8% | - | - | 1,246 |
| 1997 | 364 | 25.4% | - | - | 1,432 |
| 1998 | 459 | 26.6% | - | - | 1,724 |

# Czech Republic

*Table CZ.1   Small Entity patent counts by year, 1994 to 2003*

| Year | Individual | Small Firm | Nonprofit | Total |
|------|------------|------------|-----------|-------|
| 1994 | 0 | 0 | 0 | 0 |
| 1995 | 0 | 0 | 0 | 0 |
| 1996 | 1 | 1 | 0 | 2 |
| 1997 | 0 | 5 | 0 | 5 |
| 1998 | 3 | 1 | 0 | 4 |
| 1999 | 5 | 1 | 1 | 7 |
| 2000 | 3 | 0 | 0 | 3 |
| 2001 | 2 | 4 | 0 | 6 |
| 2002 | 5 | 3 | 0 | 8 |
| 2003 | 7 | 3 | 2 | 12 |
| 10 yrs | 26 | 18 | 3 | 47 |

*Figure CZ.1   SE counts, % change on 1996 with % change year on year*

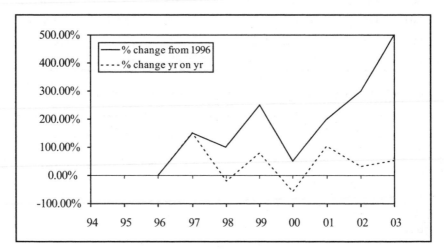

*Table CZ.2   Cited Small Entity patents, 1994 to 2002*

| Year | Cited>=1 | % >=1 | Cited >= 3 | % >= 3 | Total |
|------|----------|-------|------------|--------|-------|
| 1994 | - | - | - | - | 0 |
| 1995 | - | - | - | - | 0 |
| 1996 | 2 | 100.0% | 1 | 50.0% | 2 |
| 1997 | 3 | 60.0% | 1 | 20.0% | 5 |
| 1998 | 2 | 50.0% | 0 | 0.0% | 4 |
| 1999 | 4 | 57.1% | 2 | 28.6% | 7 |
| 2000 | 1 | 33.3% | 0 | 0.0% | 3 |
| 2001 | 1 | 16.7% | 0 | 0.0% | 6 |
| 2002 | 0 | 0.0% | 0 | 0.0% | 8 |

*Table CZ.3   Distribution of SE patents by Technology Class, 1994 to 2003*

| Year | Chem. | % Chem. | Elec. | % Elec. | Mech. | % Mech. |
|------|-------|---------|-------|---------|-------|---------|
| 1994 | 0 | 0.0% | 0 | 0.0% | 0 | 0.0% |
| 1995 | 0 | 0.0% | 0 | 0.0% | 0 | 0.0% |
| 1996 | 1 | 50.0% | 0 | 0.0% | 1 | 50.0% |
| 1997 | 1 | 20.0% | 0 | 0.0% | 4 | 80.0% |
| 1998 | 2 | 50.0% | 0 | 0.0% | 2 | 50.0% |
| 1999 | 4 | 57.1% | 0 | 0.0% | 3 | 42.9% |
| 2000 | 0 | 0.0% | 1 | 33.3% | 2 | 66.7% |
| 2001 | 2 | 33.3% | 0 | 0.0% | 4 | 66.7% |
| 2002 | 3 | 37.5% | 0 | 0.0% | 5 | 62.5% |
| 2003 | 3 | 25.0% | 3 | 25.0% | 6 | 50.0% |

*Table CZ.4   Small Entity patents lapsing at 4 yr and 8 yr stages*

| Year | Lapsed 4 | % Lapsed 4 | Lapsed 8 | % Lapsed 8 | Total |
|------|----------|------------|----------|------------|-------|
| 1994 | - | - | - | - | 0 |
| 1995 | - | - | - | - | 0 |
| 1996 | 1 | 50.0% | - | - | 2 |
| 1997 | 0 | 0.0% | - | - | 5 |
| 1998 | 0 | 0.0% | - | - | 4 |

# Denmark

*Table DK.1   Small Entity patent counts by year, 1994 to 2003*

| Year | Individual | Small Firm | Nonprofit | Total |
|------|-----------|-----------|-----------|-------|
| 1994 | 17 | 31 | 0 | 48 |
| 1995 | 30 | 34 | 1 | 65 |
| 1996 | 24 | 34 | 3 | 61 |
| 1997 | 34 | 34 | 2 | 70 |
| 1998 | 23 | 42 | 1 | 66 |
| 1999 | 26 | 61 | 3 | 90 |
| 2000 | 29 | 45 | 1 | 75 |
| 2001 | 25 | 60 | 3 | 88 |
| 2002 | 23 | 45 | 0 | 68 |
| 2003 | 18 | 61 | 1 | 80 |
| 10 yrs | 249 | 447 | 15 | 711 |

*Figure DK.1   SE counts, % change on 1994 with % change year on year*

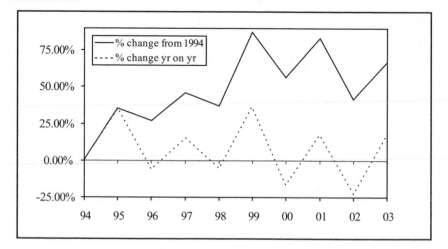

*Table DK.2   Cited Small Entity patents, 1994 to 2002*

| Year | Cited>=1 | % >=1 | Cited >= 3 | % >= 3 | Total |
|------|------|-------|-------|-------|-------|
| 1994 | 38 | 79.2% | 21 | 43.8% | 48 |
| 1995 | 53 | 81.5% | 34 | 52.3% | 65 |
| 1996 | 46 | 75.4% | 21 | 34.4% | 61 |
| 1997 | 51 | 72.9% | 24 | 34.3% | 70 |
| 1998 | 43 | 65.2% | 10 | 15.2% | 66 |
| 1999 | 44 | 48.9% | 14 | 15.6% | 90 |
| 2000 | 28 | 37.3% | 5 | 6.7% | 75 |
| 2001 | 15 | 17.0% | 0 | 0.0% | 88 |
| 2002 | 0 | 0.0% | 0 | 0.0% | 68 |

*Table DK.3   Distribution of SE patents by Technology Class, 1994 to 2003*

| Year | Chem. | % Chem. | Elec. | % Elec. | Mech. | % Mech. |
|------|-------|---------|-------|---------|-------|---------|
| 1994 | 7 | 14.6% | 5 | 10.4% | 36 | 75.0% |
| 1995 | 21 | 32.3% | 5 | 7.7% | 39 | 60.0% |
| 1996 | 15 | 24.6% | 5 | 8.2% | 41 | 67.2% |
| 1997 | 16 | 22.9% | 8 | 11.4% | 46 | 65.7% |
| 1998 | 18 | 27.3% | 7 | 10.6% | 41 | 62.1% |
| 1999 | 24 | 26.7% | 18 | 20.0% | 48 | 53.3% |
| 2000 | 16 | 21.3% | 9 | 12.0% | 50 | 66.7% |
| 2001 | 17 | 19.3% | 12 | 13.6% | 59 | 67.0% |
| 2002 | 21 | 30.9% | 7 | 10.3% | 40 | 58.8% |
| 2003 | 24 | 30.0% | 6 | 7.5% | 50 | 62.5% |

*Table DK.4   Small Entity patents lapsing at 4 yr and 8 yr stages*

| Year | Lapsed 4 | % Lapsed 4 | Lapsed 8 | % Lapsed 8 | Total |
|------|----------|------------|----------|------------|-------|
| 1994 | 9 | 18.8% | 20 | 41.7% | 48 |
| 1995 | 16 | 24.6% | - | - | 65 |
| 1996 | 18 | 29.5% | - | - | 61 |
| 1997 | 16 | 22.9% | - | - | 70 |
| 1998 | 16 | 24.2% | - | - | 66 |

# Finland

*Table FI.1  Small Entity patent counts by year, 1994 to 2003*

| Year | Individual | Small Firm | Nonprofit | Total |
|------|-----------|-----------|-----------|-------|
| 1994 | 21 | 32 | 0 | 53 |
| 1995 | 28 | 43 | 2 | 73 |
| 1996 | 45 | 40 | 1 | 86 |
| 1997 | 53 | 46 | 2 | 101 |
| 1998 | 55 | 64 | 3 | 122 |
| 1999 | 42 | 65 | 2 | 109 |
| 2000 | 37 | 63 | 1 | 101 |
| 2001 | 45 | 63 | 0 | 108 |
| 2002 | 19 | 64 | 1 | 84 |
| 2003 | 24 | 57 | 1 | 82 |
| 10 yrs | 369 | 537 | 13 | 919 |

*Figure FI.1  SE counts, % change on 1994 with % change year on year*

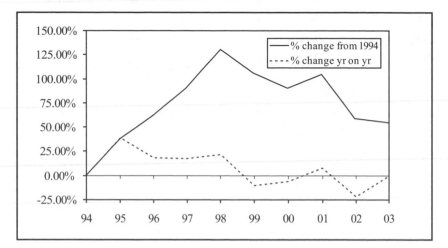

*Table FI.2  Cited Small Entity patents, 1994 to 2002*

| Year | Cited>=1 | % >=1 | Cited >= 3 | % >= 3 | Total |
|------|------|------|------|------|------|
| 1994 | 46 | 86.8% | 27 | 50.9% | 53 |
| 1995 | 60 | 82.2% | 28 | 38.4% | 73 |
| 1996 | 60 | 69.8% | 28 | 32.6% | 86 |
| 1997 | 67 | 66.3% | 25 | 24.8% | 101 |
| 1998 | 88 | 72.1% | 31 | 25.4% | 122 |
| 1999 | 53 | 48.6% | 9 | 8.3% | 109 |
| 2000 | 47 | 46.5% | 4 | 4.0% | 101 |
| 2001 | 18 | 16.7% | 1 | 0.9% | 108 |
| 2002 | 3 | 3.6% | 0 | 0.0% | 84 |

*Table FI.3  Distribution of SE patents by Technology Class, 1994 to 2003*

| Year | Chem. | % Chem. | Elec. | % Elec. | Mech. | % Mech. |
|------|------|------|------|------|------|------|
| 1994 | 9 | 17.0% | 9 | 17.0% | 35 | 66.0% |
| 1995 | 16 | 21.9% | 9 | 12.3% | 48 | 65.8% |
| 1996 | 22 | 25.6% | 11 | 12.8% | 53 | 61.6% |
| 1997 | 18 | 17.8% | 12 | 11.9% | 71 | 70.3% |
| 1998 | 25 | 20.5% | 23 | 18.9% | 74 | 60.7% |
| 1999 | 28 | 25.7% | 9 | 8.3% | 72 | 66.1% |
| 2000 | 25 | 24.8% | 19 | 18.8% | 57 | 56.4% |
| 2001 | 34 | 31.5% | 23 | 21.3% | 51 | 47.2% |
| 2002 | 23 | 27.4% | 19 | 22.6% | 42 | 50.0% |
| 2003 | 21 | 25.6% | 20 | 24.4% | 41 | 50.0% |

*Table FI.4  Small Entity patents lapsing at 4 yr and 8 yr stages*

| Year | Lapsed 4 | % Lapsed 4 | Lapsed 8 | % Lapsed 8 | Total |
|------|------|------|------|------|------|
| 1994 | 16 | 30.2% | 25 | 47.2% | 53 |
| 1995 | 14 | 19.2% | - | - | 73 |
| 1996 | 13 | 15.1% | - | - | 86 |
| 1997 | 16 | 15.8% | - | - | 101 |
| 1998 | 25 | 20.5% | - | - | 122 |

# France

*Table FR.1   Small Entity patent counts by year, 1994 to 2003*

| Year | Individual | Small Firm | Nonprofit | Total |
|------|-----------|-----------|-----------|-------|
| 1994 | 139 | 168 | 11 | 318 |
| 1995 | 150 | 203 | 8 | 361 |
| 1996 | 117 | 202 | 10 | 329 |
| 1997 | 111 | 186 | 13 | 310 |
| 1998 | 155 | 247 | 11 | 413 |
| 1999 | 142 | 235 | 12 | 389 |
| 2000 | 132 | 240 | 19 | 391 |
| 2001 | 121 | 252 | 24 | 397 |
| 2002 | 108 | 246 | 12 | 366 |
| 2003 | 89 | 248 | 12 | 349 |
| 10 yrs | 1,264 | 2,227 | 132 | 3,623 |

*Figure FR.1   SE counts, % change on 1994 with % change year on year*

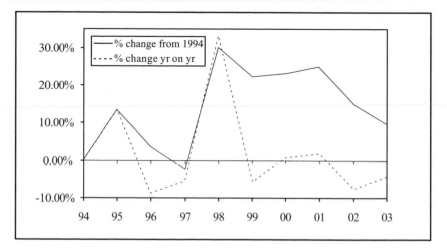

*Table FR.2   Cited Small Entity patents, 1994 to 2002*

| Year | Cited>=1 | % >=1 | Cited >= 3 | % >= 3 | Total |
|------|----------|-------|------------|--------|-------|
| 1994 | 267 | 84.0% | 162 | 50.9% | 318 |
| 1995 | 302 | 83.7% | 186 | 51.5% | 361 |
| 1996 | 270 | 82.1% | 154 | 46.8% | 329 |
| 1997 | 231 | 74.5% | 115 | 37.1% | 310 |
| 1998 | 275 | 66.6% | 117 | 28.3% | 413 |
| 1999 | 208 | 53.5% | 61 | 15.7% | 389 |
| 2000 | 147 | 37.6% | 29 | 7.4% | 391 |
| 2001 | 91 | 22.9% | 8 | 2.0% | 397 |
| 2002 | 5 | 1.4% | 0 | 0.0% | 366 |

*Table FR.3   Distribution of SE patents by Technology Class, 1994 to 2003*

| Year | Chem. | % Chem. | Elec. | % Elec. | Mech. | % Mech. |
|------|-------|---------|-------|---------|-------|---------|
| 1994 | 60 | 18.9% | 45 | 14.2% | 213 | 67.0% |
| 1995 | 75 | 20.8% | 53 | 14.7% | 233 | 64.5% |
| 1996 | 57 | 17.3% | 57 | 17.3% | 215 | 65.3% |
| 1997 | 78 | 25.2% | 35 | 11.3% | 197 | 63.5% |
| 1998 | 88 | 21.3% | 67 | 16.2% | 258 | 62.5% |
| 1999 | 100 | 25.7% | 51 | 13.1% | 238 | 61.2% |
| 2000 | 80 | 20.5% | 67 | 17.1% | 244 | 62.4% |
| 2001 | 116 | 29.2% | 51 | 12.8% | 230 | 57.9% |
| 2002 | 78 | 21.3% | 69 | 18.9% | 219 | 59.8% |
| 2003 | 85 | 24.4% | 62 | 17.8% | 202 | 57.9% |

*Table FR.4   Small Entity patents lapsing at 4 yr and 8 yr stages*

| Year | Lapsed 4 | % Lapsed 4 | Lapsed 8 | % Lapsed 8 | Total |
|------|----------|------------|----------|------------|-------|
| 1994 | 83 | 26.1% | 174 | 54.7% | 318 |
| 1995 | 86 | 23.8% | - | - | 361 |
| 1996 | 79 | 24.0% | - | - | 329 |
| 1997 | 56 | 18.1% | - | - | 310 |
| 1998 | 97 | 23.5% | - | - | 413 |

# Germany

*Table DE.1   Small Entity patent counts by year, 1994 to 2003*

| Year | Individual | Small Firm | Nonprofit | Total |
|------|-----------|-----------|-----------|--------|
| 1994 | 367 | 550 | 52 | 969 |
| 1995 | 355 | 520 | 44 | 919 |
| 1996 | 352 | 518 | 59 | 929 |
| 1997 | 425 | 549 | 62 | 1,036 |
| 1998 | 504 | 754 | 102 | 1,360 |
| 1999 | 513 | 745 | 130 | 1,388 |
| 2000 | 474 | 833 | 129 | 1,436 |
| 2001 | 510 | 829 | 84 | 1,423 |
| 2002 | 401 | 780 | 83 | 1,264 |
| 2003 | 381 | 719 | 56 | 1,156 |
| 10 yrs | 4,282 | 6,797 | 801 | 11,880 |

*Figure DE.1   SE counts, % change on 1994 with % change year on year*

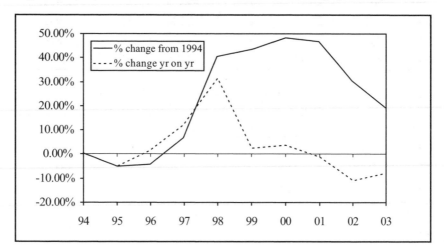

*Table DE.2   Cited Small Entity patents, 1994 to 2002*

| Year | Cited>=1 | % >=1 | Cited >= 3 | % >= 3 | Total |
|------|----------|--------|-----------|--------|-------|
| 1994 | 930 | 96.0% | 642 | 66.3% | 969 |
| 1995 | 843 | 91.7% | 559 | 60.8% | 919 |
| 1996 | 829 | 89.2% | 461 | 49.6% | 929 |
| 1997 | 845 | 81.6% | 390 | 37.6% | 1,036 |
| 1998 | 950 | 69.9% | 353 | 26.0% | 1,360 |
| 1999 | 764 | 55.0% | 212 | 15.3% | 1,388 |
| 2000 | 573 | 39.9% | 101 | 7.0% | 1,436 |
| 2001 | 272 | 19.1% | 16 | 1.1% | 1,423 |
| 2002 | 24 | 1.9% | 0 | 0.0% | 1,264 |

*Table DE.3   Distribution of SE patents by Technology Class, 1994 to 2003*

| Year | Chem. | % Chem. | Elec. | % Elec. | Mech. | % Mech. |
|------|-------|---------|-------|---------|-------|---------|
| 1994 | 178 | 18.4% | 118 | 12.2% | 673 | 69.5% |
| 1995 | 166 | 18.1% | 115 | 12.5% | 638 | 69.4% |
| 1996 | 187 | 20.1% | 118 | 12.7% | 624 | 67.2% |
| 1997 | 227 | 21.9% | 133 | 12.8% | 676 | 65.3% |
| 1998 | 278 | 20.4% | 195 | 14.3% | 887 | 65.2% |
| 1999 | 316 | 22.8% | 193 | 13.9% | 879 | 63.3% |
| 2000 | 298 | 20.8% | 204 | 14.2% | 934 | 65.0% |
| 2001 | 284 | 20.0% | 194 | 13.6% | 945 | 66.4% |
| 2002 | 297 | 23.5% | 191 | 15.1% | 776 | 61.4% |
| 2003 | 265 | 22.9% | 222 | 19.2% | 668 | 57.8% |

*Table DE.4   Small Entity patents lapsing at 4 yr and 8 yr stages*

| Year | Lapsed 4 | % Lapsed 4 | Lapsed 8 | % Lapsed 8 | Total |
|------|----------|------------|----------|------------|-------|
| 1994 | 254 | 26.2% | 507 | 52.3% | 969 |
| 1995 | 216 | 23.5% | - | - | 919 |
| 1996 | 183 | 19.7% | - | - | 929 |
| 1997 | 225 | 21.7% | - | - | 1,036 |
| 1998 | 297 | 21.8% | - | - | 1,360 |

# Greece

*Table GR.1   Small Entity patent counts by year, 1994 to 2003*

| Year | Individual | Small Firm | Nonprofit | Total |
|------|-----------|-----------|-----------|-------|
| 1994 | 7 | 1 | 2 | 10 |
| 1995 | 4 | 2 | 0 | 6 |
| 1996 | 8 | 4 | 1 | 13 |
| 1997 | 5 | 3 | 0 | 8 |
| 1998 | 5 | 3 | 2 | 10 |
| 1999 | 7 | 3 | 1 | 11 |
| 2000 | 7 | 2 | 0 | 9 |
| 2001 | 13 | 6 | 0 | 19 |
| 2002 | 4 | 5 | 1 | 10 |
| 2003 | 6 | 3 | 1 | 10 |
| 10 yrs | 66 | 32 | 8 | 106 |

*Figure GR.1   SE counts, % change on 1994 with % change year on year*

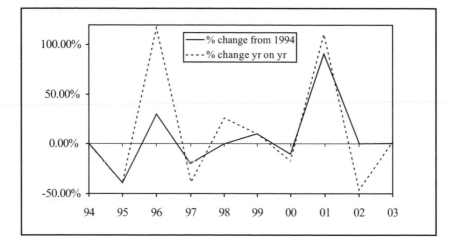

*Table GR.2   Cited Small Entity patents, 1994 to 2002*

| Year | Cited>=1 | % >=1 | Cited >= 3 | % >= 3 | Total |
|------|----------|-------|------------|--------|-------|
| 1994 | 9 | 90.0% | 6 | 60.0% | 10 |
| 1995 | 6 | 100.0% | 5 | 83.3% | 6 |
| 1996 | 11 | 84.6% | 5 | 38.5% | 13 |
| 1997 | 5 | 62.5% | 1 | 12.5% | 8 |
| 1998 | 8 | 80.0% | 2 | 20.0% | 10 |
| 1999 | 7 | 63.6% | 2 | 18.2% | 11 |
| 2000 | 2 | 22.2% | 0 | 0.0% | 9 |
| 2001 | 0 | 0.0% | 0 | 0.0% | 19 |
| 2002 | 0 | 0.0% | 0 | 0.0% | 10 |

*Table GR.3   Distribution of SE patents by Technology Class, 1994 to 2003*

| Year | Chem. | % Chem. | Elec. | % Elec. | Mech. | % Mech. |
|------|-------|---------|-------|---------|-------|---------|
| 1994 | 4 | 40.0% | 1 | 10.0% | 5 | 50.0% |
| 1995 | 1 | 16.7% | 1 | 16.7% | 4 | 66.7% |
| 1996 | 4 | 30.8% | 2 | 15.4% | 7 | 53.8% |
| 1997 | 3 | 37.5% | 2 | 25.0% | 3 | 37.5% |
| 1998 | 5 | 50.0% | 1 | 10.0% | 4 | 40.0% |
| 1999 | 1 | 9.1% | 3 | 27.3% | 7 | 63.6% |
| 2000 | 2 | 22.2% | 1 | 11.1% | 6 | 66.7% |
| 2001 | 5 | 26.3% | 3 | 15.8% | 11 | 57.9% |
| 2002 | 4 | 40.0% | 1 | 10.0% | 5 | 50.0% |
| 2003 | 6 | 60.0% | 1 | 10.0% | 3 | 30.0% |

*Table GR.4   Small Entity patents lapsing at 4 yr and 8 yr stages*

| Year | Lapsed 4 | % Lapsed 4 | Lapsed 8 | % Lapsed 8 | Total |
|------|----------|------------|----------|------------|-------|
| 1994 | 4 | 40.0% | 6 | 60.0% | 10 |
| 1995 | 2 | 33.3% | - | - | 6 |
| 1996 | 4 | 30.8% | - | - | 13 |
| 1997 | 2 | 25.0% | - | - | 8 |
| 1998 | 2 | 20.0% | - | - | 10 |

# Hungary

Table HU.1   *Small Entity patent counts by year, 1994 to 2003*

| Year | Individual | Small Firm | Nonprofit | Total |
|------|-----------|-----------|-----------|-------|
| 1994 | 6 | 2 | 1 | 9 |
| 1995 | 7 | 4 | 0 | 11 |
| 1996 | 7 | 3 | 0 | 10 |
| 1997 | 6 | 3 | 0 | 9 |
| 1998 | 6 | 6 | 0 | 12 |
| 1999 | 10 | 5 | 1 | 16 |
| 2000 | 10 | 2 | 0 | 12 |
| 2001 | 9 | 9 | 0 | 18 |
| 2002 | 11 | 5 | 0 | 16 |
| 2003 | 9 | 6 | 1 | 16 |
| 10 yrs | 81 | 45 | 3 | 129 |

Figure HU.1   *SE counts, % change on 1994 with % change year on year*

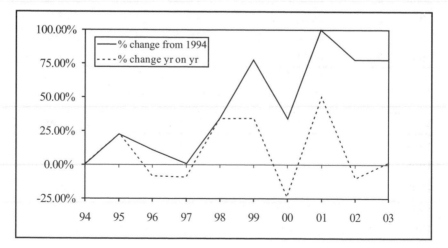

*Table HU.2   Cited Small Entity patents, 1994 to 2002*

| Year | Cited>=1 | % >=1 | Cited >= 3 | % >= 3 | Total |
|------|----------|-------|------------|--------|-------|
| 1994 | 8 | 88.9% | 4 | 44.4% | 9 |
| 1995 | 7 | 63.6% | 2 | 18.2% | 11 |
| 1996 | 8 | 80.0% | 5 | 50.0% | 10 |
| 1997 | 4 | 44.4% | 3 | 33.3% | 9 |
| 1998 | 9 | 75.0% | 3 | 25.0% | 12 |
| 1999 | 9 | 56.3% | 0 | 0.0% | 16 |
| 2000 | 4 | 33.3% | 1 | 8.3% | 12 |
| 2001 | 3 | 16.7% | 0 | 0.0% | 18 |
| 2002 | 0 | 0.0% | 0 | 0.0% | 16 |

*Table HU.3   Distribution of SE patents by Technology Class, 1994 to 2003*

| Year | Chem. | % Chem. | Elec. | % Elec. | Mech. | % Mech. |
|------|-------|---------|-------|---------|-------|---------|
| 1994 | 4 | 44.4% | 1 | 11.1% | 4 | 44.4% |
| 1995 | 4 | 36.4% | 2 | 18.2% | 5 | 45.5% |
| 1996 | 3 | 30.0% | 2 | 20.0% | 5 | 50.0% |
| 1997 | 2 | 22.2% | 0 | 0.0% | 7 | 77.8% |
| 1998 | 2 | 16.7% | 2 | 16.7% | 8 | 66.7% |
| 1999 | 4 | 25.0% | 1 | 6.3% | 11 | 68.8% |
| 2000 | 3 | 25.0% | 2 | 16.7% | 7 | 58.3% |
| 2001 | 7 | 38.9% | 5 | 27.8% | 6 | 33.3% |
| 2002 | 9 | 56.3% | 2 | 12.5% | 5 | 31.3% |
| 2003 | 3 | 18.8% | 6 | 37.5% | 7 | 43.8% |

*Table HU.4   Small Entity patents lapsing at 4 yr and 8 yr stages*

| Year | Lapsed 4 | % Lapsed 4 | Lapsed 8 | % Lapsed 8 | Total |
|------|----------|------------|----------|------------|-------|
| 1994 | 5 | 55.6% | 5 | 55.6% | 9 |
| 1995 | 4 | 36.4% | - | - | 11 |
| 1996 | 3 | 30.0% | - | - | 10 |
| 1997 | 4 | 44.4% | - | - | 9 |
| 1998 | 3 | 25.0% | - | - | 12 |

# Iceland

*Table IS.1   Small Entity patent counts by year, 1994 to 2003*

| Year | Individual | Small Firm | Nonprofit | Total |
|------|-----------|-----------|-----------|-------|
| 1994 | 3 | 0 | 0 | 3 |
| 1995 | 1 | 2 | 0 | 3 |
| 1996 | 2 | 1 | 0 | 3 |
| 1997 | 1 | 1 | 0 | 2 |
| 1998 | 2 | 2 | 0 | 4 |
| 1999 | 0 | 4 | 0 | 4 |
| 2000 | 2 | 6 | 0 | 8 |
| 2001 | 1 | 3 | 0 | 4 |
| 2002 | 1 | 2 | 0 | 3 |
| 2003 | 1 | 4 | 0 | 5 |
| 10 yrs | 14 | 25 | 0 | 39 |

*Figure IS.1   SE counts, % change on 1994 with % change year on year*

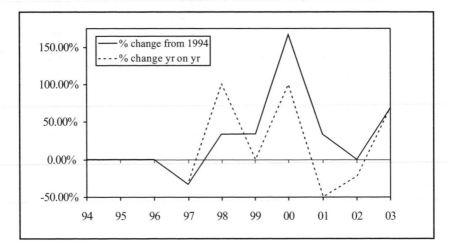

*Table IS.2   Cited Small Entity patents, 1994 to 2002*

| Year | Cited>=1 | % >=1 | Cited >= 3 | % >= 3 | Total |
|------|----------|-------|------------|--------|-------|
| 1994 | 2 | 66.7% | 2 | 66.7% | 3 |
| 1995 | 3 | 100.0% | 2 | 66.7% | 3 |
| 1996 | 2 | 66.7% | 0 | 0.0% | 3 |
| 1997 | 2 | 100.0% | 2 | 100.0% | 2 |
| 1998 | 3 | 75.0% | 3 | 75.0% | 4 |
| 1999 | 2 | 50.0% | 0 | 0.0% | 4 |
| 2000 | 5 | 62.5% | 1 | 12.5% | 8 |
| 2001 | 0 | 0.0% | 0 | 0.0% | 4 |
| 2002 | 0 | 0.0% | 0 | 0.0% | 3 |

*Table IS.3   Distribution of SE patents by Technology Class, 1994 to 2003*

| Year | Chem. | % Chem. | Elec. | % Elec. | Mech. | % Mech. |
|------|-------|---------|-------|---------|-------|---------|
| 1994 | 2 | 66.7% | - | 0.0% | 1 | 33.3% |
| 1995 | 2 | 66.7% | - | 0.0% | 1 | 33.3% |
| 1996 | 1 | 33.3% | - | 0.0% | 2 | 66.7% |
| 1997 | 1 | 50.0% | - | 0.0% | 1 | 50.0% |
| 1998 | - | 0.0% | - | 0.0% | 4 | 100.0% |
| 1999 | 1 | 25.0% | - | 0.0% | 3 | 75.0% |
| 2000 | - | 0.0% | 2 | 25.0% | 6 | 75.0% |
| 2001 | 1 | 25.0% | - | 0.0% | 3 | 75.0% |
| 2002 | 3 | 100.0% | - | 0.0% | - | 0.0% |
| 2003 | 2 | 40.0% | 1 | 20.0% | 2 | 40.0% |

*Table IS.4   Small Entity patents lapsing at 4 yr and 8 yr stages*

| Year | Lapsed 4 | % Lapsed 4 | Lapsed 8 | % Lapsed 8 | Total |
|------|----------|------------|----------|------------|-------|
| 1994 | 0 | 0.0% | 0 | 0.0% | 3 |
| 1995 | 0 | 0.0% | - | - | 3 |
| 1996 | 0 | 0.0% | - | - | 3 |
| 1997 | 0 | 0.0% | - | - | 2 |
| 1998 | 0 | 0.0% | - | - | 4 |

# Ireland

*Table IE.1    Small Entity patent counts by year, 1994 to 2003*

| Year | Individual | Small Firm | Nonprofit | Total |
|------|-----------|-----------|-----------|-------|
| 1994 | 11 | 12 | 0 | 23 |
| 1995 | 6 | 6 | 2 | 14 |
| 1996 | 6 | 14 | 1 | 21 |
| 1997 | 10 | 13 | 1 | 24 |
| 1998 | 5 | 21 | 0 | 26 |
| 1999 | 16 | 19 | 4 | 39 |
| 2000 | 20 | 19 | 7 | 46 |
| 2001 | 10 | 24 | 4 | 38 |
| 2002 | 21 | 19 | 2 | 42 |
| 2003 | 14 | 16 | 2 | 32 |
| 10 yrs | 119 | 163 | 23 | 305 |

*Figure IE.1    SE counts, % change on 1994 with % change year on year*

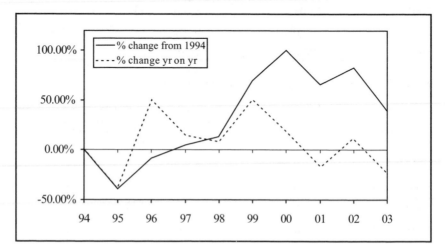

*Table IE.2    Cited Small Entity patents, 1994 to 2002*

| Year | Cited>=1 | % >=1 | Cited >= 3 | % >= 3 | Total |
|------|----------|-------|------------|--------|-------|
| 1994 | 18 | 78.3% | 15 | 65.2% | 23 |
| 1995 | 11 | 78.6% | 5 | 35.7% | 14 |
| 1996 | 18 | 85.7% | 13 | 61.9% | 21 |
| 1997 | 18 | 75.0% | 9 | 37.5% | 24 |
| 1998 | 19 | 73.1% | 9 | 34.6% | 26 |
| 1999 | 23 | 59.0% | 7 | 17.9% | 39 |
| 2000 | 19 | 41.3% | 3 | 6.5% | 46 |
| 2001 | 9 | 23.7% | 1 | 2.6% | 38 |
| 2002 | 2 | 4.8% | 0 | 0.0% | 42 |

*Table IE.3    Distribution of SE patents by Technology Class, 1994 to 2003*

| Year | Chem. | % Chem. | Elec. | % Elec. | Mech. | % Mech. |
|------|-------|---------|-------|---------|-------|---------|
| 1994 | 4 | 17.4% | 3 | 13.0% | 16 | 69.6% |
| 1995 | 5 | 35.7% | 2 | 14.3% | 7 | 50.0% |
| 1996 | 3 | 14.3% | 7 | 33.3% | 11 | 52.4% |
| 1997 | 7 | 29.2% | 2 | 8.3% | 15 | 62.5% |
| 1998 | 3 | 11.5% | 5 | 19.2% | 18 | 69.2% |
| 1999 | 9 | 23.1% | 6 | 15.4% | 24 | 61.5% |
| 2000 | 6 | 13.0% | 15 | 32.6% | 25 | 54.3% |
| 2001 | 5 | 13.2% | 8 | 21.1% | 25 | 65.8% |
| 2002 | 4 | 9.5% | 16 | 38.1% | 22 | 52.4% |
| 2003 | 7 | 21.9% | 6 | 18.8% | 19 | 59.4% |

*Table IE.4    Small Entity patents lapsing at 4 yr and 8 yr stages*

| Year | Lapsed 4 | % Lapsed 4 | Lapsed 8 | % Lapsed 8 | Total |
|------|----------|------------|----------|------------|-------|
| 1994 | 9 | 39.1% | 13 | 56.5% | 23 |
| 1995 | 3 | 21.4% | - | - | 14 |
| 1996 | 6 | 28.6% | - | - | 21 |
| 1997 | 3 | 12.5% | - | - | 24 |
| 1998 | 8 | 30.8% | - | - | 26 |

# Israel

*Table IL.1   Small Entity patent counts by year, 1994 to 2003*

| Year | Individual | Small Firm | Nonprofit | Total |
|------|-----------|-----------|-----------|-------|
| 1994 | 84 | 84 | 29 | 197 |
| 1995 | 77 | 110 | 22 | 209 |
| 1996 | 76 | 136 | 39 | 251 |
| 1997 | 95 | 161 | 33 | 289 |
| 1998 | 124 | 249 | 62 | 435 |
| 1999 | 132 | 246 | 64 | 442 |
| 2000 | 110 | 276 | 53 | 439 |
| 2001 | 84 | 350 | 54 | 488 |
| 2002 | 102 | 379 | 46 | 527 |
| 2003 | 94 | 363 | 57 | 514 |
| 10 yrs | 978 | 2,354 | 459 | 3,791 |

*Figure IL.1   SE counts, % change on 1994 with % change year on year*

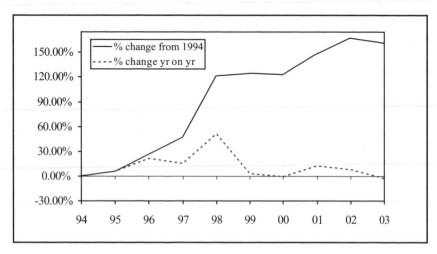

*Table IL.2   Cited Small Entity patents, 1994 to 2002*

| Year | Cited>=1 | % >=1 | Cited >= 3 | % >= 3 | Total |
|------|----------|-------|------------|--------|-------|
| 1994 | 177 | 89.8% | 129 | 65.5% | 197 |
| 1995 | 179 | 85.6% | 122 | 58.4% | 209 |
| 1996 | 201 | 80.1% | 123 | 49.0% | 251 |
| 1997 | 228 | 78.9% | 140 | 48.4% | 289 |
| 1998 | 314 | 72.2% | 167 | 38.4% | 435 |
| 1999 | 268 | 60.6% | 117 | 26.5% | 442 |
| 2000 | 215 | 49.0% | 62 | 14.1% | 439 |
| 2001 | 142 | 29.1% | 21 | 4.3% | 488 |
| 2002 | 20 | 3.8% | 0 | 0.0% | 527 |

*Table IL.3   Distribution of SE patents by Technology Class, 1994 to 2003*

| Year | Chem. | % Chem. | Elec. | % Elec. | Mech. | % Mech. |
|------|-------|---------|-------|---------|-------|---------|
| 1994 | 55 | 27.9% | 35 | 17.8% | 107 | 54.3% |
| 1995 | 56 | 26.8% | 46 | 22.0% | 107 | 51.2% |
| 1996 | 81 | 32.3% | 46 | 18.3% | 124 | 49.4% |
| 1997 | 66 | 22.8% | 65 | 22.5% | 158 | 54.7% |
| 1998 | 104 | 23.9% | 121 | 27.8% | 210 | 48.3% |
| 1999 | 127 | 28.7% | 121 | 27.4% | 194 | 43.9% |
| 2000 | 112 | 25.5% | 149 | 33.9% | 178 | 40.5% |
| 2001 | 108 | 22.1% | 158 | 32.4% | 222 | 45.5% |
| 2002 | 133 | 25.2% | 167 | 31.7% | 227 | 43.1% |
| 2003 | 120 | 23.3% | 170 | 33.1% | 224 | 43.6% |

*Table IL.4   Small Entity patents lapsing at 4 yr and 8 yr stages*

| Year | Lapsed 4 | % Lapsed 4 | Lapsed 8 | % Lapsed 8 | Total |
|------|----------|------------|----------|------------|-------|
| 1994 | 59 | 29.9% | 110 | 55.8% | 197 |
| 1995 | 50 | 23.9% | - | - | 209 |
| 1996 | 58 | 23.1% | - | - | 251 |
| 1997 | 69 | 23.9% | - | - | 289 |
| 1998 | 124 | 28.5% | - | - | 435 |

# Italy

*Table IT.1   Small Entity patent counts by year, 1994 to 2003*

| Year | Individual | Small Firm | Nonprofit | Total |
|------|-----------|-----------|-----------|-------|
| 1994 | 127 | 308 | 6 | 441 |
| 1995 | 102 | 294 | 7 | 403 |
| 1996 | 108 | 294 | 10 | 412 |
| 1997 | 114 | 320 | 14 | 448 |
| 1998 | 145 | 418 | 9 | 572 |
| 1999 | 104 | 403 | 11 | 518 |
| 2000 | 147 | 448 | 12 | 607 |
| 2001 | 140 | 364 | 10 | 514 |
| 2002 | 124 | 362 | 11 | 497 |
| 2003 | 136 | 365 | 13 | 514 |
| 10 yrs | 1,247 | 3,576 | 103 | 4,926 |

*Figure IT.1   SE counts, % change on 1994 with % change year on year*

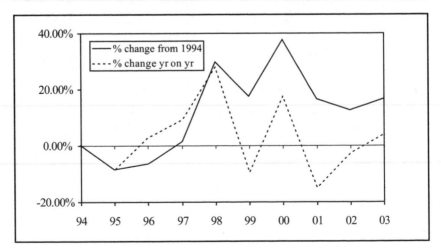

*142*

*Table IT.2   Cited Small Entity patents, 1994 to 2002*

| Year | Cited>=1 | % >=1 | Cited >= 3 | % >= 3 | Total |
|------|----------|-------|------------|--------|-------|
| 1994 | 362 | 82.1% | 207 | 46.9% | 441 |
| 1995 | 326 | 80.9% | 184 | 45.7% | 403 |
| 1996 | 317 | 76.9% | 165 | 40.0% | 412 |
| 1997 | 316 | 70.5% | 145 | 32.4% | 448 |
| 1998 | 352 | 61.5% | 131 | 22.9% | 572 |
| 1999 | 268 | 51.7% | 66 | 12.7% | 518 |
| 2000 | 217 | 35.7% | 38 | 6.3% | 607 |
| 2001 | 101 | 19.6% | 3 | 0.6% | 514 |
| 2002 | 8 | 1.6% | 0 | 0.0% | 497 |

*Table IT.3   Distribution of SE patents by Technology Class, 1994 to 2003*

| Year | Chem. | % Chem. | Elec. | % Elec. | Mech. | % Mech. |
|------|-------|---------|-------|---------|-------|---------|
| 1994 | 80 | 18.1% | 45 | 10.2% | 316 | 71.7% |
| 1995 | 82 | 20.3% | 26 | 6.5% | 295 | 73.2% |
| 1996 | 80 | 19.4% | 40 | 9.7% | 292 | 70.9% |
| 1997 | 110 | 24.6% | 33 | 7.4% | 305 | 68.1% |
| 1998 | 122 | 21.3% | 47 | 8.2% | 403 | 70.5% |
| 1999 | 124 | 23.9% | 29 | 5.6% | 365 | 70.5% |
| 2000 | 117 | 19.3% | 44 | 7.2% | 446 | 73.5% |
| 2001 | 110 | 21.4% | 44 | 8.6% | 360 | 70.0% |
| 2002 | 88 | 17.7% | 42 | 8.5% | 367 | 73.8% |
| 2003 | 93 | 18.1% | 46 | 8.9% | 375 | 73.0% |

*Table IT.4   Small Entity patents lapsing at 4 yr and 8 yr stages*

| Year | Lapsed 4 | % Lapsed 4 | Lapsed 8 | % Lapsed 8 | Total |
|------|----------|------------|----------|------------|-------|
| 1994 | 96 | 21.8% | 213 | 48.3% | 441 |
| 1995 | 88 | 21.8% | - | - | 403 |
| 1996 | 80 | 19.4% | - | - | 412 |
| 1997 | 97 | 21.7% | - | - | 448 |
| 1998 | 134 | 23.4% | - | - | 572 |

# Japan

*Table JP.1   Small Entity patent counts by year, 1994 to 2003*

| Year | Individual | Small Firm | Nonprofit | Total |
|------|-----------|-----------|-----------|-------|
| 1994 | 250 | 702 | 18 | 970 |
| 1995 | 267 | 721 | 19 | 1,007 |
| 1996 | 262 | 816 | 36 | 1,114 |
| 1997 | 253 | 805 | 28 | 1,086 |
| 1998 | 345 | 1,034 | 37 | 1,416 |
| 1999 | 312 | 1,087 | 26 | 1,425 |
| 2000 | 377 | 1,041 | 58 | 1,476 |
| 2001 | 318 | 1,129 | 53 | 1,500 |
| 2002 | 292 | 947 | 94 | 1,333 |
| 2003 | 273 | 960 | 87 | 1,320 |
| 10 yrs | 2,949 | 9,242 | 456 | 12,647 |

*Figure JP.1   SE counts, % change on 1994 with % change year on year*

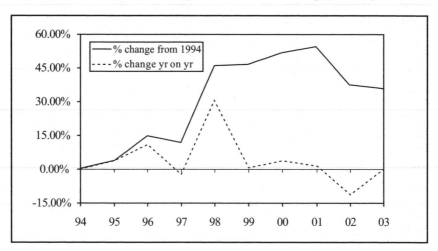

*Table JP.2   Cited Small Entity patents, 1994 to 2002*

| Year | Cited>=1 | % >=1 | Cited >= 3 | % >= 3 | Total |
|------|----------|-------|------------|--------|-------|
| 1994 | 837 | 86.3% | 570 | 58.8% | 970 |
| 1995 | 854 | 84.8% | 528 | 52.4% | 1,007 |
| 1996 | 879 | 78.9% | 504 | 45.2% | 1,114 |
| 1997 | 812 | 74.8% | 416 | 38.3% | 1,086 |
| 1998 | 993 | 70.1% | 434 | 30.6% | 1,416 |
| 1999 | 850 | 59.6% | 284 | 19.9% | 1,425 |
| 2000 | 660 | 44.7% | 133 | 9.0% | 1,476 |
| 2001 | 333 | 22.2% | 28 | 1.9% | 1,500 |
| 2002 | 37 | 2.8% | 0 | 0.0% | 1,333 |

*Table JP.3   Distribution of SE patents by Technology Class, 1994 to 2003*

| Year | Chem. | % Chem. | Elec. | % Elec. | Mech. | % Mech. |
|------|-------|---------|-------|---------|-------|---------|
| 1994 | 208 | 21.4% | 156 | 16.1% | 606 | 62.5% |
| 1995 | 249 | 24.7% | 150 | 14.9% | 608 | 60.4% |
| 1996 | 270 | 24.2% | 185 | 16.6% | 659 | 59.2% |
| 1997 | 278 | 25.6% | 165 | 15.2% | 643 | 59.2% |
| 1998 | 335 | 23.7% | 253 | 17.9% | 828 | 58.5% |
| 1999 | 352 | 24.7% | 254 | 17.8% | 819 | 57.5% |
| 2000 | 360 | 24.4% | 297 | 20.1% | 819 | 55.5% |
| 2001 | 381 | 25.4% | 272 | 18.1% | 847 | 56.5% |
| 2002 | 347 | 26.0% | 253 | 19.0% | 733 | 55.0% |
| 2003 | 318 | 24.1% | 333 | 25.2% | 668 | 50.6% |

*Table JP.4   Small Entity patents lapsing at 4 yr and 8 yr stages*

| Year | Lapsed 4 | % Lapsed 4 | Lapsed 8 | % Lapsed 8 | Total |
|------|----------|------------|----------|------------|-------|
| 1994 | 145 | 14.9% | 371 | 38.2% | 970 |
| 1995 | 162 | 16.1% | - | - | 1,007 |
| 1996 | 183 | 16.4% | - | - | 1,114 |
| 1997 | 176 | 16.2% | - | - | 1,086 |
| 1998 | 232 | 16.4% | - | - | 1,416 |

# Korea, Republic of

*Table KR.1   Small Entity patent counts by year, 1994 to 2003*

| Year | Individual | Small Firm | Nonprofit | Total |
|------|-----------|-----------|-----------|-------|
| 1994 | 68 | 25 | 21 | 114 |
| 1995 | 96 | 43 | 49 | 188 |
| 1996 | 81 | 62 | 47 | 190 |
| 1997 | 80 | 79 | 62 | 221 |
| 1998 | 133 | 146 | 90 | 369 |
| 1999 | 123 | 188 | 104 | 415 |
| 2000 | 149 | 205 | 122 | 476 |
| 2001 | 214 | 162 | 177 | 553 |
| 2002 | 207 | 214 | 198 | 619 |
| 2003 | 226 | 262 | 231 | 719 |
| 10 yrs | 1,377 | 1,386 | 1,101 | 3,864 |

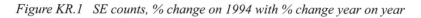

*Figure KR.1   SE counts, % change on 1994 with % change year on year*

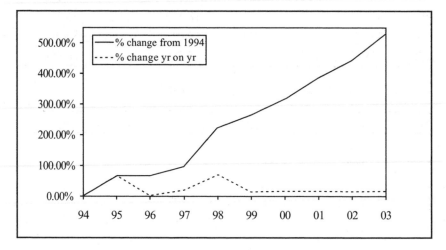

*Table KR.2   Cited Small Entity patents, 1994 to 2002*

| Year | Cited>=1 | % >=1 | Cited >= 3 | % >= 3 | Total |
|------|----------|-------|------------|--------|-------|
| 1994 | 97 | 85.1% | 72 | 63.2% | 114 |
| 1995 | 147 | 78.2% | 87 | 46.3% | 188 |
| 1996 | 147 | 77.4% | 78 | 41.1% | 190 |
| 1997 | 156 | 70.6% | 78 | 35.3% | 221 |
| 1998 | 257 | 69.6% | 113 | 30.6% | 369 |
| 1999 | 239 | 57.6% | 88 | 21.2% | 415 |
| 2000 | 210 | 44.1% | 43 | 9.0% | 476 |
| 2001 | 125 | 22.6% | 14 | 2.5% | 553 |
| 2002 | 14 | 2.3% | 0 | 0.0% | 619 |

*Table KR.3   Distribution of SE patents by Technology Class, 1994 to 2003*

| Year | Chem. | % Chem. | Elec. | % Elec. | Mech. | % Mech. |
|------|-------|---------|-------|---------|-------|---------|
| 1994 | 32 | 28.1% | 12 | 10.5% | 70 | 61.4% |
| 1995 | 66 | 35.1% | 33 | 17.6% | 89 | 47.3% |
| 1996 | 69 | 36.3% | 29 | 15.3% | 92 | 48.4% |
| 1997 | 71 | 32.1% | 54 | 24.4% | 96 | 43.4% |
| 1998 | 109 | 29.5% | 119 | 32.2% | 141 | 38.2% |
| 1999 | 146 | 35.2% | 122 | 29.4% | 147 | 35.4% |
| 2000 | 149 | 31.3% | 113 | 23.7% | 214 | 45.0% |
| 2001 | 171 | 30.9% | 137 | 24.8% | 245 | 44.3% |
| 2002 | 189 | 30.5% | 164 | 26.5% | 266 | 43.0% |
| 2003 | 191 | 26.6% | 220 | 30.6% | 308 | 42.8% |

*Table KR.4   Small Entity patents lapsing at 4 yr and 8 yr stages*

| Year | Lapsed 4 | % Lapsed 4 | Lapsed 8 | % Lapsed 8 | Total |
|------|----------|------------|----------|------------|-------|
| 1994 | 39 | 34.2% | 61 | 53.5% | 114 |
| 1995 | 54 | 28.7% | - | - | 188 |
| 1996 | 38 | 20.0% | - | - | 190 |
| 1997 | 43 | 19.5% | - | - | 221 |
| 1998 | 60 | 16.3% | - | - | 369 |

# Luxembourg

*Table LU.1   Small Entity patent counts by year, 1994 to 2003*

| Year | Individual | Small Firm | Nonprofit | Total |
|------|-----------|-----------|-----------|-------|
| 1994 | 1 | 1 | 0 | 2 |
| 1995 | 1 | 1 | 0 | 2 |
| 1996 | 0 | 1 | 0 | 1 |
| 1997 | 2 | 1 | 0 | 3 |
| 1998 | 0 | 1 | 0 | 1 |
| 1999 | 0 | 3 | 0 | 3 |
| 2000 | 1 | 5 | 0 | 6 |
| 2001 | 2 | 2 | 0 | 4 |
| 2002 | 1 | 1 | 0 | 2 |
| 2003 | 1 | 1 | 0 | 2 |
| 10 yrs | 9 | 17 | 0 | 26 |

*Figure LU.1   SE counts, % change on 1994 with % change year on year*

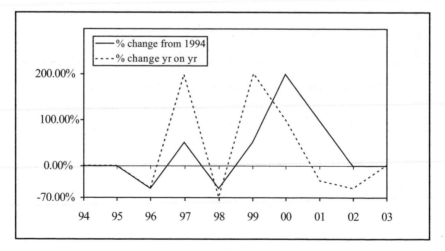

*Table LU.2   Cited Small Entity patents, 1994 to 2002*

| Year | Cited>=1 | % >=1 | Cited >= 3 | % >= 3 | Total |
|------|----------|-------|------------|--------|-------|
| 1994 | 2 | 100.0% | 1 | 50.0% | 2 |
| 1995 | 1 | 50.0% | 0 | 0.0% | 2 |
| 1996 | 1 | 100.0% | 1 | 100.0% | 1 |
| 1997 | 1 | 33.3% | 1 | 33.3% | 3 |
| 1998 | 1 | 100.0% | 1 | 100.0% | 1 |
| 1999 | 1 | 33.3% | 0 | 0.0% | 3 |
| 2000 | 2 | 33.3% | 1 | 16.7% | 6 |
| 2001 | 3 | 75.0% | 0 | 0.0% | 4 |
| 2002 | 0 | 0.0% | 0 | 0.0% | 2 |

*Table LU.3   Distribution of SE patents by Technology Class, 1994 to 2003*

| Year | Chem. | % Chem. | Elec. | % Elec. | Mech. | % Mech. |
|------|-------|---------|-------|---------|-------|---------|
| 1994 | 0 | 0.0% | 0 | 0.0% | 2 | 100.0% |
| 1995 | 0 | 0.0% | 1 | 50.0% | 1 | 50.0% |
| 1996 | 0 | 0.0% | 0 | 0.0% | 1 | 100.0% |
| 1997 | 0 | 0.0% | 0 | 0.0% | 3 | 100.0% |
| 1998 | 0 | 0.0% | 0 | 0.0% | 1 | 100.0% |
| 1999 | 1 | 33.3% | 0 | 0.0% | 2 | 66.7% |
| 2000 | 2 | 33.3% | 0 | 0.0% | 4 | 66.7% |
| 2001 | 0 | 0.0% | 1 | 25.0% | 3 | 75.0% |
| 2002 | 0 | 0.0% | 0 | 0.0% | 2 | 100.0% |
| 2003 | 0 | 0.0% | 0 | 0.0% | 2 | 100.0% |

*Table LU.4   Small Entity patents lapsing at 4 yr and 8 yr stages*

| Year | Lapsed 4 | % Lapsed 4 | Lapsed 8 | % Lapsed 8 | Total |
|------|----------|------------|----------|------------|-------|
| 1994 | 0 | 0.0% | 0 | 0.0% | 2 |
| 1995 | 1 | 50.0% | - | - | 2 |
| 1996 | 1 | 100.0% | - | - | 1 |
| 1997 | 1 | 33.3% | - | - | 3 |
| 1998 | 0 | 0.0% | - | - | 1 |

# Mexico

*Table MX.1   Small Entity patent counts by year, 1994 to 2003*

| Year | Individual | Small Firm | Nonprofit | Total |
|------|-----------|-----------|-----------|-------|
| 1994 | 19 | 6 | 3 | 28 |
| 1995 | 18 | 4 | 5 | 27 |
| 1996 | 13 | 4 | 5 | 22 |
| 1997 | 15 | 6 | 3 | 24 |
| 1998 | 27 | 6 | 1 | 34 |
| 1999 | 25 | 10 | 2 | 37 |
| 2000 | 27 | 6 | 3 | 36 |
| 2001 | 26 | 10 | 5 | 41 |
| 2002 | 22 | 7 | 3 | 32 |
| 2003 | 17 | 11 | 2 | 30 |
| 10 yrs | 209 | 70 | 32 | 311 |

*Figure MX.1   SE counts, % change on 1994 with % change year on year*

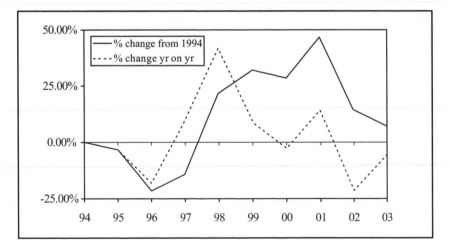

*Table MX.2   Cited Small Entity patents, 1994 to 2002*

| Year | Cited>=1 | % >=1 | Cited >= 3 | % >= 3 | Total |
|------|----------|-------|------------|--------|-------|
| 1994 | 22 | 78.6% | 12 | 42.9% | 28 |
| 1995 | 22 | 81.5% | 10 | 37.0% | 27 |
| 1996 | 13 | 59.1% | 6 | 27.3% | 22 |
| 1997 | 15 | 62.5% | 6 | 25.0% | 24 |
| 1998 | 19 | 55.9% | 7 | 20.6% | 34 |
| 1999 | 13 | 35.1% | 4 | 10.8% | 37 |
| 2000 | 13 | 36.1% | 3 | 8.3% | 36 |
| 2001 | 5 | 12.2% | 0 | 0.0% | 41 |
| 2002 | 0 | 0.0% | 0 | 0.0% | 32 |

*Table MX.3   Distribution of SE patents by Technology Class, 1994 to 2003*

| Year | Chem. | % Chem. | Elec. | % Elec. | Mech. | % Mech. |
|------|-------|---------|-------|---------|-------|---------|
| 1994 | 13 | 46.4% | 1 | 3.6% | 14 | 50.0% |
| 1995 | 12 | 44.4% | 1 | 3.7% | 14 | 51.9% |
| 1996 | 7 | 31.8% | 2 | 9.1% | 13 | 59.1% |
| 1997 | 8 | 33.3% | 3 | 12.5% | 13 | 54.2% |
| 1998 | 7 | 20.6% | 3 | 8.8% | 24 | 70.6% |
| 1999 | 9 | 24.3% | 4 | 10.8% | 24 | 64.9% |
| 2000 | 9 | 25.0% | 5 | 13.9% | 22 | 61.1% |
| 2001 | 12 | 29.3% | 5 | 12.2% | 24 | 58.5% |
| 2002 | 10 | 31.3% | 3 | 9.4% | 19 | 59.4% |
| 2003 | 11 | 36.7% | 5 | 16.7% | 14 | 46.7% |

*Table MX.4   Small Entity patents lapsing at 4 yr and 8 yr stages*

| Year | Lapsed 4 | % Lapsed 4 | Lapsed 8 | % Lapsed 8 | Total |
|------|----------|------------|----------|------------|-------|
| 1994 | 13 | 46.4% | 18 | 64.3% | 28 |
| 1995 | 8 | 29.6% | - | - | 27 |
| 1996 | 5 | 22.7% | - | - | 22 |
| 1997 | 5 | 20.8% | - | - | 24 |
| 1998 | 7 | 20.6% | - | - | 34 |

# Netherlands

*Table NL.1   Small Entity patent counts by year, 1994 to 2003*

| Year | Individual | Small Firm | Nonprofit | Total |
|------|------------|------------|-----------|-------|
| 1994 | 37 | 95 | 6 | 138 |
| 1995 | 44 | 90 | 2 | 136 |
| 1996 | 38 | 68 | 3 | 109 |
| 1997 | 40 | 77 | 10 | 127 |
| 1998 | 37 | 94 | 13 | 144 |
| 1999 | 51 | 109 | 10 | 170 |
| 2000 | 38 | 124 | 19 | 181 |
| 2001 | 36 | 138 | 10 | 184 |
| 2002 | 20 | 118 | 9 | 147 |
| 2003 | 24 | 77 | 10 | 111 |
| 10 yrs | 365 | 990 | 92 | 1,447 |

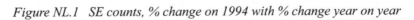

*Figure NL.1   SE counts, % change on 1994 with % change year on year*

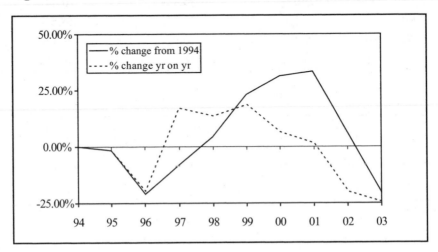

*Table NL.2   Cited Small Entity patents, 1994 to 2002*

| Year | Cited>=1 | % >=1 | Cited >= 3 | % >= 3 | Total |
|------|----------|-------|------------|--------|-------|
| 1994 | 121 | 87.7% | 88 | 63.8% | 138 |
| 1995 | 109 | 80.1% | 68 | 50.0% | 136 |
| 1996 | 95 | 87.2% | 56 | 51.4% | 109 |
| 1997 | 89 | 70.1% | 39 | 30.7% | 127 |
| 1998 | 96 | 66.7% | 37 | 25.7% | 144 |
| 1999 | 80 | 47.1% | 24 | 14.1% | 170 |
| 2000 | 71 | 39.2% | 15 | 8.3% | 181 |
| 2001 | 41 | 22.3% | 3 | 1.6% | 184 |
| 2002 | 4 | 2.7% | 0 | 0.0% | 147 |

*Table NL.3   Distribution of SE patents by Technology Class, 1994 to 2003*

| Year | Chem. | % Chem. | Elec. | % Elec. | Mech. | % Mech. |
|------|-------|---------|-------|---------|-------|---------|
| 1994 | 27 | 19.6% | 13 | 9.4% | 98 | 71.0% |
| 1995 | 32 | 23.5% | 5 | 3.7% | 99 | 72.8% |
| 1996 | 19 | 17.4% | 12 | 11.0% | 78 | 71.6% |
| 1997 | 29 | 22.8% | 15 | 11.8% | 83 | 65.4% |
| 1998 | 35 | 24.3% | 13 | 9.0% | 96 | 66.7% |
| 1999 | 44 | 25.9% | 5 | 2.9% | 121 | 71.2% |
| 2000 | 51 | 28.2% | 17 | 9.4% | 113 | 62.4% |
| 2001 | 53 | 28.8% | 17 | 9.2% | 114 | 62.0% |
| 2002 | 51 | 34.7% | 14 | 9.5% | 82 | 55.8% |
| 2003 | 28 | 25.2% | 10 | 9.0% | 73 | 65.8% |

*Table NL.4   Small Entity patents lapsing at 4 yr and 8 yr stages*

| Year | Lapsed 4 | % Lapsed 4 | Lapsed 8 | % Lapsed 8 | Total |
|------|----------|------------|----------|------------|-------|
| 1994 | 22 | 15.9% | 58 | 42.0% | 138 |
| 1995 | 28 | 20.6% | - | - | 136 |
| 1996 | 22 | 20.2% | - | - | 109 |
| 1997 | 33 | 26.0% | - | - | 127 |
| 1998 | 32 | 22.2% | - | - | 144 |

# New Zealand

*Table NZ.1  Small Entity patent counts by year, 1994 to 2003*

| Year | Individual | Small Firm | Nonprofit | Total |
|------|-----------|-----------|-----------|-------|
| 1994 | 14 | 5 | 0 | 19 |
| 1995 | 10 | 11 | 0 | 21 |
| 1996 | 23 | 8 | 0 | 31 |
| 1997 | 25 | 25 | 1 | 51 |
| 1998 | 25 | 33 | 0 | 58 |
| 1999 | 25 | 33 | 0 | 58 |
| 2000 | 21 | 35 | 2 | 58 |
| 2001 | 29 | 36 | 1 | 66 |
| 2002 | 27 | 31 | 1 | 59 |
| 2003 | 21 | 30 | 0 | 51 |
| 10 yrs | 220 | 247 | 5 | 472 |

*Figure NZ.1  SE counts, % change on 1994 with % change year over year*

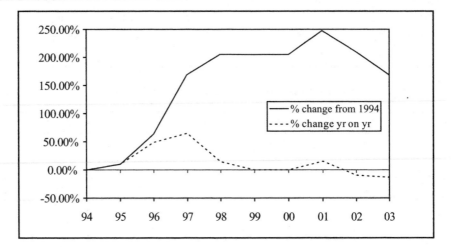

*Table NZ.2   Cited Small Entity patents, 1994 to 2002*

| Year | Cited>=1 | % >=1 | Cited >= 3 | % >= 3 | Total |
|------|----------|-------|------------|--------|-------|
| 1994 | 17 | 89.5% | 8 | 42.1% | 19 |
| 1995 | 15 | 71.4% | 7 | 33.3% | 21 |
| 1996 | 19 | 61.3% | 8 | 25.8% | 31 |
| 1997 | 38 | 74.5% | 19 | 37.3% | 51 |
| 1998 | 42 | 72.4% | 17 | 29.3% | 58 |
| 1999 | 31 | 53.4% | 12 | 20.7% | 58 |
| 2000 | 26 | 44.8% | 6 | 10.3% | 58 |
| 2001 | 15 | 22.7% | 3 | 4.5% | 66 |
| 2002 | 0 | 0.0% | 0 | 0.0% | 59 |

*Table NZ.3   Distribution of SE patents by Technology Class, 1994 to 2003*

| Year | Chem. | % Chem. | Elec. | % Elec. | Mech. | % Mech. |
|------|-------|---------|-------|---------|-------|---------|
| 1994 | 3 | 15.8% | 3 | 15.8% | 13 | 68.4% |
| 1995 | 4 | 19.0% | 2 | 9.5% | 15 | 71.4% |
| 1996 | 8 | 25.8% | 5 | 16.1% | 18 | 58.1% |
| 1997 | 6 | 11.8% | 8 | 15.7% | 37 | 72.5% |
| 1998 | 6 | 10.3% | 12 | 20.7% | 40 | 69.0% |
| 1999 | 12 | 20.7% | 3 | 5.2% | 43 | 74.1% |
| 2000 | 19 | 32.8% | 11 | 19.0% | 28 | 48.3% |
| 2001 | 8 | 12.1% | 17 | 25.8% | 41 | 62.1% |
| 2002 | 19 | 32.2% | 12 | 20.3% | 28 | 47.5% |
| 2003 | 9 | 17.6% | 6 | 11.8% | 36 | 70.6% |

*Table NZ.4   Small Entity patents lapsing at 4 yr and 8 yr stages*

| Year | Lapsed 4 | % Lapsed 4 | Lapsed 8 | % Lapsed 8 | Total |
|------|----------|------------|----------|------------|-------|
| 1994 | 3 | 15.8% | 9 | 47.4% | 19 |
| 1995 | 3 | 14.3% | - | - | 21 |
| 1996 | 16 | 51.6% | - | - | 31 |
| 1997 | 14 | 27.5% | - | - | 51 |
| 1998 | 13 | 22.4% | - | - | 58 |

# Norway

*Table NO.1   Small Entity patent counts by year, 1994 to 2003*

| Year | Individual | Small Firm | Nonprofit | Total |
|------|------------|------------|-----------|-------|
| 1994 | 24 | 20 | 0 | 44 |
| 1995 | 17 | 26 | 0 | 43 |
| 1996 | 30 | 24 | 0 | 54 |
| 1997 | 27 | 22 | 0 | 49 |
| 1998 | 37 | 36 | 0 | 73 |
| 1999 | 35 | 35 | 0 | 70 |
| 2000 | 34 | 49 | 1 | 84 |
| 2001 | 33 | 45 | 0 | 78 |
| 2002 | 28 | 54 | 0 | 82 |
| 2003 | 30 | 48 | 2 | 80 |
| 10 yrs | 295 | 359 | 3 | 657 |

*Figure NO.1   SE counts, % change on 1994 with % change year on year*

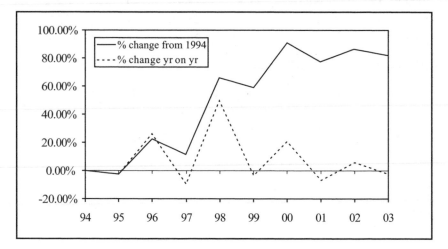

*Table NO.2   Cited Small Entity patents, 1994 to 2002*

| Year | Cited>=1 | % >=1 | Cited >= 3 | % >= 3 | Total |
|------|----------|-------|------------|--------|-------|
| 1994 | 33 | 75.0% | 20 | 45.5% | 44 |
| 1995 | 33 | 76.7% | 19 | 44.2% | 43 |
| 1996 | 41 | 75.9% | 25 | 46.3% | 54 |
| 1997 | 34 | 69.4% | 14 | 28.6% | 49 |
| 1998 | 47 | 64.4% | 12 | 16.4% | 73 |
| 1999 | 28 | 40.0% | 4 | 5.7% | 70 |
| 2000 | 31 | 36.9% | 7 | 8.3% | 84 |
| 2001 | 14 | 17.9% | 1 | 1.3% | 78 |
| 2002 | 1 | 1.2% | 0 | 0.0% | 82 |

*Table NO.3   Distribution of SE patents by Technology Class, 1994 to 2003*

| Year | Chem. | % Chem. | Elec. | % Elec. | Mech. | % Mech. |
|------|-------|---------|-------|---------|-------|---------|
| 1994 | 9 | 20.5% | 5 | 11.4% | 30 | 68.2% |
| 1995 | 4 | 9.3% | 3 | 7.0% | 36 | 83.7% |
| 1996 | 10 | 18.5% | 4 | 7.4% | 40 | 74.1% |
| 1997 | 8 | 16.3% | 5 | 10.2% | 36 | 73.5% |
| 1998 | 12 | 16.4% | 7 | 9.6% | 54 | 74.0% |
| 1999 | 12 | 17.1% | 11 | 15.7% | 47 | 67.1% |
| 2000 | 17 | 20.2% | 7 | 8.3% | 60 | 71.4% |
| 2001 | 16 | 20.5% | 10 | 12.8% | 52 | 66.7% |
| 2002 | 20 | 24.4% | 10 | 12.2% | 52 | 63.4% |
| 2003 | 16 | 20.0% | 8 | 10.0% | 56 | 70.0% |

*Table NO.4   Small Entity patents lapsing at 4 yr and 8 yr stages*

| Year | Lapsed 4 | % Lapsed 4 | Lapsed 8 | % Lapsed 8 | Total |
|------|----------|------------|----------|------------|-------|
| 1994 | 14 | 31.8% | 24 | 54.5% | 44 |
| 1995 | 12 | 27.9% | - | - | 43 |
| 1996 | 7 | 13.0% | - | - | 54 |
| 1997 | 8 | 16.3% | - | - | 49 |
| 1998 | 15 | 20.5% | - | - | 73 |

# Poland

*Table PL.1   Small Entity patent counts by year, 1994 to 2003*

| Year | Individual | Small Firm | Nonprofit | Total |
|------|-----------|-----------|-----------|-------|
| 1994 | 1 | 3 | 0 | 4 |
| 1995 | 1 | 0 | 0 | 1 |
| 1996 | 2 | 3 | 1 | 6 |
| 1997 | 0 | 0 | 2 | 2 |
| 1998 | 2 | 5 | 1 | 8 |
| 1999 | 2 | 4 | 1 | 7 |
| 2000 | 0 | 3 | 2 | 5 |
| 2001 | 3 | 2 | 2 | 7 |
| 2002 | 2 | 0 | 2 | 4 |
| 2003 | 1 | 4 | 3 | 8 |
| 10 yrs | 14 | 24 | 14 | 52 |

*Figure PL.1   SE counts, % change on 1994 with % change year on year*

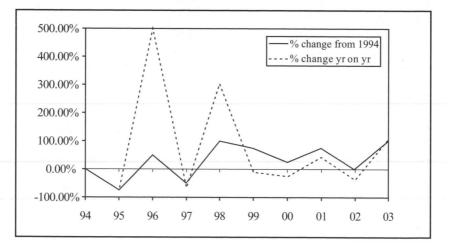

*Table PL.2   Cited Small Entity patents, 1994 to 2002*

| Year | Cited>=1 | % >=1 | Cited >= 3 | % >= 3 | Total |
|------|----------|--------|------------|---------|-------|
| 1994 | 4 | 100.0% | 2 | 50.0% | 4 |
| 1995 | 1 | 100.0% | 0 | 0.0% | 1 |
| 1996 | 4 | 66.7% | 2 | 33.3% | 6 |
| 1997 | 2 | 100.0% | 2 | 100.0% | 2 |
| 1998 | 3 | 37.5% | 1 | 12.5% | 8 |
| 1999 | 1 | 14.3% | 0 | 0.0% | 7 |
| 2000 | 0 | 0.0% | 0 | 0.0% | 5 |
| 2001 | 2 | 28.6% | 0 | 0.0% | 7 |
| 2002 | 0 | 0.0% | 0 | 0.0% | 4 |

*Table PL.3   Distribution of SE patents by Technology Class, 1994 to 2003*

| Year | Chem. | % Chem. | Elec. | % Elec. | Mech. | % Mech. |
|------|-------|---------|-------|---------|-------|---------|
| 1994 | 2 | 50.0% | 0 | 0.0% | 2 | 50.0% |
| 1995 | 1 | 100.0% | 0 | 0.0% | 0 | 0.0% |
| 1996 | 3 | 50.0% | 0 | 0.0% | 3 | 50.0% |
| 1997 | 2 | 100.0% | 0 | 0.0% | 0 | 0.0% |
| 1998 | 4 | 50.0% | 2 | 25.0% | 2 | 25.0% |
| 1999 | 3 | 42.9% | 1 | 14.3% | 3 | 42.9% |
| 2000 | 3 | 60.0% | 0 | 0.0% | 2 | 40.0% |
| 2001 | 4 | 57.1% | 1 | 14.3% | 2 | 28.6% |
| 2002 | 3 | 75.0% | 1 | 25.0% | 0 | 0.0% |
| 2003 | 2 | 25.0% | 1 | 12.5% | 5 | 62.5% |

*Table PL.4   Small Entity patents lapsing at 4 yr and 8 yr stages*

| Year | Lapsed 4 | % Lapsed 4 | Lapsed 8 | % Lapsed 8 | Total |
|------|----------|------------|----------|------------|-------|
| 1994 | 1 | 25.0% | 3 | 75.0% | 4 |
| 1995 | 1 | 100.0% | - | - | 1 |
| 1996 | 0 | 0.0% | - | - | 6 |
| 1997 | 0 | 0.0% | - | - | 2 |
| 1998 | 3 | 37.5% | - | - | 8 |

# Portugal

*Table PT.1   Small Entity patent counts by year, 1994 to 2003*

| Year | Individual | Small Firm | Nonprofit | Total |
|------|-----------|-----------|-----------|-------|
| 1994 | 3 | 3 | 0 | 6 |
| 1995 | 1 | 0 | 0 | 1 |
| 1996 | 1 | 0 | 0 | 1 |
| 1997 | 3 | 1 | 0 | 4 |
| 1998 | 2 | 2 | 1 | 5 |
| 1999 | 2 | 2 | 0 | 4 |
| 2000 | 4 | 4 | 0 | 8 |
| 2001 | 2 | 4 | 0 | 6 |
| 2002 | 2 | 3 | 0 | 5 |
| 2003 | 3 | 4 | 0 | 7 |
| 10 yrs | 23 | 23 | 1 | 47 |

*Figure PT.1   SE counts, % change on 1994 with % change year on year*

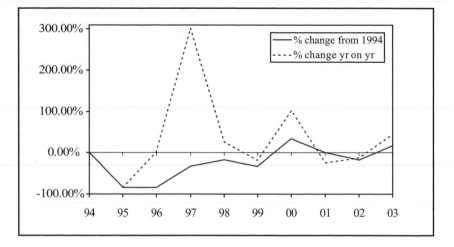

*Table PT.2 Cited Small Entity patents, 1994 to 2002*

| Year | Cited>=1 | % >=1 | Cited >= 3 | % >= 3 | Total |
|------|----------|-------|------------|--------|-------|
| 1994 | 4 | 66.7% | 1 | 16.7% | 6 |
| 1995 | 0 | 0.0% | 0 | 0.0% | 1 |
| 1996 | 0 | 0.0% | 0 | 0.0% | 1 |
| 1997 | 3 | 75.0% | 1 | 25.0% | 4 |
| 1998 | 1 | 20.0% | 1 | 20.0% | 5 |
| 1999 | 0 | 0.0% | 0 | 0.0% | 4 |
| 2000 | 2 | 25.0% | 0 | 0.0% | 8 |
| 2001 | 2 | 33.3% | 2 | 33.3% | 6 |
| 2002 | 0 | 0.0% | 0 | 0.0% | 5 |

*Table PT.3 Distribution of SE patents by Technology Class, 1994 to 2003*

| Year | Chem. | % Chem. | Elec. | % Elec. | Mech. | % Mech. |
|------|-------|---------|-------|---------|-------|---------|
| 1994 | 2 | 33.3% | 0 | 0.0% | 4 | 66.7% |
| 1995 | 0 | 0.0% | 0 | 0.0% | 1 | 100.0% |
| 1996 | 1 | 100.0% | 0 | 0.0% | 0 | 0.0% |
| 1997 | 1 | 25.0% | 0 | 0.0% | 3 | 75.0% |
| 1998 | 3 | 60.0% | 0 | 0.0% | 2 | 40.0% |
| 1999 | 2 | 50.0% | 0 | 0.0% | 2 | 50.0% |
| 2000 | 3 | 37.5% | 1 | 12.5% | 4 | 50.0% |
| 2001 | 2 | 33.3% | 3 | 50.0% | 1 | 16.7% |
| 2002 | 2 | 40.0% | 1 | 20.0% | 2 | 40.0% |
| 2003 | 3 | 42.9% | 2 | 28.6% | 2 | 28.6% |

*Table PT.4 Small Entity patents lapsing at 4 yr and 8 yr stages*

| Year | Lapsed 4 | % Lapsed 4 | Lapsed 8 | % Lapsed 8 | Total |
|------|----------|------------|----------|------------|-------|
| 1994 | 2 | 33.3% | 2 | 33.3% | 6 |
| 1995 | 1 | 100.0% | - | - | 1 |
| 1996 | 0 | 0.0% | - | - | 1 |
| 1997 | 2 | 50.0% | - | - | 4 |
| 1998 | 1 | 20.0% | - | - | 5 |

# Slovakia

*Table SK.1   Small Entity patent counts by year, 1994 to 2003*

| Year | Individual | Small Firm | Nonprofit | Total |
|------|-----------|-----------|-----------|-------|
| 1994 | 0 | 0 | 0 | 0 |
| 1995 | 0 | 0 | 0 | 0 |
| 1996 | 0 | 1 | 0 | 1 |
| 1997 | 2 | 0 | 0 | 2 |
| 1998 | 0 | 2 | 0 | 2 |
| 1999 | 1 | 1 | 0 | 2 |
| 2000 | 3 | 0 | 0 | 3 |
| 2001 | 0 | 0 | 0 | 0 |
| 2002 | 1 | 3 | 0 | 4 |
| 2003 | 4 | 0 | 0 | 4 |
| 10 yrs | 11 | 7 | 0 | 18 |

*Figure SK.1   SE counts, % change on 1996*

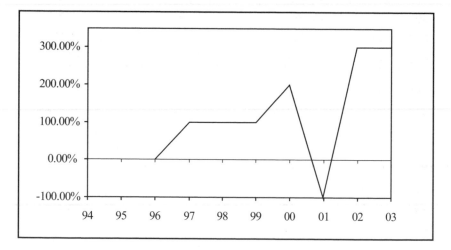

*Table SK.2   Cited Small Entity patents, 1994 to 2002*

| Year | Cited>=1 | % >=1 | Cited >= 3 | % >= 3 | Total |
|------|----------|-------|-----------|--------|-------|
| 1994 | 0 | 0.0% | 0 | 0.0% | 0 |
| 1995 | 0 | 0.0% | 0 | 0.0% | 0 |
| 1996 | 0 | 0.0% | 0 | 0.0% | 1 |
| 1997 | 1 | 50.0% | 0 | 0.0% | 2 |
| 1998 | 0 | 0.0% | 0 | 0.0% | 2 |
| 1999 | 1 | 50.0% | 0 | 0.0% | 2 |
| 2000 | 0 | 0.0% | 0 | 0.0% | 3 |
| 2001 | 0 | 0.0% | 0 | 0.0% | 0 |
| 2002 | 0 | 0.0% | 0 | 0.0% | 4 |

*Table SK.3   Distribution of SE patents by Technology Class, 1994 to 2003*

| Year | Chem. | % Chem. | Elec. | % Elec. | Mech. | % Mech. |
|------|-------|---------|-------|---------|-------|---------|
| 1994 | 0 | 0.0% | 0 | 0.0% | 0 | 0.0% |
| 1995 | 0 | 0.0% | 0 | 0.0% | 0 | 0.0% |
| 1996 | 0 | 0.0% | 0 | 0.0% | 1 | 100.0% |
| 1997 | 0 | 0.0% | 0 | 0.0% | 2 | 100.0% |
| 1998 | 0 | 0.0% | 0 | 0.0% | 2 | 100.0% |
| 1999 | 0 | 0.0% | 0 | 0.0% | 2 | 100.0% |
| 2000 | 1 | 33.3% | 1 | 33.3% | 1 | 33.3% |
| 2001 | 0 | 0.0% | 0 | 0.0% | 0 | 0.0% |
| 2002 | 1 | 25.0% | 0 | 0.0% | 3 | 75.0% |
| 2003 | 1 | 25.0% | 0 | 0.0% | 3 | 75.0% |

*Table SK.4   Small Entity patents lapsing at 4 yr and 8 yr stages*

| Year | Lapsed 4 | % Lapsed 4 | Lapsed 8 | % Lapsed 8 | Total |
|------|----------|------------|----------|------------|-------|
| 1994 | 0 | 0.0% | 0 | 0.0% | 0 |
| 1995 | 0 | 0.0% | - | - | 0 |
| 1996 | 1 | 100.0% | - | - | 1 |
| 1997 | 2 | 100.0% | - | - | 2 |
| 1998 | 2 | 100.0% | - | - | 2 |

# Spain

*Table ES.1   Small Entity patent counts by year, 1994 to 2003*

| Year | Individual | Small Firm | Nonprofit | Total |
|------|------------|------------|-----------|-------|
| 1994 | 42 | 42 | 2 | 86 |
| 1995 | 38 | 49 | 3 | 90 |
| 1996 | 31 | 41 | 6 | 78 |
| 1997 | 46 | 44 | 6 | 96 |
| 1998 | 52 | 67 | 9 | 128 |
| 1999 | 52 | 48 | 7 | 107 |
| 2000 | 60 | 49 | 8 | 117 |
| 2001 | 37 | 57 | 11 | 105 |
| 2002 | 51 | 74 | 14 | 139 |
| 2003 | 44 | 52 | 7 | 103 |
| 10 yrs | 453 | 523 | 73 | 1,049 |

*Figure ES.1   SE counts, % change on 1994 with % change year on year*

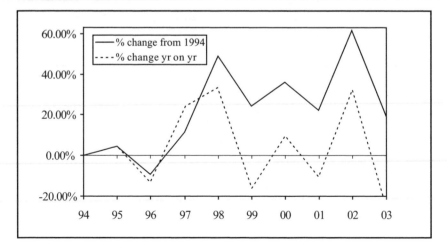

*Table ES.2   Cited Small Entity patents, 1994 to 2002*

| Year | Cited>=1 | % >=1 | Cited >= 3 | % >= 3 | Total |
|------|----------|-------|-----------|--------|-------|
| 1994 | 68 | 79.1% | 36 | 41.9% | 86 |
| 1995 | 65 | 72.2% | 31 | 34.4% | 90 |
| 1996 | 50 | 64.1% | 24 | 30.8% | 78 |
| 1997 | 56 | 58.3% | 25 | 26.0% | 96 |
| 1998 | 74 | 57.8% | 31 | 24.2% | 128 |
| 1999 | 43 | 40.2% | 10 | 9.3% | 107 |
| 2000 | 48 | 41.0% | 9 | 7.7% | 117 |
| 2001 | 27 | 25.7% | 4 | 3.8% | 105 |
| 2002 | 5 | 3.6% | 0 | 0.0% | 139 |

*Table ES.3   Distribution of SE patents by Technology Class, 1994 to 2003*

| Year | Chem. | % Chem. | Elec. | % Elec. | Mech. | % Mech. |
|------|-------|---------|-------|---------|-------|---------|
| 1994 | 17 | 19.8% | 8 | 9.3% | 61 | 70.9% |
| 1995 | 19 | 21.1% | 5 | 5.6% | 66 | 73.3% |
| 1996 | 20 | 25.6% | 6 | 7.7% | 52 | 66.7% |
| 1997 | 21 | 21.9% | 12 | 12.5% | 63 | 65.6% |
| 1998 | 30 | 23.4% | 17 | 13.3% | 81 | 63.3% |
| 1999 | 27 | 25.2% | 7 | 6.5% | 73 | 68.2% |
| 2000 | 22 | 18.8% | 14 | 12.0% | 81 | 69.2% |
| 2001 | 28 | 26.7% | 13 | 12.4% | 64 | 61.0% |
| 2002 | 32 | 23.0% | 15 | 10.8% | 92 | 66.2% |
| 2003 | 28 | 27.2% | 11 | 10.7% | 64 | 62.1% |

*Table ES.4   Small Entity patents lapsing at 4 yr and 8 yr stages*

| Year | Lapsed 4 | % Lapsed 4 | Lapsed 8 | % Lapsed 8 | Total |
|------|----------|------------|----------|------------|-------|
| 1994 | 30 | 34.9% | 56 | 65.1% | 86 |
| 1995 | 18 | 20.0% | - | - | 90 |
| 1996 | 20 | 25.6% | - | - | 78 |
| 1997 | 27 | 28.1% | - | - | 96 |
| 1998 | 35 | 27.3% | - | - | 128 |

# Sweden

*Table SE.1   Small Entity patent counts by year, 1994 to 2003*

| Year | Individual | Small Firm | Nonprofit | Total |
|------|-----------|-----------|-----------|-------|
| 1994 | 82 | 85 | 7 | 174 |
| 1995 | 81 | 89 | 3 | 173 |
| 1996 | 56 | 85 | 4 | 145 |
| 1997 | 68 | 91 | 4 | 163 |
| 1998 | 111 | 151 | 5 | 267 |
| 1999 | 108 | 151 | 3 | 262 |
| 2000 | 97 | 185 | 6 | 288 |
| 2001 | 112 | 218 | 5 | 335 |
| 2002 | 93 | 209 | 5 | 307 |
| 2003 | 61 | 194 | 1 | 256 |
| 10 yrs | 869 | 1,458 | 43 | 2,370 |

*Figure SE.1   SE counts, % change on 1994 with % change year on year*

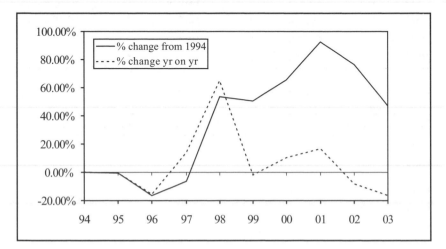

*Table SE.2   Cited Small Entity patents, 1994 to 2002*

| Year | Cited>=1 | % >=1 | Cited >= 3 | % >= 3 | Total |
|------|----------|-------|------------|--------|-------|
| 1994 | 147 | 84.5% | 98 | 56.3% | 174 |
| 1995 | 138 | 79.8% | 73 | 42.2% | 173 |
| 1996 | 108 | 74.5% | 57 | 39.3% | 145 |
| 1997 | 114 | 69.9% | 57 | 35.0% | 163 |
| 1998 | 160 | 59.9% | 60 | 22.5% | 267 |
| 1999 | 137 | 52.3% | 36 | 13.7% | 262 |
| 2000 | 102 | 35.4% | 13 | 4.5% | 288 |
| 2001 | 59 | 17.6% | 4 | 1.2% | 335 |
| 2002 | 6 | 2.0% | 0 | 0.0% | 307 |

*Table SE.3   Distribution of SE patents by Technology Class, 1994 to 2003*

| Year | Chem. | % Chem. | Elec. | % Elec. | Mech. | % Mech. |
|------|-------|---------|-------|---------|-------|---------|
| 1994 | 31 | 17.8% | 27 | 15.5% | 116 | 66.7% |
| 1995 | 26 | 15.0% | 21 | 12.1% | 126 | 72.8% |
| 1996 | 24 | 16.6% | 14 | 9.7% | 107 | 73.8% |
| 1997 | 44 | 27.0% | 14 | 8.6% | 105 | 64.4% |
| 1998 | 45 | 16.9% | 41 | 15.4% | 181 | 67.8% |
| 1999 | 54 | 20.6% | 38 | 14.5% | 170 | 64.9% |
| 2000 | 58 | 20.1% | 43 | 14.9% | 187 | 64.9% |
| 2001 | 70 | 20.9% | 56 | 16.7% | 208 | 62.1% |
| 2002 | 86 | 28.0% | 61 | 19.9% | 160 | 52.1% |
| 2003 | 54 | 21.1% | 60 | 23.4% | 142 | 55.5% |

*Table SE.4   Small Entity patents lapsing at 4 yr and 8 yr stages*

| Year | Lapsed 4 | % Lapsed 4 | Lapsed 8 | % Lapsed 8 | Total |
|------|----------|------------|----------|------------|-------|
| 1994 | 34 | 19.5% | 78 | 44.8% | 174 |
| 1995 | 23 | 13.3% | - | - | 173 |
| 1996 | 26 | 17.9% | - | - | 145 |
| 1997 | 26 | 16.0% | - | - | 163 |
| 1998 | 51 | 19.1% | - | - | 267 |

# Switzerland

*Table CH.1   Small Entity patent counts by year, 1994 to 2003*

| Year | Individual | Small Firm | Nonprofit | Total |
|------|-----------|-----------|-----------|-------|
| 1994 | 97 | 174 | 3 | 274 |
| 1995 | 90 | 135 | 4 | 229 |
| 1996 | 105 | 145 | 5 | 255 |
| 1997 | 86 | 149 | 8 | 243 |
| 1998 | 90 | 169 | 6 | 265 |
| 1999 | 83 | 176 | 8 | 267 |
| 2000 | 85 | 188 | 8 | 281 |
| 2001 | 82 | 199 | 15 | 296 |
| 2002 | 57 | 157 | 5 | 219 |
| 2003 | 50 | 144 | 16 | 210 |
| 10 yrs | 825 | 1,636 | 78 | 2,539 |

*Figure CH.1   SE counts, % change on 1994 with % change year on year*

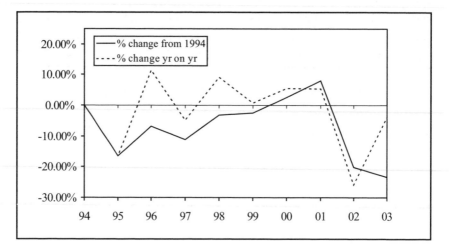

*Table CH.2   Cited Small Entity patents, 1994 to 2002*

| Year | Cited>=1 | % >=1 | Cited >= 3 | % >= 3 | Total |
|------|----------|-------|------------|--------|-------|
| 1994 | 234 | 85.4% | 139 | 50.7% | 274 |
| 1995 | 189 | 82.5% | 122 | 53.3% | 229 |
| 1996 | 204 | 80.0% | 88 | 34.5% | 255 |
| 1997 | 183 | 75.3% | 91 | 37.4% | 243 |
| 1998 | 179 | 67.5% | 77 | 29.1% | 265 |
| 1999 | 169 | 63.3% | 54 | 20.2% | 267 |
| 2000 | 118 | 42.0% | 17 | 6.0% | 281 |
| 2001 | 69 | 23.3% | 7 | 2.4% | 296 |
| 2002 | 6 | 2.7% | 0 | 0.0% | 219 |

*Table CH.3   Distribution of SE patents by Technology Class, 1994 to 2003*

| Year | Chem. | % Chem. | Elec. | % Elec. | Mech. | % Mech. |
|------|-------|---------|-------|---------|-------|---------|
| 1994 | 47 | 17.2% | 21 | 7.7% | 206 | 75.2% |
| 1995 | 42 | 18.3% | 27 | 11.8% | 160 | 69.9% |
| 1996 | 38 | 14.9% | 37 | 14.5% | 180 | 70.6% |
| 1997 | 51 | 21.0% | 32 | 13.2% | 160 | 65.8% |
| 1998 | 65 | 24.5% | 29 | 10.9% | 171 | 64.5% |
| 1999 | 58 | 21.7% | 28 | 10.5% | 181 | 67.8% |
| 2000 | 59 | 21.0% | 24 | 8.5% | 198 | 70.5% |
| 2001 | 68 | 23.0% | 30 | 10.1% | 198 | 66.9% |
| 2002 | 50 | 22.8% | 31 | 14.2% | 138 | 63.0% |
| 2003 | 49 | 23.3% | 39 | 18.6% | 122 | 58.1% |

*Table CH.4   Small Entity patents lapsing at 4 yr and 8 yr stages*

| Year | Lapsed 4 | % Lapsed 4 | Lapsed 8 | % Lapsed 8 | Total |
|------|----------|------------|----------|------------|-------|
| 1994 | 59 | 21.5% | 123 | 44.9% | 274 |
| 1995 | 49 | 21.4% | - | - | 229 |
| 1996 | 65 | 25.5% | - | - | 255 |
| 1997 | 43 | 17.7% | - | - | 243 |
| 1998 | 63 | 23.8% | - | - | 265 |

# Taiwan

*Table TW.1   Small Entity patent counts by year, 1994 to 2003*

| Year | Individual | Small Firm | Nonprofit | Total |
|------|-----------|-----------|-----------|-------|
| 1994 | 982 | 165 | 73 | 1,220 |
| 1995 | 990 | 173 | 34 | 1,197 |
| 1996 | 1,135 | 214 | 15 | 1,364 |
| 1997 | 1,112 | 225 | 16 | 1,353 |
| 1998 | 1,537 | 342 | 39 | 1,918 |
| 1999 | 1,585 | 458 | 36 | 2,079 |
| 2000 | 1,737 | 551 | 40 | 2,328 |
| 2001 | 1,822 | 740 | 46 | 2,608 |
| 2002 | 1,692 | 830 | 40 | 2,562 |
| 2003 | 1,594 | 894 | 42 | 2,530 |
| 10 yrs | 14,186 | 4,592 | 381 | 19,159 |

*Figure TW.1   SE counts, % change on 1994 with % change year on year*

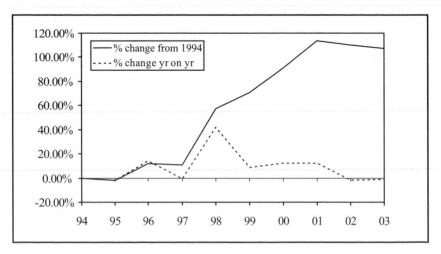

*Table TW.2   Cited Small Entity patents, 1994 to 2002*

| Year | Cited>=1 | % >=1 | Cited >= 3 | % >= 3 | Total |
|------|----------|-------|------------|--------|-------|
| 1994 | 1,042 | 85.4% | 718 | 58.9% | 1,220 |
| 1995 | 1,031 | 86.1% | 696 | 58.1% | 1,197 |
| 1996 | 1,168 | 85.6% | 726 | 53.2% | 1,364 |
| 1997 | 1,078 | 79.7% | 645 | 47.7% | 1,353 |
| 1998 | 1,450 | 75.6% | 766 | 39.9% | 1,918 |
| 1999 | 1,350 | 64.9% | 546 | 26.3% | 2,079 |
| 2000 | 1,203 | 51.7% | 351 | 15.1% | 2,328 |
| 2001 | 856 | 32.8% | 124 | 4.8% | 2,608 |
| 2002 | 137 | 5.3% | 4 | 0.2% | 2,562 |

*Table TW.3   Distribution of SE patents by Technology Class, 1994 to 2003*

| Year | Chem. | % Chem. | Elec. | % Elec. | Mech. | % Mech. |
|------|-------|---------|-------|---------|-------|---------|
| 1994 | 90 | 7.4% | 188 | 15.4% | 942 | 77.2% |
| 1995 | 83 | 6.9% | 199 | 16.6% | 915 | 76.4% |
| 1996 | 72 | 5.3% | 224 | 16.4% | 1,068 | 78.3% |
| 1997 | 65 | 4.8% | 250 | 18.5% | 1,038 | 76.7% |
| 1998 | 125 | 6.5% | 389 | 20.3% | 1,403 | 73.1% |
| 1999 | 139 | 6.7% | 394 | 19.0% | 1,546 | 74.4% |
| 2000 | 139 | 6.0% | 485 | 20.8% | 1,702 | 73.1% |
| 2001 | 183 | 7.0% | 544 | 20.9% | 1,881 | 72.1% |
| 2002 | 185 | 7.2% | 650 | 25.4% | 1,727 | 67.4% |
| 2003 | 170 | 6.7% | 702 | 27.7% | 1,658 | 65.5% |

*Table TW.4   Small Entity patents lapsing at 4 yr and 8 yr stages*

| Year | Lapsed 4 | % Lapsed 4 | Lapsed 8 | % Lapsed 8 | Total |
|------|----------|------------|----------|------------|-------|
| 1994 | 616 | 50.5% | 955 | 78.3% | 1,220 |
| 1995 | 576 | 48.1% | - | - | 1,197 |
| 1996 | 676 | 49.6% | - | - | 1,364 |
| 1997 | 710 | 52.5% | - | - | 1,353 |
| 1998 | 904 | 47.1% | - | - | 1,918 |

# Turkey

*Table TR.1   Small Entity patent counts by year, 1994 to 2003*

| Year | Individual | Small Firm | Nonprofit | Total |
|------|-----------|-----------|-----------|-------|
| 1994 | 1 | 0 | 1 | 2 |
| 1995 | 0 | 0 | 0 | 0 |
| 1996 | 1 | 0 | 0 | 1 |
| 1997 | 1 | 0 | 0 | 1 |
| 1998 | 0 | 0 | 0 | 0 |
| 1999 | 1 | 0 | 1 | 2 |
| 2000 | 2 | 2 | 0 | 4 |
| 2001 | 1 | 2 | 2 | 5 |
| 2002 | 4 | 0 | 1 | 5 |
| 2003 | 1 | 2 | 0 | 3 |
| 10 yrs | 12 | 6 | 5 | 23 |

*Figure TR.1   SE counts, % change on 1994*

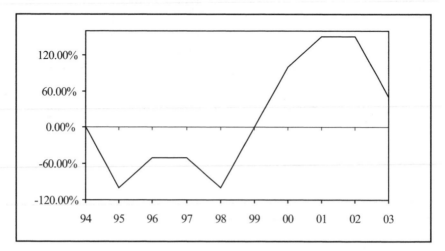

*Table TR.2   Cited Small Entity patents, 1994 to 2002*

| Year | Cited>=1 | % >=1 | Cited >= 3 | % >= 3 | Total |
|------|----------|-------|------------|--------|-------|
| 1994 | 2 | 100.0% | 0 | 0.0% | 2 |
| 1995 | 0 | 0.0% | 0 | 0.0% | 0 |
| 1996 | 1 | 100.0% | 0 | 0.0% | 1 |
| 1997 | 0 | 0.0% | 0 | 0.0% | 1 |
| 1998 | 0 | 0.0% | 0 | 0.0% | 0 |
| 1999 | 2 | 100.0% | 1 | 50.0% | 2 |
| 2000 | 0 | 0.0% | 0 | 0.0% | 4 |
| 2001 | 0 | 0.0% | 0 | 0.0% | 5 |
| 2002 | 1 | 20.0% | 0 | 0.0% | 5 |

*Table TR.3   Distribution of SE patents by Technology Class, 1994 to 2003*

| Year | Chem. | % Chem. | Elec. | % Elec. | Mech. | % Mech. |
|------|-------|---------|-------|---------|-------|---------|
| 1994 | 1 | 50.0% | 0 | 0.0% | 1 | 50.0% |
| 1995 | 0 | 0.0% | 0 | 0.0% | 0 | 0.0% |
| 1996 | 0 | 0.0% | 0 | 0.0% | 1 | 100.0% |
| 1997 | 0 | 0.0% | 0 | 0.0% | 1 | 100.0% |
| 1998 | 0 | 0.0% | 0 | 0.0% | 0 | 0.0% |
| 1999 | 0 | 0.0% | 0 | 0.0% | 2 | 100.0% |
| 2000 | 2 | 50.0% | 0 | 0.0% | 2 | 50.0% |
| 2001 | 2 | 40.0% | 1 | 20.0% | 2 | 40.0% |
| 2002 | 0 | 0.0% | 1 | 20.0% | 4 | 80.0% |
| 2003 | 2 | 66.7% | 0 | 0.0% | 1 | 33.3% |

*Table TR.4   Small Entity patents lapsing at 4 yr and 8 yr stages*

| Year | Lapsed 4 | % Lapsed 4 | Lapsed 8 | % Lapsed 8 | Total |
|------|----------|------------|----------|------------|-------|
| 1994 | 1 | 50.0% | 2 | 100.0% | 2 |
| 1995 | 0 | 0.0% | - | - | 0 |
| 1996 | 1 | 100.0% | - | - | 1 |
| 1997 | 1 | 100.0% | - | - | 1 |
| 1998 | 0 | 0.0% | - | - | 0 |

# United Kingdom

*Table GB.1   Small Entity patent counts by year, 1994 to 2003*

| Year | Individual | Small Firm | Nonprofit | Total |
|------|-----------|-----------|-----------|-------|
| 1994 | 156 | 215 | 21 | 392 |
| 1995 | 167 | 246 | 23 | 436 |
| 1996 | 169 | 281 | 28 | 478 |
| 1997 | 175 | 287 | 33 | 495 |
| 1998 | 237 | 415 | 62 | 714 |
| 1999 | 240 | 414 | 54 | 708 |
| 2000 | 265 | 428 | 50 | 743 |
| 2001 | 231 | 466 | 58 | 755 |
| 2002 | 217 | 423 | 66 | 706 |
| 2003 | 201 | 426 | 44 | 671 |
| 10 yrs | 2,058 | 3,601 | 439 | 6,098 |

*Figure GB.1   SE counts, % change on 1994 with % change year on year*

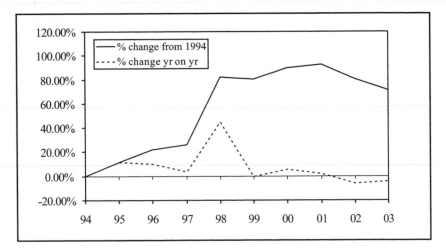

*Table GB.2   Cited Small Entity patents, 1994 to 2002*

| Year | Cited>=1 | % >=1 | Cited >= 3 | % >= 3 | Total |
|------|----------|-------|------------|--------|-------|
| 1994 | 342 | 87.2% | 223 | 56.9% | 392 |
| 1995 | 378 | 86.7% | 243 | 55.7% | 436 |
| 1996 | 388 | 81.2% | 213 | 44.6% | 478 |
| 1997 | 373 | 75.4% | 204 | 41.2% | 495 |
| 1998 | 474 | 66.4% | 231 | 32.4% | 714 |
| 1999 | 393 | 55.5% | 136 | 19.2% | 708 |
| 2000 | 317 | 42.7% | 55 | 7.4% | 743 |
| 2001 | 158 | 20.9% | 12 | 1.6% | 755 |
| 2002 | 15 | 2.1% | 0 | 0.0% | 706 |

*Table GB.3   Distribution of SE patents by Technology Class, 1994 to 2003*

| Year | Chem. | % Chem. | Elec. | % Elec. | Mech. | % Mech. |
|------|-------|---------|-------|---------|-------|---------|
| 1994 | 64 | 16.3% | 75 | 19.1% | 253 | 64.5% |
| 1995 | 80 | 18.3% | 61 | 14.0% | 295 | 67.7% |
| 1996 | 107 | 22.4% | 81 | 16.9% | 290 | 60.7% |
| 1997 | 128 | 25.9% | 74 | 14.9% | 293 | 59.2% |
| 1998 | 200 | 28.0% | 120 | 16.8% | 394 | 55.2% |
| 1999 | 198 | 28.0% | 105 | 14.8% | 405 | 57.2% |
| 2000 | 181 | 24.4% | 117 | 15.7% | 445 | 59.9% |
| 2001 | 191 | 25.3% | 129 | 17.1% | 435 | 57.6% |
| 2002 | 186 | 26.3% | 138 | 19.5% | 382 | 54.1% |
| 2003 | 168 | 25.0% | 130 | 19.4% | 373 | 55.6% |

*Table GB.4   Small Entity patents lapsing at 4 yr and 8 yr stages*

| Year | Lapsed 4 | % Lapsed 4 | Lapsed 8 | % Lapsed 8 | Total |
|------|----------|------------|----------|------------|-------|
| 1994 | 113 | 28.8% | 206 | 52.6% | 392 |
| 1995 | 96 | 22.0% | - | - | 436 |
| 1996 | 130 | 27.2% | - | - | 478 |
| 1997 | 112 | 22.6% | - | - | 495 |
| 1998 | 180 | 25.2% | - | - | 714 |

# United States

*Table US.1   Small Entity patent counts by year, 1994 to 2003*

| Year | Individual | Small Firm | Nonprofit | Total |
| --- | --- | --- | --- | --- |
| 1994 | 11,725 | 8,717 | 1,572 | 22,014 |
| 1995 | 11,631 | 8,688 | 1,644 | 21,963 |
| 1996 | 12,401 | 9,732 | 2,022 | 24,155 |
| 1997 | 11,749 | 10,369 | 2,336 | 24,454 |
| 1998 | 14,776 | 13,667 | 3,015 | 31,458 |
| 1999 | 15,117 | 13,738 | 3,119 | 31,974 |
| 2000 | 14,629 | 13,966 | 2,760 | 31,355 |
| 2001 | 13,702 | 13,696 | 2,830 | 30,228 |
| 2002 | 12,044 | 12,646 | 2,652 | 27,342 |
| 2003 | 11,254 | 12,929 | 2,659 | 26,842 |
| 10 yrs | 129,028 | 118,148 | 24,609 | 271,785 |

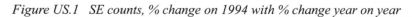

*Figure US.1   SE counts, % change on 1994 with % change year on year*

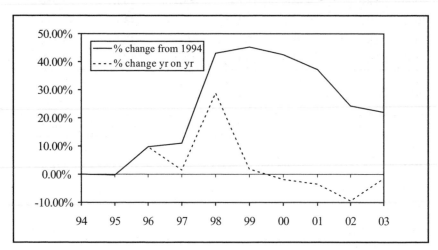

*Table US.2   Cited Small Entity patents, 1994 to 2002*

| Year | Cited>=1 | % >=1 | Cited >= 3 | % >= 3 | Total |
|------|----------|-------|-----------|--------|-------|
| 1994 | 20,110 | 91.4% | 15,063 | 68.4% | 22,014 |
| 1995 | 19,773 | 90.0% | 14,259 | 64.9% | 21,963 |
| 1996 | 21,103 | 87.4% | 14,321 | 59.3% | 24,155 |
| 1997 | 20,398 | 83.4% | 12,631 | 51.7% | 24,454 |
| 1998 | 24,394 | 77.5% | 13,059 | 41.5% | 31,458 |
| 1999 | 21,458 | 67.1% | 8,812 | 27.6% | 31,974 |
| 2000 | 16,250 | 51.8% | 4,493 | 14.3% | 31,355 |
| 2001 | 8,825 | 29.2% | 1,171 | 3.9% | 30,228 |
| 2002 | 832 | 3.0% | 24 | 0.1% | 27,342 |

*Table US.3   Distribution of SE patents by Technology Class, 1994 to 2003*

| Year | Chem. | % Chem. | Elec. | % Elec. | Mech. | % Mech. |
|------|-------|---------|-------|---------|-------|---------|
| 1994 | 3,636 | 16.5% | 3,258 | 14.8% | 15,120 | 68.7% |
| 1995 | 3,860 | 17.6% | 3,499 | 15.9% | 14,603 | 66.5% |
| 1996 | 4,628 | 19.2% | 4,017 | 16.6% | 15,510 | 64.2% |
| 1997 | 5,563 | 22.7% | 4,132 | 16.9% | 14,758 | 60.4% |
| 1998 | 6,963 | 22.1% | 5,732 | 18.2% | 18,763 | 59.6% |
| 1999 | 7,206 | 22.5% | 5,666 | 17.7% | 19,097 | 59.7% |
| 2000 | 6,678 | 21.3% | 5,911 | 18.9% | 18,765 | 59.8% |
| 2001 | 6,777 | 22.4% | 5,837 | 19.3% | 17,613 | 58.3% |
| 2002 | 6,115 | 22.4% | 5,624 | 20.6% | 15,602 | 57.1% |
| 2003 | 5,749 | 21.4% | 5,733 | 21.4% | 15,349 | 57.2% |

*Table US.4   Small Entity patents lapsing at 4 yr and 8 yr stages*

| Year | Lapsed 4 | % Lapsed 4 | Lapsed 8 | % Lapsed 8 | Total |
|------|----------|-----------|----------|-----------|-------|
| 1994 | 6,086 | 27.6% | 11,269 | 51.2% | 22,014 |
| 1995 | 5,367 | 24.4% | - | - | 21,963 |
| 1996 | 5,669 | 23.5% | - | - | 24,155 |
| 1997 | 5,623 | 23.0% | - | - | 24,454 |
| 1998 | 7,494 | 23.8% | - | - | 31,458 |

# Appendix A: Extract from the USPTO Manual of Patent Examining Procedure

**§ 1.27 Definition of small entities and establishing status as a Small Entity to permit payment of Small Entity fees; when a determination of entitlement to Small Entity status and notification of loss of entitlement to Small Entity status are required; fraud on the Office.**

(a) *Definition of small entities.* A Small Entity as used in this chapter means any party (person, small business concern, or nonprofit organization) under paragraphs (a)(1) through (a)(3) of this section.

(1) Person. A person, as used in paragraph (c) of this section, means any inventor or other individual (e.g., an individual to whom an inventor has transferred some rights in the invention), who has not assigned, granted, conveyed, or licensed, and is under no obligation under contract or law to assign, grant, convey, or license, any rights in the invention. An inventor or other individual who has transferred some rights, or is under an obligation to transfer some rights in the invention to one or more parties, can also qualify for Small Entity status if all the parties who have had rights in the invention transferred to them also qualify for Small Entity status either as a person, small business concern, or nonprofit organization under this section.

(2) Small business concern. A small business concern, as used in paragraph (c) of this section, means any business concern that:

(i) Has not assigned, granted, conveyed, or licensed, and is under no obligation under contract or law to assign, grant, convey, or license, any rights in the invention to any person, concern, or organization which would not qualify for Small Entity status as a person, small business concern, or nonprofit organization.

(ii) Meets the standards set forth in 13 CFR part 121 to be eligible for reduced patent fees. Questions related to standards for a small business concern may be directed to: Small Business Administration, Size Standards Staff, 409 Third Street, S.W., Washington, D.C. 20416.

(3) Nonprofit Organization. A nonprofit organization, as used in paragraph (c) of this section, means any nonprofit organization that:

(i) Has not assigned, granted, conveyed, or licensed, and is under no obligation under contract or law to assign, grant, convey, or license, any rights in the invention to any person, concern, or organization which would not qualify as a person, small business concern, or a nonprofit organization, and

(ii) Is either:

(A) A university or other institution of higher education located in any country;

(B) An organization of the type described in section 501(c)(3) of the Internal Revenue Code of 1986 (26 U.S.C. 501(c)(3)) and exempt from taxation under section 501(a) of the Internal Revenue Code (26 U.S.C. 501(a));

(C) Any nonprofit scientific or educational organization qualified under a nonprofit organization statute of a state of this country (35 U.S.C. 201(i)); or

(D) Any nonprofit organization located in a foreign country which would qualify as a nonprofit organization under paragraphs (a)(3)(ii)(B) of this section or (a)(3)(ii)(C) of this section if it were located in this country.

(4) License to a Federal agency.

(i) For persons under paragraph (a)(1) of this section, a license to the Government resulting from a rights determination under Executive Order 10096 does not constitute a license so as to prohibit claiming Small Entity status.

(ii) For small business concerns and nonprofit organizations under paragraphs (a)(2) and (a)(3) of this section, a license to a Federal agency resulting from a funding agreement with that agency pursuant to 35 U.S.C. 202(c)(4) does not constitute a license for the purposes of paragraphs (a)(2)(i) and (a)(3)(i) of this section.

(b) *Establishment of Small Entity status permits payment of reduced fees.* A Small Entity, as defined in paragraph (a) of this section, who has properly asserted entitlement to Small Entity status pursuant to paragraph (c) of this section will be accorded Small Entity status by the Office in the particular application or patent in which entitlement to Small Entity status was asserted. Establishment of Small Entity status allows the payment of certain reduced patent fees pursuant to 35 U.S.C. 41(h).

# Appendix B: A list of the major Class numbers with the corresponding Technology Class groups

Class groups as defined by USPTO Patent Technology Monitoring Division

| Class | Class Group | Class | Class Group |
| --- | --- | --- | --- |
| 1 | Missing | 42 | Mechanical |
| 2 | Mechanical | 43 | Mechanical |
| 4 | Mechanical | 44 | Chemical |
| 5 | Mechanical | 47 | Mechanical |
| 7 | Mechanical | 48 | Chemical |
| 8 | Chemical | 49 | Mechanical |
| 12 | Mechanical | 51 | Chemical |
| 14 | Mechanical | 52 | Mechanical |
| 15 | Mechanical | 53 | Mechanical |
| 16 | Mechanical | 54 | Mechanical |
| 19 | Mechanical | 55 | Chemical |
| 23 | Chemical | 56 | Mechanical |
| 24 | Mechanical | 57 | Mechanical |
| 26 | Mechanical | 59 | Mechanical |
| 27 | Mechanical | 60 | Mechanical |
| 28 | Mechanical | 62 | Mechanical |
| 29 | Mechanical | 63 | Mechanical |
| 30 | Mechanical | 65 | Chemical |
| 33 | Mechanical | 66 | Mechanical |
| 34 | Mechanical | 68 | Mechanical |
| 36 | Mechanical | 69 | Mechanical |
| 37 | Mechanical | 70 | Mechanical |
| 38 | Mechanical | 71 | Chemical |
| 40 | Mechanical | 72 | Mechanical |

| Class | Class Group | Class | Class Group |
| --- | --- | --- | --- |
| 73 | Mechanical | 122 | Mechanical |
| 74 | Mechanical | 123 | Mechanical |
| 75 | Chemical | 124 | Mechanical |
| 76 | Mechanical | 125 | Mechanical |
| 79 | Mechanical | 126 | Mechanical |
| 81 | Mechanical | 127 | Chemical |
| 82 | Mechanical | 128 | Mechanical |
| 83 | Mechanical | 131 | Mechanical |
| 84 | Mechanical | 132 | Mechanical |
| 86 | Mechanical | 134 | Mechanical |
| 87 | Mechanical | 135 | Mechanical |
| 89 | Mechanical | 136 | Chemical |
| 91 | Mechanical | 137 | Mechanical |
| 92 | Mechanical | 138 | Mechanical |
| 95 | Chemical | 139 | Mechanical |
| 96 | Chemical | 140 | Mechanical |
| 99 | Mechanical | 141 | Mechanical |
| 100 | Mechanical | 142 | Mechanical |
| 101 | Mechanical | 144 | Mechanical |
| 102 | Mechanical | 147 | Mechanical |
| 104 | Mechanical | 148 | Chemical |
| 105 | Mechanical | 149 | Chemical |
| 106 | Chemical | 150 | Mechanical |
| 108 | Mechanical | 152 | Mechanical |
| 109 | Mechanical | 156 | Chemical |
| 110 | Mechanical | 157 | Mechanical |
| 111 | Mechanical | 159 | Chemical |
| 112 | Mechanical | 160 | Mechanical |
| 114 | Mechanical | 162 | Chemical |
| 116 | Mechanical | 163 | Mechanical |
| 117 | Chemical | 164 | Mechanical |
| 118 | Mechanical | 166 | Mechanical |
| 119 | Mechanical | 168 | Mechanical |

| Class | Class Group | Class | Class Group |
|-------|-------------|-------|-------------|
| 169 | Mechanical | 210 | Chemical |
| 171 | Mechanical | 211 | Mechanical |
| 172 | Mechanical | 212 | Mechanical |
| 173 | Mechanical | 213 | Mechanical |
| 174 | Electrical | 215 | Mechanical |
| 175 | Mechanical | 216 | Chemical |
| 177 | Mechanical | 217 | Mechanical |
| 178 | Electrical | 218 | Electrical |
| 180 | Mechanical | 219 | Electrical |
| 181 | Mechanical | 220 | Mechanical |
| 182 | Mechanical | 221 | Mechanical |
| 184 | Mechanical | 222 | Mechanical |
| 185 | Mechanical | 223 | Mechanical |
| 186 | Mechanical | 224 | Mechanical |
| 187 | Mechanical | 225 | Mechanical |
| 188 | Mechanical | 226 | Mechanical |
| 190 | Mechanical | 227 | Mechanical |
| 191 | Electrical | 228 | Mechanical |
| 192 | Mechanical | 229 | Mechanical |
| 193 | Mechanical | 231 | Mechanical |
| 194 | Mechanical | 232 | Mechanical |
| 196 | Chemical | 234 | Mechanical |
| 198 | Mechanical | 235 | Electrical |
| 199 | Mechanical | 236 | Mechanical |
| 200 | Electrical | 237 | Mechanical |
| 201 | Chemical | 238 | Mechanical |
| 202 | Chemical | 239 | Mechanical |
| 203 | Chemical | 241 | Mechanical |
| 204 | Chemical | 242 | Mechanical |
| 205 | Chemical | 244 | Mechanical |
| 206 | Mechanical | 245 | Mechanical |
| 208 | Chemical | 246 | Mechanical |
| 209 | Chemical | 248 | Mechanical |

| Class | Class Group | Class | Class Group |
|-------|-------------|-------|-------------|
| 249 | Mechanical | 297 | Mechanical |
| 250 | Electrical | 298 | Mechanical |
| 251 | Mechanical | 299 | Mechanical |
| 252 | Chemical | 300 | Mechanical |
| 254 | Mechanical | 301 | Mechanical |
| 256 | Mechanical | 303 | Mechanical |
| 257 | Electrical | 305 | Mechanical |
| 258 | Mechanical | 307 | Electrical |
| 260 | Chemical | 310 | Electrical |
| 261 | Chemical | 312 | Mechanical |
| 264 | Chemical | 313 | Electrical |
| 266 | Mechanical | 314 | Electrical |
| 267 | Mechanical | 315 | Electrical |
| 269 | Mechanical | 318 | Electrical |
| 270 | Mechanical | 320 | Electrical |
| 271 | Mechanical | 322 | Electrical |
| 273 | Mechanical | 323 | Electrical |
| 276 | Mechanical | 324 | Electrical |
| 277 | Mechanical | 326 | Electrical |
| 278 | Mechanical | 327 | Electrical |
| 279 | Mechanical | 328 | Electrical |
| 280 | Mechanical | 329 | Electrical |
| 281 | Mechanical | 330 | Electrical |
| 283 | Mechanical | 331 | Electrical |
| 285 | Mechanical | 332 | Electrical |
| 289 | Mechanical | 333 | Electrical |
| 290 | Electrical | 334 | Electrical |
| 291 | Mechanical | 335 | Electrical |
| 292 | Mechanical | 336 | Electrical |
| 293 | Mechanical | 337 | Electrical |
| 294 | Mechanical | 338 | Electrical |
| 295 | Mechanical | 340 | Electrical |
| 296 | Mechanical | 341 | Electrical |

| Class | Class Group | Class | Class Group |
|-------|-------------|-------|-------------|
| 342 | Electrical | 378 | Electrical |
| 343 | Electrical | 379 | Electrical |
| 345 | Electrical | 380 | Electrical |
| 346 | Electrical | 381 | Electrical |
| 347 | Mechanical | 382 | Electrical |
| 348 | Electrical | 383 | Electrical |
| 349 | Electrical | 384 | Mechanical |
| 351 | Mechanical | 385 | Mechanical |
| 352 | Mechanical | 386 | Electrical |
| 353 | Mechanical | 388 | Electrical |
| 354 | Electrical | 392 | Electrical |
| 355 | Electrical | 395 | Electrical |
| 356 | Mechanical | 396 | Electrical |
| 358 | Electrical | 398 | Electrical |
| 359 | Mechanical | 399 | Electrical |
| 360 | Electrical | 400 | Mechanical |
| 361 | Electrical | 401 | Mechanical |
| 362 | Electrical | 402 | Mechanical |
| 363 | Electrical | 403 | Mechanical |
| 364 | Electrical | 404 | Mechanical |
| 365 | Electrical | 405 | Mechanical |
| 366 | Mechanical | 406 | Mechanical |
| 367 | Electrical | 407 | Mechanical |
| 368 | Electrical | 408 | Mechanical |
| 369 | Electrical | 409 | Mechanical |
| 370 | Electrical | 410 | Mechanical |
| 371 | Electrical | 411 | Mechanical |
| 372 | Electrical | 412 | Mechanical |
| 373 | Electrical | 413 | Mechanical |
| 374 | Mechanical | 414 | Mechanical |
| 375 | Electrical | 415 | Mechanical |
| 376 | Chemical | 416 | Mechanical |
| 377 | Electrical | 417 | Mechanical |

| Class | Class Group | Class | Class Group |
|-------|-------------|-------|-------------|
| 418 | Mechanical | 460 | Mechanical |
| 419 | Chemical | 462 | Mechanical |
| 420 | Chemical | 463 | Mechanical |
| 422 | Chemical | 464 | Mechanical |
| 423 | Chemical | 470 | Mechanical |
| 424 | Chemical | 472 | Mechanical |
| 425 | Mechanical | 473 | Mechanical |
| 426 | Chemical | 474 | Mechanical |
| 427 | Chemical | 475 | Mechanical |
| 428 | Chemical | 476 | Mechanical |
| 429 | Chemical | 477 | Mechanical |
| 430 | Chemical | 482 | Mechanical |
| 431 | Mechanical | 483 | Mechanical |
| 432 | Mechanical | 492 | Mechanical |
| 433 | Mechanical | 493 | Mechanical |
| 434 | Mechanical | 494 | Mechanical |
| 435 | Chemical | 501 | Chemical |
| 436 | Chemical | 502 | Chemical |
| 437 | Electrical | 503 | Electrical |
| 438 | Chemical | 504 | Chemical |
| 439 | Mechanical | 505 | Electrical |
| 440 | Mechanical | 507 | Chemical |
| 441 | Mechanical | 508 | Chemical |
| 442 | Chemical | 510 | Chemical |
| 445 | Mechanical | 512 | Chemical |
| 446 | Mechanical | 514 | Chemical |
| 449 | Mechanical | 516 | Chemical |
| 450 | Mechanical | 518 | Chemical |
| 451 | Mechanical | 520 | Chemical |
| 452 | Mechanical | 521 | Chemical |
| 453 | Mechanical | 522 | Chemical |
| 454 | Mechanical | 523 | Chemical |
| 455 | Electrical | 524 | Chemical |

| Class | Class Group | Class | Class Group |
|-------|-------------|-------|-------------|
| 525 | Chemical | 702 | Electrical |
| 526 | Chemical | 703 | Electrical |
| 527 | Chemical | 704 | Electrical |
| 528 | Chemical | 705 | Electrical |
| 530 | Chemical | 706 | Electrical |
| 532 | Chemical | 707 | Electrical |
| 534 | Chemical | 708 | Electrical |
| 536 | Chemical | 709 | Electrical |
| 540 | Chemical | 710 | Electrical |
| 544 | Chemical | 711 | Electrical |
| 546 | Chemical | 712 | Electrical |
| 548 | Chemical | 713 | Electrical |
| 549 | Chemical | 714 | Electrical |
| 552 | Chemical | 715 | Electrical |
| 554 | Chemical | 716 | Electrical |
| 556 | Chemical | 717 | Electrical |
| 558 | Chemical | 718 | Electrical |
| 560 | Chemical | 719 | Electrical |
| 562 | Chemical | 725 | Electrical |
| 564 | Chemical | 800 | Chemical |
| 568 | Chemical | 901 | Mechanical |
| 570 | Chemical | 902 | Electrical |
| 585 | Chemical | 930 | Chemical |
| 588 | Chemical | 935 | Chemical |
| 600 | Mechanical | 968 | Mechanical |
| 601 | Mechanical | 976 | Chemical |
| 602 | Mechanical | 984 | Mechanical |
| 604 | Mechanical | 987 | Chemical |
| 606 | Mechanical | | |
| 607 | Mechanical | | |
| 623 | Mechanical | | |
| 700 | Electrical | | |
| 701 | Electrical | | |

# Appendix C: A random sample taken from the Chemical classes, 1994 to 2003

| Patent No. | Title |
|---|---|
| 5277766 | Separation of n-heptane from vinyl acetate by extractive dist. |
| 5288550 | Production method of non-fitting type capsule |
| 5312647 | Method and apparatus of vacuum deposition |
| 5314567 | Modular apparatus for preparing articles to be mailed |
| 5340662 | Emergency battery system with an infinite shelf life |
| 5342461 | High speed continuous conveyor printer/applicator |
| 5362731 | Use of piribedil derivatives and analogs for the treatment of hyperactive or unstable bladders |
| 5371006 | Isolated DNA encoding the NotI restriction endonuclease |
| 5384263 | Method to produce immunodiagnostic reagents |
| 5399197 | Bismuth phosphovanadate and/or bismuth silicovanadate based yellow pigments and processes |
| 5403405 | Spectral control for thermophotovoltaic generators |
| 5429645 | Solid fuel and process for combustion of the solid fuel |
| 5434170 | Method for treating neurocognitive disorders |
| 5437982 | Methods of identifying specific inactivation gate inhibitors of the sodium channel |
| 5439570 | Water soluble texaphyrin metal complexes for singlet oxygen production |
| 5449520 | Pharmaceutical composition for rectal administration of active principles exhibiting a prevalently topical medication action at the colon level |
| 5449795 | Process for synthesis of steroidal allylic tert. alcohols |
| 5472881 | Thiol labeling of DNA for attachment to gold surfaces |
| 5518849 | Ferrite carrier for electrophotographic developer and developer using said carrier |
| 5545744 | Cyano naphthalene compounds |

| Patent No. | Title |
|---|---|
| 5569345 | Flexible iron-on patch for soft clothing |
| 5571399 | Electrostatic fluid filter and system |
| 5610072 | Detection of caffeine in beverages |
| 5635265 | Apparatus for decorative mounting of planar articles |
| 5643450 | Filter apparatus for fluids, in particular for thermoplastic synthetic plastics material fluid |
| 5665779 | Pharmaceutical composition for inhibiting the infection with AIDS virus |
| 5683586 | Method and apparatus for magnetically treating a fluid |
| 5684149 | Metal complexes for promoting catalytic cleavage of RNA by transesterification |
| 5690861 | Coupling of polymers made by cationic polymerization |
| 5698763 | Transgenic animals lacking prion proteins |
| 5716594 | Biotin compounds for targetting tumors and sites of infection |
| 5723332 | Translational enhancer DNA |
| 5728422 | Ratiometric fluorescence method of making for measuring oxygen |
| 5728483 | System for storing and utilizing hydrogen |
| 5741697 | Bacteriophage of chlamydia psittaci |
| 5756048 | Modernization of a reactor |
| 5756282 | Oligonucleotides for the diagnosis of papillomavirus |
| 5773077 | Abrasion-protective convertible window |
| 5834185 | Formation of triple helix complexes of single stranded nucleic acids using nucleoside oligomers which comprise pyrimidine analogs, triple helix complexes formed thereby |
| 5834591 | Polypeptides and antibodies useful for the diagnosis and treatment of pathogenic neisseria and other microorganisms having type 4 pilin |
| 5837424 | Optical storage medium and process |
| 5861161 | Chimeric proteins comprising a Vpr/Vpx virion incorporation domain for targeting into HIV-1 or HIV-2 virions |
| 5897816 | Concrete corner form |
| 5902585 | Methods of inducing T cell unresponsiveness to donor tissue or organ in a recipient with GP39 antagonists |
| 5914393 | Human Jak2 kinase |

| Patent No. | Title |
|---|---|
| 5919460 | Composition for administration to patients with chronic fatigue syndrome and acquired immune deficiency syndrome |
| 5928409 | Method and apparatus for gas removal by cyclic flow swing membrane permeation |
| 5959093 | Bovine rotavirus genes |
| 5962089 | Automotive trim panel and method of making same |
| 5980861 | Chelator compositions and methods of synthesis thereof |
| 5985446 | Acetylenic carbon allotrope |
| 5985577 | Protein conjugates containing multimers of green fluorescent protein |
| 6004387 | Fire resistant liquid, process for preparing it and fireproof building material and fire resistant adhesive |
| 6004436 | Processes for the chemical modification of inorganic aerogels |
| 6013278 | Liposomal antineoplaston therapies with markedly improved antineoplastic activity |
| 6025355 | Pharmaceutically active compounds and methods of use |
| 6051615 | Use of C.sub.16 -C.sub.18 alkyl polyglycosides as defoamers in cleaning compositions |
| 6074445 | Polymeric fuel additive and method of making the same |
| 6103189 | Method of removing microbial contamination |
| 6140108 | Wine yeast cultures |
| 6149824 | Continuous filtration system using single pump, venturi, and flow control valve |
| 6156498 | "Establishment of HHV-8.sup.+ lymphoma cell line, virus produced, antibody, diagnostic method and kit for detecting HHV-8 infection" |
| 6183684 | Apparatus and method for producing non-woven webs with high filament velocity |
| 6200486 | Fluid jet cavitation method and system for efficient decontamination of liquids |
| 6210894 | Method and apparatus for conducting an array of chemical reactions on a support surface |
| 6221255 | Ultrasound-assisted filtration system |
| 6221263 | Treatment system for fire protection sprinkler system |
| 6264981 | Oral transmucosal drug dosage using solid solution |
| 6287817 | Fusion proteins for protein delivery |

| Patent No. | Title |
| --- | --- |
| 6291387 | Transition metal-free olefin polymerization catalyst |
| 6293988 | Inoculant and inoculant method for gray and ductile cast irons |
| 6299775 | Waste and wastewater treatment and recycling system |
| 6333188 | Lactic acid bacteria preparation having biopurification activity |
| 6342611 | Fluorogenic or fluorescent reporter molecules and their applications for whole-cell fluorescence screening assays for capsases and other enzymes and the use thereof |
| 6362392 | Nude mouse model for the growth and treatment of human neurally-derived tumors |
| 6368544 | Method and apparatus for accelerating the manufacture of molded particleboard parts |
| 6379648 | Biodegradable glass compositions and methods for radiation therapy |
| 6380377 | Nucleic acid hairpin probes and uses thereof |
| 6383491 | Prevention of infectious diseases with hsp90-peptide complexes |
| 6410334 | Method for determining the immune defense of blood and test kit for the same and use of a suitable blood sampling system |
| 6416794 | Methods and compositions for treating cataracts using substances derived from yeast or saltbush |
| 6440670 | Allele of human histamine H2 receptor and methods of detection of H2 receptor variants |
| 6506381 | Modified red blood cell that has surface molecules that neutralize chemical agents |
| 6524478 | Apparatus for filtering and separating particularly biologically organic fluids |
| 6565792 | Apparatus and method for use in molding a composite structure |
| 6592888 | Composition for wound dressings safely using metallic compounds to produce anti-microbial properties |
| 6608180 | B7-specific antibodies |
| 6613211 | Capillary electrokinesis based cellular assays |
| 6627400 | Multiplexed measurement of membrane protein populations |
| 6638973 | Taxane formulations |
| 6649615 | Method for inhibiting fibrogenesis |
| 6652750 | Externally mounted bilge water filter and methods therefor |
| 6653085 | Celiac antigen |

# Appendix D: Countries with fewer than 18 SE patents between 1994 and 2003 (Group E)

| Country | Count | Country | Count | Country | Count |
|---|---|---|---|---|---|
| Albania | 1 | F. Polynesia | 2 | Neth. Antilles | 6 |
| Algeria | 1 | Georgia | 10 | New Guinea | 1 |
| Andorra | 6 | Guatemala | 8 | Nicaragua | 1 |
| Anquilla | 1 | Guinea | 1 | Nigeria | 13 |
| Antigua | 6 | Haiti | 2 | Pakistan | 4 |
| Arab Emirates | 9 | Honduras | 7 | Panama | 9 |
| Armenia | 3 | Indonesia | 17 | Paraguay | 1 |
| Aruba | 4 | Iran | 4 | Qatar | 1 |
| Azerbaijan | 2 | Jamaica | 8 | San Marino | 2 |
| Bahrain | 3 | Jordan | 4 | Sri Lanka | 7 |
| Bangladesh | 1 | Kazakhstan | 12 | St Kitts/Nevis | 8 |
| Barbados | 3 | Kenya | 9 | St Vincent | 1 |
| Bermuda | 17 | Korea, N. | 1 | Suriname | 2 |
| Bolivia | 5 | Kyrgyzstan | 3 | Syria | 3 |
| Bosnia/Herz. | 2 | Latvia | 5 | Trinidad/Tob. | 12 |
| Congo | 1 | Lebanon | 15 | Turks & Caicos I. | 6 |
| Cook Islands | 1 | Lithuania | 7 | Uganda | 2 |
| Cyprus | 7 | Macau | 4 | Uruguay | 15 |
| Dominica | 3 | Malta | 12 | Uzbekistan | 8 |
| Dominican Rep. | 5 | Marshall I. | 2 | Vietnam | 1 |
| Ecuador | 11 | Mauritius | 2 | Virgin I. | 8 |
| El Salvador | 6 | Moldova | 2 | Yemen | 1 |
| Estonia | 6 | Morocco | 4 | Zimbabwe | 5 |
| Fiji | 2 | Myanmar | 1 | | |

# Index